The Afterlife of King James IV

Otherworld legends of the Scottish king

The Afterlife of King James IV

Otherworld legends of the Scottish king

Keith J. Coleman

Winchester, UK
Washington, USA

First published by Chronos Books, 2019
Chronos Books is an imprint of John Hunt Publishing Ltd., No. 3 East St., Alresford,
Hampshire SO24 9EE, UK
office1@jhpbooks.net
www.johnhuntpublishing.com

For distributor details and how to order please visit the 'Ordering' section on our website.

ISBN: 978 1 78904 117 0
978 1 78904 118 7 (ebook)
Library of Congress Control Number: 2018942282

A CIP catalogue record for this book is available from the British Library.

Design: Stuart Davies

Printed and bound by CPI Group (UK) Ltd, Croydon, CR0 4YY, UK

Contents

Dedicated to B and John Coleman

Acknowledgements

I would like to thank the following people for very kindly assisting me with queries: Morna Annandale (Museums Collection Unit, St Andrews University), Rev. Jenny Earl, Lisa Jemison at the University of Toronto Press for permission to quote from the Adages of Erasmus, Lizzie Macgregor (Assistant Librarian, Scottish Poetry Library), Roddy Martine, Robert Noel (Lancaster Herald), Dr Helen C. Rawson (Co-Director, Museum Collections Unit, of St Andrews University), James Smith, Marion Whyte. During the long course of research into this subject and allied subjects I have used the services of the following libraries and would like to thank the staff: The National Library of Scotland, Bristol City Libraries, Cornwall County Libraries.

Introduction

One of the major gateways into the daunting Scottish psyche is through the underground tradition beyond mainstream literature: its supernatural fiction, legend and folklore. The pivotal point for adventurers seeking insight into these recesses comes in an inconspicuous story embedded in Sir Walter Scott's novel *Redgauntlet* (1824).[1] The narrator of 'Wandering Willie's Tale' relates a supposed tradition of his own father, a tenant on a 17th century Scottish estate, who was driven to abnormal extremes by the threat of financial ruin. He had paid his rent as usual to the old laird, Sir Robert Redgauntlet, but when his master suddenly died there was no sign of the money or a receipt to prove that it had been paid. The laird's son, Sir John, demonstrated scant sympathy for his plight and demanded either hard cash or proof that the debt had been honoured. Facing this crisis, the tenant – Steenie Steenson – blindly called upon the powers of darkness to assist him. One dark night soon afterwards he met on the road a nameless messenger who led him to a house which he recognised as a simulacrum of the late laird's mansion. But the place appeared strangely transformed to his vexed senses. Old Redgauntlet was there sure enough, large as life, showing no detrimental effects from his recent demise. But things have altered in this Otherworld.

The old laird was keeping uproarious but uneasy company in death with a group of ambivalent figures from Scottish history. These characters would have been familiar to the unfortunate mortal intruder (and to Scott's readers), but some of them are now mere shadowy names, devoid of their former notoriety. Among the group were the infamous Bloody Advocate Mackenzie, General Tam Dalyell, and John Graham of Claverhouse (Viscount Dundee), important men who had spilled much blood in their time. The gauze of good humour which may have fooled the visitor into thinking the frightful revelry was joyful was torn away by the description of Dundee:

> And there was Claverhouse, as beautiful as when he lived, with his long, dark, curled locks streaming down over his laced buff-coat, and his left hand always on his right spule-blade, to hide the wound that the silver bullet had made. He sat apart from them all, and looked at them with a melancholy, haughty countenance; while the rest hallooed, and sung, and laughed, that the room rang. But their smiles were fearfully contorted from time to time; and their laughter passed into such wild sounds, as made my gudesire's very nails grow blue, and chilled the marrow in his banes.[2]

The ambivalence of Claverhouse in this particular afterlife reflects an uncertainty echoing down from Scotland's past: it may have vanished, but there remain unresolved residual issues haunting the realm. Scottish history, for Sir Walter Scott as well as the hapless Steenie Steenson, intrudes into everyday consciousness in a manner far removed from nostalgic reflection.

The old laird of Redgauntlet remains a frightening embodiment of history unleashed, the ultimate devolved power in the land. His son, on the other hand, is a pallid creature with a cold eye fixed on the present, who has sold his soul in favour of the economic bonanza proposed by the Union of England and Scotland. There is a facet of the bygone age which is more tangible than today, though it may be neither warm nor welcoming, and Scott's fable demonstrates the craving for this darker, more fulfilling age. It also puts into context the unease of Scotland's shadowy post-independence identity. Even Sir Walter Scott, a supporter of the United Kingdom, knew that his beloved country, despite its robustly unique institutions, survived only in a semi-autonomous twilight. Echoing this were the dead, those great and the not-so-good, stuck in an afterlife limbo which is a misshaped mirror of the present. In that place political and moral issues are unresolved until some cataclysmic day of national reckoning. Scottish folk tradition recognises the existence of an indefinite border zone, distinct from either heaven or hell, found for example in the poem and later ballad of 'Thomas the Rhymer', where the great poet and seer is escorted into this arcane plane of existence by the Faerie Queen.[3]

There are other national figures that inhabit that imaginary, uproarious stately home on the moorland edge of the Scottish mind, not only those sentenced to a peculiar purgatory for the sake of their violent, forgotten causes. If one of the qualifications for entry was a wholesale denial of that individual's death, then the subject of this book would certainly be resident there. The traditions surrounding the fate of one of Scotland's best loved kings merit examination for the insight they provide about the man, his times, and how an individual's reputation can act as a surrogate presence to be used and misused for many years after their death.

King James IV was one of Scotland's most successful rulers, his achievements made abundantly clear by historians of different hues who wrote about him in the century after his death. His accomplishments can be judged firstly in terms of the order he managed to impose on his own domains, most notably in the fractious Highlands and the Border region. He succeeded to a large extent in imposing the rule of law that his ancestor King James I ardently wished for.[4] That first royal James, like the fourth, died a dramatic and violent death, but on Scottish soil and at the hands of his own subjects. Similarities between the two men can be drawn also from the miasma of legend surrounding their deaths. The assassination of King James I inspired a poetical work entitled *The Dethe of the King of Scots*[5], and his demise was said to have been foretold by an Irish or Highland seeress.[6] A man of the arts and a righteous ruler, he was perceived by some in a martyr. Both men were part of a legend which portrays the royal Stewarts/Stuarts as a perversely attractive, fatally flawed lineage, which ultimately came to ruin through a combination of their own inherent weaknesses and the incessant ill-will of fate against them.[7] Their own, ill chosen acts – sometimes against their own kin – seemed to damn them. The resonance of guilt over the battlefield death of James III marked his son James IV with guilt, justified or not. The premature death of James V following the battle of Solway Moss in 1542 was linked, in the mind of one English writer at least, with the more bloody disaster of Flodden twenty-nine years earlier, albeit James V died broken in his own bed.[8]

The fables associated with the death of James IV are more complex and intriguing that any that have survived about previous kings, though the earlier stories still compel attention. Over two hundred and twenty years before the death of James IV at the battle of Flodden, his ancestor King Alexander III, seen by some as the last 'Celtic' king of Scotland, was thrown to his death by a horse at Kinghorn in Fife. Even though Alexander's death was a quite ordinary accident there were soon two versions of the event, quite different English and Scottish accounts.[9] There were also many legends associated with the fateful circumstances of Alexander's demise.

The stories which arose after the death of James IV surpass any of those associated with his ancestors. For breadth and interest, the only comparable group are those tales linked with Macbeth, who died in 1057. Differing legends about him arose from disparate and geographically distant sources, such as Norse saga (a culture which saw him as a racial, military enemy), and from mainstream ecclesiastic tradition in Fife, a region where he sought to ingratiate himself into legitimate Scottish society by richly endowing the church.[10] But there is no possibility of actually unearthing the real character of the man through these stories, fascinating though they are. Macbeth inhabited too remote a past, and the information we possess about him is both too biased and too incoherent to be fully unravelled.

King James IV, on the other hand, stands on the threshold of the modern world. He introduced the printing press into Scotland, studied new scientific manufacturing processes for artillery and warships and seemed for a time to be able to swim comfortably in the shark ridden waters of European diplomacy. Scotland in his reign appeared to be steering a course which would guarantee its integrity and independence, maintaining its traditional alliance with France while keeping a wary peace with England. In the end the political tensions consumed the king, forcing him to favour the older French alliance and go to war with England. Ironically, his marital alliance with King Henry VII's daughter eventually led to the union of crowns, and after the massive defeat at Flodden, Scotland was never again so resolute or independent.

The belief that King James IV survived the battle of Flodden in 1513 was one immediate, spontaneous response of a crushed nation. Nobody can question that it was the scale of the calamity of Flodden as well as the reaction to the death of a single, charismatic leader that gave birth to his survival legends. He was the first Scottish monarch to have led his nation onto the battlefield and perished there since King Malcolm III in the 11th century, and became the last king of any British nation to have died in battle. Rumours about his fate were traded after Flodden, and the tales became a component in the political infighting during the minority of his son, James V. The figure of the dead king was an active ingredient in the tumult of the leaderless country, and doubts over his fate were even used as a political weapon by his widow over a decade later.The traditions of the undying king were not just cynical gossip manipulated by the ruling class, any more than they were merely sentimental delusions of the 'common folk' or literary legends fabricated long after the fact.

Whispers about James IV defying fate and living on after his catastrophic last battle were a widespread reflex to unexpected tragedy common with many countries. Other kings are said to have cheated death and gone into hiding, or become religious penitents who went to Jerusalem or Rome. Some of these lost leaders shared another of the king's rumoured fates: murdered by some person they knew and trusted. But very few have been believed to be actually resident in another, supernatural dimension, as one tradition of James IV insisted. This was the destiny of the truly elite, such as the primal warlord Arthur. No ruler, not even the great emperor Charlemagne, attracted so many diverse tales about himself so immediately after his apparent death.

Some individuals prominent in Scotland after the Flodden disaster manipulated the fable of the lost king to damn their political opponents. The Scottish nobleman Lord Home was accused of not helping the king on the battlefield, but also of murdering him after the battle. Englishman Lord Dacre claimed to have found the king's body at Flodden, though perhaps his claim was based on an urgent need to redeem himself with the authorities who were suspicious of him. Accusations of inaction and open treachery touched these men in the aftermath of the battle of Flodden as they struggled to retain power. Even non combatants like Andrew, Bishop of Moray, faced accusations of causing the Anglo-Scottish war. James IV's widow also involved herself in trading rumours about the fate of her late husband, possibly as an act of desperation to be rid of her second partner, the Earl of Angus. In the end it was the late king's cousin, the Duke of Albany, who had to juggle with the sharp edged, shattered remnants of Scottish society. The figure of King James IV was a ghostly presence in the manoeuvrings of all of these damaged individuals after his death and their actions and intentions are a central part of this story.

Chapter 1

The Measure of a Monarch

The personal fame of King James IV arose from his subjects seeing him travelling tirelessly about his kingdom, dispensing justice, going on pilgrimages to his favourite shrines of St Ninian at Whithorn and St Duthac at Tain, or on other adventures. This gregarious manner of life contrasted markedly with the supposed sedentary lifestyle of his father James III, who was accused of being in the thrall of a small circle of inappropriate and ignoble favourites. His son may have learned from his father's supposed inability to embrace the manly activities of hunting and hawking, but James IV was also following his own restless instincts by being constantly physically active. King James IV was not merely visible to his subjects; he was seen engaged in activities which won the approval of Scots. It is ironic then that so conspicuous a king should be the focus of superstitious rumour after his death. Or perhaps the stories came from the trauma that his sudden physical absence generated.

James was energetic in his observance of religion, and even considered the possibility of going on pilgrimage or launching a crusade to the Holy Land. More than this, his actions and character sat well with peasantry and nobility alike. Later Protestant and Catholic historians lauded the king; though to different extents and with varying reservations, especially when it came to blaming him for apparently throwing his life away at Flodden. Some writers, like Lindsay of Pitscottie, make a direct connection between the perceived fornication of the king with his untimely death. To ordinary Scots the king's amorous adventures were a proof of his potency and understandable humanity. And while the monarch was no intellectual, a fact pertinently noted by the scholar George Buchanan[1], he did have an array of imaginative interests which led to active involvement in the spheres of surgery, alchemy, poetry, and naval and military technology.

If we look for a proliferation of legends surrounding the youth of the king as a pattern for those which surrounded him later in life, and in death, there are scant clues. James was born on St Patrick's Day, 17 March 1473, and it was said that a comet visible in January and February was a portent of this or another momentous event.[2] Even before his birth his father was manipulated by courtiers who took advantage of his superstitious mind and turned him against his own family. King James III had the misfortune to have two adult brothers who were more widely admired than himself, according to accounts written in the following century. One credible detail in the supernatural drama which followed was that it was grounded in a prosaic dispute: a disagreement about rents claimed both by the king's brother, Alexander, Duke of Albany, and a leading family, the Homes in the eastern border area. Playing on the king's weakness, the Homes and their allies the Hepburns recruited one of James's favourites, Robert Cochrane, who found a witch who told the monarch that he would be killed by one of his close kin. Rumours about this prophecy became so persuasive and were repeated so often that the monarch came to suspect his brothers. Albany grew mistrustful of the king and fled to his castle of Dunbar, but the younger brother John, Earl of Mar, met a suspicious death, though details of his demise are vague. Mar may have been beheaded or, according to others, he was allowed to choose the manner of his end and opted for opening his veins in a warm bath. Apart from these legends, a prosaic version maintains that he took a sudden fever and, during his delirium, tore his bandages off after the royal doctors bled him, hastening his own death. The historian Robert Lindsay of Pitscottie, writing three quarters of a century later, stated that the young prince was murdered in a bath in the Canongate, though he did not identify the perpetrator or the exact motive.[3] Another historian, John Lesley, believed that Mar was taken during the night to Craigmillar Castle, just outside Edinburgh, and convicted by the king of conspiracy against him by magic. Then his captors bled him to death in the Canongate, Edinburgh, in December 1480. Lesley adds that witches and warlocks implicated in Mar's conspiracy against the king were burnt for their crimes in Edinburgh, an event confirmed without this elaboration by other sources. There was evidently a climate of supernatural hysteria operating in Scotland at this time.[4] Albany, meanwhile, made a dramatic escape from Edinburgh Castle in the spring of 1485 and fled to France.[5] He later made an abortive attempt to oust his brother from the throne with English assistance, but eventually returned to France, where he ended his days and fathered a son who was to play a large part in his native land after his nephew's death.

The story of Mar's supernatural guilt and dramatic execution is dubious; not least because it is suspiciously similar to the tale of another prince who came to a dreadful end in this period. George, Duke of Clarence, brother of King Edward IV of England, was a similar character to Albany: popular, larger than life and ambitious for more power. In 1478 he changed from being a mere dynastic nuisance to a traitor when he was charged with conspiring to kill his royal brother by means of magic and poison.[6] Clarence suffered a bizarre, private execution, drowned in either a bath or in a vat of malmsey wine.[7]

James III may really have been a believer in the threat of the occult against himself, but it is just as likely to be a creation of writers informed by those powerful magnates who brought him down. But he did, like other rulers who wanted to hedge their bets, have recourse to arcane areas of knowledge in his own court. When Scottish ambassadors went to Flanders to address trade issues, they encountered an astrologer named Andreas who impressed them with his knowledge of future events.

One of his famous, later predictions was the death of Emperor Charles the Bold, who died at the Battle of Nancy in 1477. Andreas was invited by the envoys to come to Scotland and first appeared at the Scottish court in 1471.[8] He quickly became a fixture among King James III's close associates.[9] In one version of events it was this seer (rather than a witch) who is alleged to have played into the hands of the king's enemies, and perhaps his own nature, when he foretold that the monarch would meet his death by means of his nearest and dearest: 'the lion should be devoured by his whelps'. This superstitious weakness damaged James's reputation, despite his variety of positive qualities.The intellectual king had a widerange of interests, which reflected in his egalitarian choice of companions: architects, musicians, writers. But he could not accommodate his nobles within the compass of his activities and, fatally, he did not have the redeeming compensation of being popular with his ordinary subjects. Even some of those ministers in the highest ranks of his administration were tainted with the suspicion of being corrupted by supernatural influence, such as the Archbishop of St Andrews, William Schevez.[10]

Although James III survived the humiliation and physical danger of the hanging of most of his close associates by a lynch mob of noblemen at Lauder Bridge in 1483,[11] he could not prevent the uprising which led to his final downfall, on 11 June 1488. James III's death was painted by a later generation as both poignant and pathetic, but lack of contemporary facts ensures it remains an obscure event. The picture remains of a fate that was pre-ordained. The king raised an army to fight the rebels, but the final contest was far from glorious. At the end of a confused skirmish this most reserved and un-martial ruler was left alone, stumbling over a bleak moor like a foot soldier, unsure of what had befallen him after his horse had thrown him into the dirt; a literal fall from grace. It was not just any bleak landscape which played host to his inept last hours:

this was close to the site of Bannockburn, scene of the greatest military triumph of the Scottish nation. The lost king managed to pathetically cling onto his weapon, the sword once owned by Robert Bruce, whose ghost the chroniclers may have imagined hovered close by him. His death was rumoured to be both sordid and uncertainly accomplished. Injured by his fall, he staggered into the mill of Bannockburn, where he responded to the enquiry of the miller and his wife about his identity with the ominous, prophetic phrase, 'I was your king this day at morn.'[12] Possibly sensing his extremity, when he called out for a cleric to make his confession a passing man entered the mill and announced, 'Here I am, a priest.' Bending over the monarch, he drew out a dirk and repeatedly stabbed him. Then the ungodly cleric vanished into the night without a trace. Despite enquiries about his identity, the assassin was never found. The officially sponsored version of events declared that the king had been murdered by anonymous cut throats,[13] and though suspicion fell on supporters of Patrick, Lord Gray, no prosecutions were made.[14] The whole messy last fray was so ignominious an event that the battle did not even acquire a fixed name until long afterwards (being called Bannockburn, the Field of Stirling, and finally, Sauchieburn). The poet Sir David Lindsay, summarised the bizarrely swift and ill fated end of James III in a poem addressed to his grandson, King James V:

> At morne ane king, with sceptour, sweird, and croun;
> At evin, ane dede deformit carioun![15]

The rhyme reflects the merciless, arbitrary nature of kingship, which was part of the inheritance of James IV. Later commentators gave the impression that James III's death was a heaven sent punishment for his sins of abandonment to sensual pleasures and enchantment.[16] To cap his crimes he was accused later of being a tyrant, and therefore his violent death was entirely just.[17]

But even without the need to believe that this king was doomed by his own weakness, his death can still be seen as a cathartic occurrence that was necessary for the harmony of the whole realm to be restored.[18] The fatality of James III was a regicide which ushered in the birth of modern Scotland. The final irony was that his son and heir was crowned king of Scots on 24 June, the anniversary of the Battle of Bannockburn.

Major historians of the 16th century ensured that James III, who ruled for a creditable twenty-nine years, had the record of his reign overwritten by rumours of his ineffectiveness, but no contemporary historian gave the melodramatic version of his inept last hours on the battlefield. The suggestion that he was slain by treachery was certainly raised by contemporaries, albeit in allegorical form, as direct accusation would have been dangerous. The deadly conspiracy of his nobles was alluded to by Robert Henryson in his poem *The Taill of the Lyoun and the Mous*, where he hints that the king, symbolised by the lion in his verse, met a cruel and unnatural end, caught suddenly in an outstretched net by nameless hunters.[19]

If the reign of James IV compared with that of his father seems like light following darkness, it was an image encouraged by those who composed the national histories.[20] But the portrayal of him as a guileless rebel, who becomes a sorrowful young king forced to wake up to reality in the political jungle partially reflected reality. Coming to the throne more or less as an adult, James was able to grasp the reigns of political power after only a short period of uncertainty, unlike some of his unfortunate predecessors. The young king's instinct was turned towards consideration of his subjects, and one of his primary talents, which helped him find his feet and survive, was an ability to involve all classes of Scots in his leadership. Although he was accused after his death of being a romantic dreamer it has been argued that James IV's early dealings with adversity in fact made him an able ruler, whereas his English counterpart, Henry VIII, had a cosseted upbringing which did not equip him with the characteristics for getting the best out of people.[21]

The moment when the fifteen year old king's naivety ended can perhaps be pinpointed, if we are prepared to believe the testimony of Pitscottie. Shortly after the battle of Sauchieburn the victorious forces saw two warships belonging to the mariner Andrew Wood, the *Flower* and the *Yellow Carval,* anchored ominously in the Firth of Forth. Wood was staunchly loyal to James III and in the post-battle confusion some people thought that the king had escaped and found his way onto one of Wood's vessels. The captain wisely refused to come ashore unless several hostages from the rebel forces remained on his ship while the meeting took place. After this was arranged, Captain Wood met the young prince and his lords at Leith. As soon as James set eyes on the seafarer he asked him plaintively if he was his father, whom he had not seen for a long time.

The story, if not actually invented by Pitscottie, reads like a piece of popular oral tradition passed down to his time. The young man's pathetic question immediately affected Wood, who began to cry and said that he was not his father, but his father's true servant and the enemy of those who cast him down. The embarrassed rebel nobles asked Wood if he knew the location of the king. But the captain said the king was not on one of his ships; if he had been he would be kept safe from all those who had apparently murdered him. He taunted his interrogators by boldly stating he hoped to see the day when all those traitors were hung and drawn for their crime.[22]

James IV's rule commenced under shadows of remorse and dread. The young prince had allegedly only agreed to participate in the battle if it was agreed amongst the rebels that no-one would lay violent hands on the king.[23] His reaction to his father's death was one of immediate and long-lasting guilt, according to most chroniclers. The new king commissioned an iron chain or belt to be made, which he wore beneath his clothes as a stark physical reminder of his personal remorse.[24] After the solemn internment of the slain monarch at Cambuskenneth Abbey, his successor went sadly to Stirling and passed his days reflectively in the Chapel Royal, listening to mourning prayers and lamenting his father. King James asked the dean of the chapel how he could placate his conscience. The dean carefully consoled the king, avoiding accusing him of patricide, mindful that it would be unwise to suggest that the fifteen year old had his own father's blood on his hands. Following this, the king came up with the concept of the iron belt, though it may have originally been suggested by his confessor Patrick Ranwick (or Ranny).[25]

The very existence of this startling object which looms large in the legend of the king has been doubted by some writers.[26] Despite the private pain it symbolised, the iron belt literally weighed down the king for life and it was a penance not kept hidden from his subjects. Several likenesses of the king show him wearing a chain of metal links about his middle.[27] There are treasury accounts of the cost of weights purchased for the king's belt, and on 26 January 1506-7 there is an entry in the accounts for worsted padding 'for the Kingis iron belt'.[28] It may have been worn outside of his clothes, at least on occasion, a symbol of repentance for all to see. The chain tethered the king down to the heavy responsibilities of religious observance, showing another side of his character than the pleasure-loving man of the world. The sincerity of his public show of faith and guilt, was also shown in the king's constant progress to pilgrimage sites at Tain (a collegiate church founded by his father in 1487) and Whithorn. But in the case of his own private remorse for his father it is noteworthy that, while he began immediately to pay for masses for the soul of his mother, it was not until 1494 that he paid for similar masses for his father.[29]

The young king may not have been quite the intellectual equal of his father, but his keen intelligence inspired surprisingly wide interests, spurred on by restless curiosity. The Spanish envoy Dom Pedro de Ayala, Bishop of the Canaries, who visited Scotland in July 1496 on a mission to reconcile Scotland with England, left a famously glowing description of the young monarch. After a flattering physical account of the king, Dom Pedro gives a suspiciously long list of languages twenty-five-year-old James was fluent in: Latin, French, German, Flemish, Italian, Spanish and Gaelic. The king's religious piety is recorded by Ayala in the conventional terms expected for a ruler, with his noted fondness for the Friars Observant. The new king pointedly visited the convent of the Observant Friars at Stirling during Holy Week each year.

After this the Spaniard offers an insight into the king's character which acts as a sad marker to his future destiny:

> He is courageous, even more so than a King should be. I am a good witness of it. I have seen him often undertake most dangerous things in the last wars. I sometimes clung to his skirts, and succeeded in keeping him back. On such occasions he does not take the least care of himself. He is not a good captain, because he begins to fight before he has given his orders. He said to me that his subjects serve him with their persons and goods, in just and unjust quarrels, exactly as he likes, and that, therefore, he does not think it right to begin any warlike undertaking without being himself the first in danger. His deeds are as good as his words. For this reason, and because he is a very humane prince, he is much loved.[30]

De Ayala was documenting his personal experiences of going into battle, when King James led his troops into Northumberland in support of the pretender Perkin Warbeck in 1496. The king's future nemesis, the Earl of Surrey, raised an army and went north to confront the Scots and this claimant for the English throne. But full warfare and disaster were averted when the Scottish horde withdrew. Ayala notes that the king 'loves war so much that I fear, judging by the provocation he receives, the peace will not last long'. Such impetuosity and disregard for his own safety on the battlefield was one of the primary reasons for his death at Flodden. There was no doubt that this king, when he stated that he wanted to lead a Christian army against the Infidel, intended that he would be with that army in the front rank.

Further insight into the king's success was his willingness to consider the views of all his counsellors before taking important decisions, which explained his successful judgements, until he disregarded this source of advice on the eve of his last, fatal battle. The country's stability was supported by the king's readiness to dispense justice to rich and poor alike. But there was also a stark observation that the king thought he was the lord of the whole world. The Spaniard also did not shirk from describing the king's fondness for the opposite sex, which indeed was no secret in Scotland or abroad. But he put much of the blame of those in the government who deliberately led the king into licentiousness when he was a minor to keep him under their control. This policy of appeasement through pleasure was repeated in the case of his son, King James V, who was controlled in this manner for much of his minority by the Douglas family.

But the claim by Dom Pedro that, after keeping one lady as a mistress in a castle and impregnating another, he had given up his lovemaking for the fear of God and public scandal, was wishful thinking. The lady in the castle (of Stirling) was Marion Drummond, the middle of a trio of royal mistresses whom James openly lived with before his union with Margaret, daughter of King Henry VII.[31] The number of his illegitimate children actually outnumbered those born to him by his wife.[32]

One argument in favour of the accuracy of Dom Pedro's eulogy is that it was meant for the private attention of his royal Spanish master and mistress. But when he wrote his description of James and Scotland on 25 July 1498 in London, a year after his visit, it was inevitably tainted by hindsight. The picture of Scotland and its king was so affirmative that the ambassador was told off by his royal Spanish masters for being gullible.[33] Dom Pedro's primary duty was to support Spanish foreign policy by persuading James that he should make peace with England. Queen Isabella and King Ferdinand admitted to their English ambassador De Puebla that they were stringing King James along with hints of a Spanish alliance, via marriage, yet they chided Dom Pedro when he was found to be promising the hand of an Infanta and not a lesser born bride for James.[34] Yet Ayala could not resist the Scottish king's charm and struck up a friendship with him. He was a type of character still recognisable today: someone who basked in the reflected aura of royalty, almost to the point of sycophancy. The two men were also bound together by their somewhat unfocused intelligence. Ayala was described by Polydore Vergil in terms similar to those used by Buchanan about the king: 'not learned but very clever and exceedingly discreet'.[35] His assessment of Henry VII is insightful and less flattering than his characterisation of James IV, focusing on Henry's unpopularity, meanness with money and the undue influence his mother had over him.[36] But his praise of James can also only be judged if seen in the light of similar communications from other diplomats about other rulers. The Venetian ambassador to England, Sebastian Giustinian, heaped acclaim on Henry VIII in a missive sent back to his homeland that recalls the Spaniard's eulogy. In it, young Henry is lauded for his dazzling physical attributes, his skills in hunting and playing music, and his piety. Part of the role of men like Giustinian and Ayala was undoubtedly to lavish admiration almost indiscriminately upon royalty if discretion demanded.[37]

The picture of Scotland during the king's reign shows an uncommon degree of domestic peace, if we can judge from the lack of recorded turbulence. There are few incidents of intrigue or internecine conflict among the fractious Scottish nobility during the period. Contemporary documents show a gregarious king, devoted to entertainment and accustomed to paying generously for it. Among more prosaic entries the Treasurer's Accounts periodically refer to payments to fiddlers, minstrels, diverse musicians and story-tellers, which can give a false sense of familiarity with the king and a notion that he spent much of his time being passively receptive to frivolity. Yet the human detail in these sombre accounts leaps out at the reader. One reciter of tales in December 1496 was Wedderspoon the Foular, who brought his majesty wild birds as well as stories one evening and formed a double bill with 'Watschod the tale tellare' the next evening.[38] Away from court, the king was open to his people and generous to many of those he encountered, giving money to the poor, infirm and others. And who could fail to be intrigued by the story behind an entry in the accounts (18 August 1491) which probably records a unique incident of unparalleled frivolity: 'Item, til a wyfe at Baythcat bog, at the King revit a rong fra [wrestled a stick from], 18 shillings.'[39]

The question of whether the king consciously constructed his own legend is difficult to assess. The few folk tales and legends associated with his lifetime focus on his human characteristics. One of the best stories, as reported by Robert Lindsay of Pitscottie, gives an insight into public perception of the king several generations later. Pitscottie says that the king ordered a dumb woman and her two infants be confined to the island of Inchkeith in the Firth of Forth, providing them with all necessary food and clothing, but depriving them of communication with anyone who had the power of speech. The king wanted to know what language the children would speak naturally in the course of time. Some people reported that the children's first words were in Hebrew, but the historian expressed his doubts.[40]

The story shows the intellectual curiosity of the king, and also has an undercurrent which gently mocks the misuse of power which his wrongheaded inquisitiveness led him into. Sadly

– or thankfully – the story of the incarceration of the hapless family is probably untrue, albeit that Inchkeith had a strange and unhappy reputation. In 1497 it was suggested as a place of incarceration for those unfortunates who had contracted the first Scottish cases of 'grandgore', or syphilis, which had likely been imported by the motley foreign retainers of the pretender Perkin Warbeck.[41]

The legend of first language acquisition is also told about many other intelligent rulers, including King Frederick II of Sweden and the Mogul emperor Akbar. The earliest mention of it was probably recorded by Herodotus in the 5th century B.C. His version states that the pharaoh Psammetichus wished to disprove Phrygian claims that they had the oldest language and culture, so he had a herdsman raise two poor children in seclusion in the wilderness. That experiment proved his certainty of Egyptian primacy, since the first word the children uttered was *bekos*, Egyptian for bread.[42]

True or not, the story accords with his famed curiosity. It is arguable whether the king's more esoteric activities contributed towards his later reputation. His interest in alchemy appears misguided to modern thinking, but in the context of the era it was an acceptable activity among rulers. James IV also had an active curiosity about medicine; state records show him at various times practising dentistry, drawing blood, treating wounds and setting broken bones. When James himself operated, he compassionately paid the patients rather than demanding a fee, and his victims included his own barber, who got 13 shillings for allowing the king to yank out his rotten tooth.[43] Pitscottie recorded the king's fame as a surgeon, saying that others of that profession would travel to consult him on medical matters, which may be more due to their flattery than his expertise.[44] Buchanan says he shared his medical skills with his royal predecessors and many of the nobility, who found that such skill was necessary on the field of battle.[45] The Treasurer's Accounts record various payments made to patients of the royal medical hobby, and also payments for tooth pulling instruments bought for the king.[46]

At the royal court there were various 'experts' who encouraged their master in his more exotic interests, such as Fullertone, who professed to make precious stones, and Dr Ogilvy who tried to find the elusive secrets of alchemy.[47] The king's chief accomplice in alchemical research was one John Damian (de Falcusis), first recorded as a physician in the royal household in 1501 or 1502.[48] The state records call him the 'French leech', but other sources state he was either Flemish or an Italian from Lombardy. The king had furnaces set up in Edinburgh and in Stirling for the difficult task of transmuting base material into gold, with the latter furnace being tended by a servant named Caldwell.[49] It would be presumptuous to guess what his exact motives were for spending so much time and money over this unrewarding process. The record of expenses for alchemical purposes continues for year after year. But a fascination with the technical aspects of alchemy came perhaps from the same source that gave him an abiding obsession with the technology involved in building cannons, great warships, or the scientific principles of warfare. Also, the pot of gold promised at the end of the process was a glittering temptation for a ruler who spent well beyond his means throughout his reign.

Alchemy, as a magical art or philosophical pursuit, was not simply concerned with changing worthless material into something materially valuable. The transmutation had a parallel process of change within the practitioner himself, leading to a deep, occult knowledge, the possession of the Philosopher's Stone and the Elixir of Life, the *quinta essentia*. Whether King James IV was mostly interested in these recondite aspects of alchemy is uncertain, but he did consult written authorities on the art of alchemy. He wrote a letter in 1508 to James Inglis, who had been keeping rare books on alchemy on his behalf, and said he was sending James Merchenistoun to collect them for him.[50] The recognition of these esoteric beliefs certainly would have aroused enmity among some quarters in Scotland. The most formidable poet at court, William Dunbar, regarded John Damian as a scurrilous creature. Partly this was due to Damian's appointment to the abbacy of Tungland (now Tongland) in Kircudbrightshire, which Dunbar as a cleric would rightly condemn, especially as Damian declined to perform the religious duties associated with the benefice. Also, Damian was a court rival for honour and esteem and the king's hard cash. Mostly, though, Dunbar saw an open goal and put the boot in, since here was someone so absurd that it would be a sin not to ridicule him.

The poet wrote two poems satirising John Damian: *A Ballat of the Abbot of Tungland* (otherwise called *Ane Ballat of the Fenȝeit Freir of Tungland*), and *Lucina shyning in silence of the nycht* (also known as *The Ballad of the Antichrist*).[51] The first poem paints its subject as coming from the East, killing a monk in Lombardy and fleeing with his habit to France. It then mocks the abbot for his ludicrous attempt in September 1507 to fly from the battlements of Stirling Castle, using a pair of feathered wings he had constructed. His flying lesson resulted in him plunging ignominiously down into a heap of dung, which the sceptical observers may have thought the ideal place for him. Dunbar's poem, and the incident as reported, have a tragicomic basis, but underlying it is the warning, like the tale's template, the story of Icarus, that some knowledge is beyond the reach of man and should not be reached for. Whatever Damian's true intentions, and there seems little doubt that the story had been reconstructed or severely embellished by his enemies, there could be serious, symbolic alchemical intention in his attempt to mimic the secret of flight.[52]

John Lesley relates a version of this incident, apparently sourced from oral tradition; people in his time were still laughing about it.[53] According to Lesley – another disapproving churchman – the alchemical boasts of Damian hoodwinked the king and his only true skill was in milking purses. Certain payments which he borrowed from the royal treasury were never repaid and were written off as bad debts.[54] In Lesley's version of the story Damian saw that his popularity was on the wane so he resorted to the drastic boast that he arrive in France before the two Scottish envoys who left the country by sea on 27 September 1507. To accomplish this journey he adopted a pair of wings and tried to soar from the ramparts of Stirling Castle. But instead of flying he plummeted to the ground and broke his thigh bone. He was reported to have blamed his failure on the fact that he included hens' feathers in his wings, obviously birds which cannot fly.[55]

It is unlikely that King James would have fostered an interest in alchemy if he truly believed it ran counter to his orthodox Catholicism. Perhaps the most revealing thing about the king's association with Damian is that he continued to support him even after he became a public laughing stock and the efficacy of alchemical efforts proved illusory. Damian was paid a considerable sum again in 1513, this time to go to the mine at Crawford Moor, where gold had been discovered.[56] His purpose in this exercise, and his subsequent history, are obscure. But the trust the king placed in this dubious individual raises the question about how credulous he was, especially as he sponsored various charlatans and frauds in his court. The major figure who falls into this category is Perkin Warbeck, who passed himself off as the Duke of York, son of King Edward IV of England, one of the Princes in the Tower who in all likelihood died unnaturally during the reign of their uncle King Richard III. By the time that Perkin came to Scotland in November 1495 he was already a highly polished fraudster with the whole weight of the powerful Yorkist faction behind his ambitions. He had also impressed a string of European rulers who acknowledged his royal blood. Whether James believed him, half-believed him, or allowed himself to be fooled by a dreamy fairy tale is unknown. True, James paired Perkin off with the well-bred Catherine Gordon, daughter of the Earl of Huntly, but this may have been the act of a shrewd politician seeking to bolster his young and useful protégé. He used Warbeck as a pretext for his invasion of England, where the pretender proved himself to be lamentably un-martial. When the young man expressed weak dismay about the depredation the Scots were perpetrating on 'his' people, King James replied by stating that it seemed to him that Perkin was 'meddling in other people's business and not his own...Thereafter, as time went on, he paid less and less attention to him.'[57] James IV soon realised which way the wind blew with regard to this would-be ruler. The Scots had few qualms about saying goodbye to Perkin Warbeck as he continued his desultory quest for a throne in 1497. The ship in which he was despatched to Ireland was called the *Cuckoo*, and perhaps the king chose the vessel for the aptness of its name and suitability for its passenger.[58]

The poet William Dunbar described the exotic mix of legitimate and esoteric professions vying for attention at the court of James IV, in his 'Remonstrance to the King', which opens with the outwardly dazzling array of those found at court:

> Kirkmen, courtmen, and craftismen fyne;
> Doctouris in jure, and medicyne;
> Divinouris, rethoris, and philosophouris,
> Astrologis, artistis, and oratouris...[59]

But the picture of energetic diversity soon changes into contempt for those dubious characters, domestic and foreign, who compete for royal benefice:

> Fenyeouris, fleichouris, and flatteraris;
> Cryaris, craikaris, and clatteraris;
> Soukaris, gronkaris, gledaris, gunnaris...[60]

And so on, until over fifty classes of hanger-on are detailed, by no means not all of which were legitimate professions. Dunbar's attitude is affected by his need to stand out among these over-coloured competitors and by his opinion that jostling with these parasitic court appendages were beneath his dignity, both as a makar – a man of letters – and as a probable descendant of the aristocratic family of Dunbar. The king, for all his artistic sensibilities, mysteriously never made the best poet of his age a personal favourite; perhaps because Dunbar found a more willing patron in Queen Margaret. Eventually Dunbar's harping neediness wore down the reservations of the king and he succeeded in obtaining better financial support, but not to the extent he felt he deserved.

Dunbar and other sources show James IV striving to uphold the public face of kingship through extravagance. He also ensured that his reputation was enhanced, at home and abroad, through the staging of magnificent tournaments – a programme of public extravagance which Henry VIII later emulated.[61] For some of his tournaments the king sent his heralds and messengers into foreign countries to invite brave knights to come and test their skills at spectacular public events. One of the reasons for these lavish events, one suspects, was a desire by the king to expend his apparently boundless reserves of energy in public display. The tournaments seem excessive to modern eyes. King James was prone to meeting all comers in single combat, fighting as an anonymous knight, perhaps to ensure that his opponents did not flatter him with false restraint. In a tournament in Edinburgh the king decided to perform as the Wild Knight, a legendary hero of King Arthur's court brought up in the woods, whose ferociousness and courtliness expressed an image cultivated by the king.[62] This figure appeared in Edinburgh in a tournament honouring the Black Lady, one of nine Moorish women captured by Scottish sailors from a Portuguese vessel in 1504. At this event, in 1507, the lady herself rode in a triumphal chariot and the competitors fought for a prize she was to give.[63] The tournament was so successful that another similar event was held the following year, when the captured foreign lady was decked out in splendid clothes and spectators were amazed by a whole troop of Wild Men wearing goat skins and stag horns and arriving on dragons.[64] It was probably after witnessing these events that William Dunbar penned a none too subtle tribute to the lady titled *Of Ane Black-Moir*, replete with sexual imagery revelling in the lady's exotic physical appearance.[65]

Attempting to find the man in the sometimes bizarre legends recorded about his reign is asking to be led astray. There are few incidents during his time which point to the looming tragedy of Flodden, even if it later seemed that the catastrophe was inevitable. Despite his restlessness, James kept his house in order to the extent that he eliminated the ancient threat from the over mighty Lords of the Isles in the Highlands, attempted to pacify the lawless borders and generally kept his nobility at peace. On the wider stage, his personal prestige and usually canny diplomacy gave Scotland a higher profile in European than it merited. His marriage to King Henry VII's daughter Margaret in 1502 ran counter to the ancient alliance with France and prefigured disaster. But the marriage also ultimately led to the union of crowns and the creation of the British state.

While this treaty of marriage was being negotiated a 'monster of a new and strange shape was born in Scotland, near the city of Glasgow'. Two co-joined infants came to life at a time when the ancient national enemies were striving to deal with the difficulties of finally contemplating a political union. The male twins, who were joined at the waist, were lucky enough to be sponsored by the compassionate and curious king, who ensured they were taught the arts of playing music. They also mirrored the monarch's alleged polyglotism, speaking seven languages. In the spirit of the time there may have been some who likened this unheard of physical union with the inevitable marriage of Scotland and England, especially given their contrary but complimentary natures: 'They had differing passions, and diverse wills, often chiding others for disorder in their behaviour and actions: after much deliberation, embracing that unto which they both contented.'[66] Yet the twins actually existed, and were not merely symbols of an impending national partnership. They lived to the age of twenty-eight, when one of them died before the other.[67]

In reality there were few wonders which showed the strange avenue of fate which was waiting for the king. His ultimate failure came because he could not work out how to reconcile the traditional Franco-Scots alliance with the new peace agreement made with his father-in-law, Henry VII. The 'Treaty of Perpetual Peace' in 1502, was associated with his marriage to Princess Margaret Tudor.[68] The alliance with France was ratified again in the spring of 1513, almost a death warrant for this monarch.[69] The reported panic among some contemporary Englishmen that the kingdom would be inherited by Scots was cannily countered by Henry VII. The English king wisely pointed out that if, God forbid, his own line should fail and England was ruled by a royal Stewart, Scotland and her rulers would be subsumed into England, rather than the other way about. He cited the example of Normandy inheriting the English crown. The story, recorded by John Lesley later in the 16th century, sits in the category of anecdotes which should be true even if they did not actually happen.[70]

James IV's reign initiated the turning point between medieval credulity and modern scepticism. An anachronistic appreciation of his sovereignty as a golden era before a long decline underpins some of the positive pictures of his character and achievement. This longing for a perfect past is similar to the backward looking chronicler who later idealised the reign of King Alexander III (1249-1286) as an age of abundance in 'ale and brede',[71] shortly before the country was exploded by the Wars of Independence.

But contemporary sources did not especially regard his reign as golden.[72] Even as late as the age of James IV the figure of the king was intimately linked to the wellbeing of the land in a primal sense. This is seen in the concept of the success of the reign bringing about fertile abundance in the land, something attributed in a praise poem associated with Macbeth.[73] James IV's early reign seemed equally blessed by providence. The flowering of arts, the peacefulness of the kingdom, extinction of internal dissent and war, all seemed to be products of the king's charismatic rule. But even when his luck turned, the king's charisma remained. Some vestige of this characteristic lingered long in the legends which proliferated around him following his death. The relationship between those legends and the events in the kingdom after his death are one fascinating aspect of his legacy.

Chapter 2

The Vision in the Kirk and the Summons of Pluto

Two sensational public events in the weeks before the war with England summed up the foreboding in Scotland and the opposition of supernatural forces to planned military action. One evening in late summer 1513, when the king was in St Michael's kirk at Linlithgow waiting for his army to muster, there was a dramatic disruption:

> The King came to *Lithgow,* where he happened to be for the Time at the Council, very sad and dolorous, making his Devotion to God to send him good Chance and Fortune in his Voyage. In this mean Time, there came a Man clad in a blue Gown in at the Kirk-Door, and belted about him in a Roll of Linen-Cloth; a Pair of Brotikins on his Feet, to the Great of his Legs, with all other Hose and Clothes conform thereto; but he had nothing on his Head, but syde yellow Hair behind, and on his Haffits, which wan down to his Shoulders; but his Forehead was bald and bare. He seemed to be a Man of two and fifty Years, with a great Pyke-Staff in his Hand, and came first forward among the Lords, crying and speiring for the King, saying, He desired to speak with him. While, at the last, he came where the King was sitting in the Desk at his Prayers: But when he saw the King, he made him little Reverence or Salutation, but leaned down groflins on the Desk before him, and said to him in this Manner, as after follows. *Sir King, my Mother hath send me to you, desiring you not to pass, at this Time, where thou are purposed; for, if thou does, thou wilt not fare well in thy Journey, nor none that passeth with thee. Further, she bade thee mell with no Woman, nor use their Counsel, nor let them touch*

> *thy Body, nor thou theirs; for, if thou do it, thou wilt be confounded and brought to Shame.*
>
> By this Man had spoken thir Words unto the King's Grace, the Even-Song was near done; and the King paused on thir Words, studying to give him an Answer: But, in the mean Time, before the King's Eyes, and in Presence of all the Lords that were about him for the Time, this Man vanished away, and could noways be seen nor comprehended, but vanished away as he had been a Blink of the Sun, or a Whip of the Whirlwind, and could no more be seen. I heard say, Sir *David Lindesay* Lyon Herauld, and *John Inglis* the Marshal, who were, at that Time, young Men, and special Servants of the King's Grace, were standing presently beside the King, who thought to have laid Hands on this Man, that they might have speared further Tidings at him: But all for nought; they could not touch him; for he vanished away betwixt them, and was no more seen.[1]

This electrifying appearance still raises questions about the identity of this apparition and the 'mother' who had prompted him to confront the king. If the event actually happened and is not dismissed as a fiction or delusion, then who was behind it and what was their intention? By this time the decision to invade England had been made by the king, so any hope of calling off the inevitable conflict was forlorn. If Linlithgow's staged apparition conveyed an anti-war message, it was possibly a token gesture or a foolhardy protest rather than a serious attempt to prevent impending hostilities.

The setting of the kirk was likely carefully chosen for the demonstration. Linlithgow, west of Edinburgh, provided a useful point for the peripatetic court to stop on its way to and from the next major royal centre of Stirling. St Michael's church has occupied the site next to the beautiful palace of Linlithgow from the 12th century. It was not exclusively a chapel royal, but a parish church, yet its proximity to the palace ensured that the king and court frequently worshipped here when in residence,[2] making it a public place of worship uniquely associated with royalty. The king's personal chair was in the southern transept of the church, dedicated to St Catherine of Siena (a 14th century mystic who was, significantly, prone to holy visions), and it was here that the dramatic episode is supposed to have taken place. Sir Walter Scott states that the monarch was surrounded here by twelve stalls set aside for fellow knights of the Thistle, but that chivalric order did not have had a designated area here at this period (and may not even have been in existence yet).[3] But the church would still have been amply populated by courtiers and attendants. If the event involved a human actor, there could have been plenty of conspirators who allowed him make a ready escape. Historians have long suspected that it was a colourful hoax devised by someone close to the king, perhaps even Queen Margaret, anxious to prevent her husband going to war against her country of birth.[4]

The objections which Margaret gave to her husband against an English invasion, as put forward by Pitscottie, sound plausible. She argued with the king that his dynasty was hanging by a thread: just one infant son would remain to succeed if he should perish in battle. If he was still determined to pursue the war against England, why not delay it until they had more children? Another reason she was opposed to the campaign was her natural sisterly love for the king of England.[5] Drummond of Hawthornden later added the story that Margaret, in desperation, tried to influence James by relating nightmares she was having about the imminent conflict. She dreamed that her jewels had turned to pearls, which was evidently an ominous sign, and had a vision of falling down from a great height and losing one of her eyes. Her husband dismissed these as mere delusions caused by the actions of the day. But Margaret would not be consoled and told him, 'It is no dream that ye are to fight a mighty people.'[6]

On the other hand, James's most recent biographer doubts that there was any agitation from a pro-English party at work in the event, and believes that Margaret demonstrated no deep concern at the forthcoming war.[7] She was also involved in a bitter dispute with Henry VIII concerning jewellery which she believed had been promised to her by their father. But there is also the testimony of the English ambassador, Dr West to consider. Though he could get no firm statement from the Scottish king regarding his intentions towards a war with England at a meeting with Queen Margaret at Linlithgow on Sunday 10 June 1513, she acknowledged that her brother now was in the right and her husband was in the wrong.[8] Despite this evidence, the most telling doubt against believing that Margaret personally orchestrated the event is that it involved a level of sophisticated imagination which she never demonstrated on any previous or subsequent occasion. Following her husband's death she sometimes took advantage of common rumours to further her cause (such as accusing the Duke of Albany of poisoning her child), but it is clear that she was not capable of actively inventing propaganda to further her own ends.

If there was a human instigator behind the incident in St Michael's, he or she deliberately designed the performance to be in tune with the ostentatious temperament of the monarch. The apparition first appeared, or was noticed, among the king's powerful lords and mysteriously vanished among them. The event might be seen as a dramatic public anti-war display couched in terms which the showman king would readily comprehend. Staged public performances and shows were familiar to James. His spectacular tournaments brought competitors from around Europe to compete in the shows, ensuring that they returned home with tales of the magnificence of the Scottish king.[9] The king's great public spectaculars were also a symbolic way of channelling away natural aggression which would ordinarily have been expended in warfare against the English.[10] But even at the height of the extravagant pomp of the tournaments there was ambivalence from the king about how he chose to view himself. James appeared several times in these events incognito, which may have arisen from the same empathy with Everyman that saw him on occasion wandering unrecognised through the countryside.[11]

The first published account of the Vision in the Kirk story was by George Buchanan, whose work was completed in 1579 and published in 1582. He probably used some of the same sources for the tale as Pitscottie (who wrote earlier, but did not reach print until 1728). Buchanan names his source as an actual eyewitness: one of the most notable Scots of the age, Sir David Lindsay of the Mount, whom he praises for his academic brilliance and honesty, adding that 'in the course of his life he abhorred lying'. Aware that the anecdote sounded unbelievable, he writes that if he had not personally heard this story from Lindsay vouched as absolute truth, he would have discarded it as being a romance invented by vulgar people. But he omits the detail (mentioned by Pitscottie) that David Lindsay was one of two bystanders who somehow let the mysterious man vanish from the kirk.[12]

David Lindsay, who became Lord Lyon King of Arms in 1542, was a noted poet and courtier who performed in theatrical events for the royal court as early as 1511, when he staged an entertainment to divert Queen Margaret's mind from the death of her mother.[13] Lindsay's qualities (notwithstanding his truthfulness) make him a prime suspect for the originator of the St Michael's apparition. His best known work, *Ane Pleasant Satyre of the Thrie Estaitis*, a play first publicly performed in 1552, is a comedic blast at the morality of the establishment, written by a fearless insider, so he was accustomed to using drama as a political tool. He was well-versed in more humble native supernatural traditions as well as classical learning, as he relates in *The Dreme*, where he recounts folk tales and legends he used to entertain the young James V: *'The Propheceis of Rymour, Beid, and Marlyng, And of mony uther pleasand storye...'*[14] Sir David Lindsay was also a relation of the historian Robert Lindsay of Pitscottie, who must have used him as a valuable source when he wrote his history, even though the poet died in 1555, when Pitscottie was twenty-three (coincidentally the age that the historian's witness to the strange events in 1513 was).

The evidence which can now be seen to definitely link Sir David Lindsay to involvement in the Linlithgow incident is found in one of his final and most important poems, *'Ane Dialog betuix Experience and Ane Courteour, Off the Miserabyll Estait of the Warld (The Monarche)'*, published in 1554. The opening lines are haunted by a familiar, ancient figure:

In to that Park I sawe appeir
One ageit Man, quhilk drew me neir,
Quhose beird wes weill thre quarter lang;
His hair doun ouer his schulders hang,
The quhilk as ony snaw wes quhyte;
Quhome to behald I thocht delyte;
His habitt Angellyke of hew,
Of culloure lyke the sapheir blew...
I did hym saluss reverendlye;
Sa did he me, rycht courteslye.
To sitt down he requeistit me,
Onder the schaddow of that tre,
To saif me frome the sonnis heit,
Amangis the floweris softe and sweit;
For I wes werye for walking.
Than we began to fall in talking:
I sperit his name, with reverence?
I am, said he, EXPERIENCE.[15]

Was Lindsay reworking the memory of a mysterious figure he

recalled hearing about in his youth, or had even seen himself? It is impossible to say, but the mysterious old man in blue is undoubtedly a double of the being which materialised before the king in flesh or phantom form. The *Dialog* was composed before the histories of Pitscottie and Buchanan. It is possible that both these visitants – in the poem and in the kirk – were creations of Sir David's fertile mind at different periods, summoned up to serve different purposes. Lindsay the poet and courtier had a long-standing relationship with the Scottish monarchy, and he may have been anxious to do something to prevent the English war. Carol Edinton has pointed out that Lindsay and Buchanan must have discussed the event in the mid 1530s, when both men were at court. The story, she says, was invented in the years, 'born out of Flodden but fostered by subsequent – abortive – attempts to rouse the country against England in the 1520s... designed to deter not James IV but his son from the vices of the flesh and the adoption of a bellicose foreign policy'.[16]

But Lindsay of course was not the only one who might have been against the campaign, although there was no substantial anti-war party in Scotland as such. There were enough strange artistic and theatrical characters hanging around the royal court to make the matter of finding a convincing actor to play the part of an apparition relatively easy. Even those within the inner circle of the royals were talented in this area. There was, for example, the prelate and diplomat Andrew Forman, Bishop of Moray (later Archbishop of St Andrews), who allegedly enlivened the royal tournament of 1509 by performing conjuring tricks, spectacularly summoning a cloud out of the roof of the hall at the time of the tournament which featured the black lady.[17] But Forman was not inclined to prevent the king fighting against England; on the contrary, he was so much in favour of war that he was afterwards made one of the scapegoats for the result of the Flodden campaign.

Neither Buchanan nor Pitscottie admit that the apparition

could have been a human in ghostly garb, and neither conjecture what its speech actually meant. Most later writers supposed that the figure represented an apostle, though they disagree on which one. One guess is that he was supposed to be Saint James, the adopted brother of Jesus, on the basis that the figure mentions his mother, alluding to the Virgin Mary, though other sources suggest he represents either Saint John or Saint Andrew.[18] But whichever saint the actor was meant to be, the episode seems ill-conceived and under rehearsed, a rushed pantomime display, more pathetic than frightening. The tolerant king, who was safe in his certain dignity, could have simply shrugged it off.

But there is another possibility: that the king was fully involved in the episode, or that it was actually devised for his amusement. Perhaps the incident was actually a satirical, off the cuff sketch devised by his courtiers, mocking the suggestion there could be any heavenly protest at Scotland's right to go to war with England. In the light of the calamitous result of Flodden, it may have been misremembered by subsequent historians as a genuine portent of doom. It would not have been the first time a light hearted incident was distorted and seen through a glass darkly after it happened.

But if it was a seriously staged masquerade, we must return to examining Queen Margaret as the second major suspect behind it. She may have given her royal assent to the event even if she was not involved in the execution of it. As for motive, if Margaret was not concerned by war with England, she may have been motivated by plain jealousy. One focus of her envy was Anne of Brittany, Queen of France, who cynically appealed to James's chivalrous instincts by urging him to attack England for her sake. According to Pitscottie, Queen Anne wrote King James a love letter, stating that she had suffered much rebuke defending him, and that she was sure he would repay her by advancing with his army three feet into England. To ensure that this appeal to his chivalry was even more enticing, she sent him the large ring off her finger and fourteen thousand glittering French crowns.[19] Margaret was allegedly resentful of Anne, and taunted James with the fact that he would never meet her, attacking her for being twice-married, divorced and involved in a near incestuous relationship with the French monarch, Louis XII.[20] Another scheming woman whom Lindsay blames for making the monarch take his eye off the political ball was Lady Heron, the wicked lady of Ford Castle in Northumberland, with whom Pitscottie accuses James of indulging in fornication with immediately prior to the battle of Flodden.[21] The woman referred to in the ghostly speech may also have been one of the many mistresses or liaisons who took up so much of James's time. But by this late date the queen would surely have been inured against the run of the mill romantic dalliances of the king. Nevertheless, Margaret may still have been involved in the charade for her own, now unknown reasons, abetted by David Lindsay or others.

Subsequent historians have avoided fully analysing the Linlithgow incident. Closely following the accounts of Buchanan and Pitscottie, Drummond of Hawthornden and Ralph Holinshed state that the king calmly waited until evensong was over to look for the intruder, by which time there was obviously no sign of him.[22] Although James may have not wanted to interrupt the evening prayer service for the sake of a foolish protester it is unlikely there would have been no attempt whatever to apprehend him until later. As mentioned, the event is located by later writers near the porch in St Catherine's Aisle in the kirk.[23] This is the small southern transept of the church,[24] and a difficult place to make an escape from. A protestor causing a disturbance here would have soon been within arm's length of any attendant close to the king. The transept is on the opposite side of the church from the palace and the most direct route for any demonstrator to flee is across the south aisle, nave, north aisle and out of the door, now blocked up, which was the entrance used by the royal family coming to and from the palace. He would have had to make his way through a crowd of courtiers and cover the few intervening metres between kirk and royal residence. Local tradition, recorded in the 19th century, says that the mysterious man escaped by going through a curtain into an upper part of the building, from where he was seen leaving the kirk and entering Linlithgow Palace by a small door under the chapel window, and it was asserted that he was a servant of Queen Margaret.[25] Both this tradition and the historians' accounts of the incident leave a lot to be desired in terms of quality and quantity of information.

But parallels with the Linlithgow event can be found further afield. The theme of a king being warned about his impending death by an apostle is reminiscent of an incident involving Edward the Confessor, when he was cautioned of his coming death by a pilgrim who himself had the information from a vision of St John the Evangelist.[26] But the conspirators behind the St Michaels incident may have taken direct inspiration from a story presented in the *Scotichronicon* of the previous century. This book contains an episode which is said to have occurred after the second marriage of King Alexander III to Yolande of Dreux at Jedburgh Abbey in October 1285. At the wedding feast there was a procession of musicians before the guests, followed by a company of dancers. Then revellers noticed a mysterious form following the dancers, and it was impossible to say whether it was a man or an apparition. When the revellers noticed the unbidden, gliding figure, the music and dancing stopped, then the figure was seen no more.[27] Whether or not the intruder intentionally represented death, it prefigured Alexander's demise the following year and a period of national misery for Scotland. The event does not feature in the earlier, gossipy and notably anti-Scottish *Chronicle of Lanercost*, so it is appears to be a 15th century invention designed to heighten the sense that Alexander's reign was doomed by supernatural intervention.

Another story about a spectral apparition in a church occurs in a 13th century tale concerning the death of King William Rufus of England. The unpopular son of the Conquerer, Rufus met his death in an ill-fated shooting accident in the New Forest in 1100. His death was surrounded by mystery and prefigured by omens, including a dream in which he forsaw his own doom. One of his principal political opponents was Archbishop Anselm of Canterbury, who had been forced into exile in Europe. At the time of the king's death he was in Lyons where one of his retinue encountered a strange figure after matins. An unknown young man appeared in the lodgings of the English monks and addressed Brother Adam by name, saying that the dispute between Anselm and King William was now at an end. When the startled monk looked up at the figure, he found himself alone. The next evening another monk was chanting matins in the church when someone handed the listening archbishop a slip of paper which had written on it 'King William is dead'. The touch of the paper startled him and he opened his eyes and read the words, but when he looked up there was no one present. A short while later two monks came to him and reported that the king was dead and he was free to return to his see.[28]

Did the plotters behind the St Michael's incident think that the king's well known piety would predispose him to believe an extraordinary spectacle staged in a church? Any unusual event which took place in a religious setting could easily have been misconstrued or magnified into something mysterious or prophetic. One example of this is the English Observant monk named Peto who became incensed with King Henry VIII's marriage to Anne Boleyn and denounced him from the pulpit at Greenwich. Friar Peto quoted from the twenty- second chapter of the third *Book of Kings*: 'even where the dogs licked thy blood also, O king...take good heed lest, being seduced, you find Ahab's punishment, which was to have his blood licked up by dogs'. For his criticism of the king, Peto and an associate were exiled. When the English king died over a decade later, stray dogs allegedly licked the blood that dripped from the corrupt body of the monarch, fulfilment of Peto's supposed prediction.[29] Macabre coincidence turned Peto's biblical castigation into a prophecy darkly fulfilled.

The Linlithgow vision was recorded within a generation and probably had its root in some actual occurrence. Barring the suggestion that it was a misinterpreted prank by some courtier, it may be best seen as a fumbled attempt by persons unknown to give public voice to urgent concerns about the impending war. There may have been no other way of showing popular feeling about the matter as it was well known by this stage that King James was adamant about war with England and would accept no objections. The only facet of the demonstration that appears well planned is its timing, evening in a barely lit church being a point in the day when shadows are likely to distort and hide all sorts of things. The fact that the apparition was able to vanish like a will-o'-the-wisp suggests collusion with several members of the royal entourage. But the rather garbled speech given by the blue gowned man signifies that he either fluffed his lines or he gave insufficient thought to the contents of his speech.

The second public supernatural event happened soon after the Vision in the Kirk, this time in the heart of Edinburgh, after King James removed the heavy cannon named the Seven Sisters from the Castle and retired to Holyrood Abbey:

> there was a Cry heard at the Market-Cross of *Edinburgh*, at the Hour of Midnight, proclaiming as it had been a Summons, which was named and called by the Proclaimer thereof, *The Summons* of Plotock; which desired all Men, *To compear, both Earl and Lord, and Baron and Gentleman, and all honest Gentlemen within the Town* (every Man specified by his own Name) *to compear, within the Space of forty Days, before his Master, where it should happen him to appoint, and be for the Time, under the Pain of Disobedience*. But whether this Summons was

> proclaimed by vain Persons, Night-Walkers, or drunk Men, for their Pastime, or if it was but a Spirit, I cannot tell truly: But it was shewn to me, That an Indweller of the Town, Mr. *Richard Lawson*, being evil-disposed, ganging in his Galley-Stair foreanent the Cross, hearing this Voice, proclaiming this Summons, thought Marvel what it should be, cried on his Servant to bring him his Purse; and when he had brought him it, he took out a Crown, and cast over the Stair, saying, *I appeal from that Summons, Judgement and Sentence thereof, and takes me all whole in the Mercy of God, and* Christ Jesus *his Son*. Verily the Author of this, that caused me write the Manner of the Summons, was a landed Gentleman, who was, at that Time, twenty Years of Age, and was in the Town the Time of the said Summons; and thereafter, when the Field was stricken, he swore to me, there was no Man that escaped that was called in this Summons, but that one Man alone, which made his Protection, and appealed from the said Summons; but all the Lave were perished in the Field with the King.[30]

But James again disregarded the intervention of the unknown, which came to his attention because the whole town was electrified by this strange disturbance. He left Edinburgh Castle and joined his forces at the Burgh Muir, then marched with them to Esk Tower. Whoever sought to put the brakes on the king had misjudged their man. He was not someone who seriously heeded the words of witches and oracles, unlike his father, even though it was said he had a favourite seer, one 'Liddell the Prophet'. However there are no surviving records to show that Liddell was frequently consulted.[31] Ironically, beyond the supernatural threat, death was already secretly travelling with the Scottish host in the form of the plague, which the contingent from Edinburgh brought into the heart of the Scottish army.[32]

Richard Lowson, who heard this Summons of Pluto, was a member of the Lords of Council and twice provost of

Edinburgh (in 1492 and 1504), so theoretically he was a man of similar integrity to Sir David Lindsay. The suggestion that he was unwell when he heard the Summons gives the incident the quality of a fever dream. Lowson's cool and canny act of forestalling death with a payment of gold reads like an episode in a folk tale. But even Pitscottie is uncharacteristically reluctant to accept this incident as supernatural, preferring to blame it on drunks or disreputable tricksters. On a practical level it is impossible to believe that the orator would have time to name all those prospective combatants (or even just lairds, lords, and earls) he thought were present in the vicinity of Edinburgh. The speaker notably did not have the temerity to announce that the king himself was destined to die, showing a human regard for avoiding open treason. The act seems to be a mocking echo of the monarch's recent summoning of his army to the Burgh Muir, and even if there was a political element to it the speaker made sure he waited until dead of night and did not dare to make his identity known. The unnamed, landed gentleman aged twenty who told Pitscottie about this event may well again have been the young David Lindsay of the Mount. It is interesting to note that David Lindsay is recorded as acquiring a tenement property in the very vicinity where the event happened, Edinburgh High Street, in March 1513.[33]

The Mercat Cross, symbol of the ancient burgh, still stands in the High Street of Edinburgh, though it was shifted further up the street in the early 17th century when the small elaborate building supporting it was rebuilt. But the structure may be substantially the same; an ornate, arched building with a doorway and internal stair leading to a platform on which stood the column (the actual Mercat Cross), surmounted by the heraldic Scottish unicorn. It was a traditional place for making public announcements and a space for nobles to celebrate on public occasions. King James VI sat here in 1600 and listened to a sermon by a famous preacher. Anyone who called loudly from this platform in the still of night would have known their words would echo and resound through the closely packed wynds and closes of the old town. A mere gang of drunks, however, would have had difficulty reaching the platform as the internal stair was barred by a locked door. Perhaps some disaffected burgh official colluded with the supposedly supernatural speaker.[34]

The Summons of Pluto story suggests an atmosphere of a city under supernatural siege which resonates down the centuries, and it remains easy to imagine what dread the midnight proclamation engendered among the teeming inhabitants of the capital, whether they gave it credence or not. But the perpetrators of the stunt were playing a dangerous game, since the city authorities were noticeably on edge and had begun to control movement of people on the streets. On 25 August 1513 fruit sellers and others were forbidden to appear at the Mercat Cross and other places. Vagrants were banned from gathering at the city gates. The authorities also prevented unauthorised people from appearing in the town after nine at night. Undesirables discovered in the streets after dark were liable to be detained and brought before provost and bailies next day.[35] It was not just disorder or the spread of rumour which the town's officials feared, though deserters from the king's army may have been causing both. Movement had to be controlled because of an outbreak of plague, which was noted in the regulation which closed down the stalls of food sellers in the same month.[36] The mysterious announcement at the Cross was therefore an expression of the double headed fear of war and pestilence.

The Edinburgh incident received mixed attention from later historians. George Buchanan does not mention it at all, while Drummond of Hawthornden was sceptical. He emphasised the lack of effect the incident had on the supposedly romantic and credulous ruler: 'Nothing was the king moved by those advertisements, thinking them scenic pieces, acted by those who hated the French, and favoured the English faction: being so boldly and to the life personated, that they appealed and struck with fear ordinary and vulgar judgements, as tragic-comedies of the spirits...'[37]

But the dramatically occult nature of the episode made it a favourite, repeated without criticism by some writers, such as George Sinclair, in his supernatural compendium *Satan's Invisible World Discovered* (1685).[38] Pitscottie's 19th century editor Æneas Mackay shrewdly observed that 'Plutock' must have acquired a sound working knowledge of Scots Law, in which forty days was the standard time allowed to answer a summons.[39] The standard length of service which the king of Scots could demand that his subjects was also forty days; again linking the ghostly speech with the royal summons to war.[40]

The figure of Plutock, or Pluto, is equated with Satan, but in contemporary poetry he is often synonymous with the King of the Fairies, and as such he appears in Chaucer's *Marchand's Tale*, and later in William Dunbar's poem *The Goldyn Targe*, where he figures among other supernatural figures: 'Thare was Pluto, the elrich incubus, In cloke of grene'.[41] In the light of other legendary material, it may be closer to the mark to have the Scottish monarch and his subjects being summoned by the ruler of fairyland rather than being sent to eternal perdition. There was a later living tradition in the country that James was taken away to the half lit land of the fairies, rather than to hell as some of his more strident English enemies may have wished. The Mercat Cross incident was a protest dressed up in supernatural clothes, and it seems more likely to have been a spontaneous effusion of discontent rather than a staged event sponsored by an upper class anti-war party, like the spectacle in the kirk. But we will never know if the groups of conspirators from Linlithgow and Edinburgh overlapped. Whoever they were, they risked a great deal and failed to accomplish anything.

The sense that the huge human disaster of Flodden was inexplicable, or had been irreversibly fated by occult design, created a vacuum in which explanations had to be manufactured. Pitscottie's work, though full of invention and colour, is notably free of supernatural set pieces until it comes to these two spectacular incidents presaging national disaster. He leads up to his description of the battle of Flodden with a sequence of incidents showing earthly and otherworldly forces combining to curse the campaign against England. He sets the scene by emphasising the king's pensive and absorbed mood as he sat in St Michael's kirk. The concentrated melancholy and possible foreknowledge of death make the king's vigil a type of personal Gethsemane. The intensity of his melancholy in the church recalls that prolonged state of self-doubt and guilt which followed his father's death twenty-five years before. That time, the background for the king's intense soul searching was also in a church, the Chapel Royal at Stirling, and he was rescued from his dangerous introspection by the dean of the chapel, George Vaus, Bishop of Galloway.[42] The bishop counselled the king, and the idea for the penitential belt came either from James himself or from his confessor, Patrick Ranwick, Provincial and warden of the Stirling house of Franciscan Observants.[43] The mental isolation of the king before Flodden, which prompted the two pseudo-supernatural events, contrasts markedly with the fact that he was one of the most visible and accessible of all Scottish monarchs. The fact that the instigators felt they had to resort to outlandish demonstrations against the war shows how frighteningly unapproachable the king had become.

After entering England the Scottish forces attacked Norham and Etam Castles. But James met his match, according to Pitscottie, when he came to Ford Castle and encountered Lady Heron, who was determined not to let her home be destroyed and was also hoping to convince the king to set free her husband, Sir William Heron, who was a prisoner in Scotland. King James supposedly became instantly besotted with this woman, perhaps fulfilling the warning of the Vision in the Kirk at Linlithgow. Not only did this distraction drain the momentum of the Scottish forces, who were forced to stay there for nearly three weeks, but the lady then secretly went to the English camp at York and informed them about the Scottish army. Pitscottie uses this dubious tale to rouse himself into a furious temper about the king's slack morals where women were concerned. The story about a temptress – and moreover an *English* temptress, doubly deceitful because of her nationality and sex – playing on the fatal weakness of a distracted man was hackneyed even in Pitscottie's time. He heightens the sleaze level by stating that the king's illegitimate son, Alexander, Archbishop of St Andrews, disgraced himself sexually with Lady Ford's daughter. Unfortunately, several 19th century writers pointed out that there was no daughter at Ford Castle in King James's time.[44] Ford Castle was actually substantially damaged by the Scots, and King James had pertinent, personal reasons for attacking it. Lady Ford's husband was being held at Fastcastle in Scotland as a hostage for his lawless brother, known as the Bastard Heron. The latter was the murderer of a royal favourite, the Warden Sir Robert Kerr. It is likely that King James occupied Ford Castle in an act of revenge against the family.[45]

The days before the battle of Flodden on 9 September were filled with omens which should have shown King James that his cause went against the prevailing divine order. The English historian Ralph Holinshed stated that there were signs in the Scottish camp presaging disaster. When the king and his lords were discussing the order of battle a hare started among them and, despite having a thousand arrows loosed after it, escaped unharmed. The next day the king's tent was found to be marked with a blood coloured stain and the leather straps on his helmet had been gnawed away by mice.[46] Pitscottie has the stress of mounting tension causing the king to use the desperate tactic of going in disguise to spy upon the Scottish lords who were meeting to discuss the merits of military action.[47] The lords' spokesman was Patrick, Lord Lindsay of the Byres, Pitscottie's own grandfather. After he made himself known to the nobles, James asserted that he would fight against England that day despite them and threatened to hang Lindsay at his own gate. The anecdote seems obviously a family tradition of the Fife branch of the Lindsays.

The theme of King James in disguise echoes other folktales about his travelling the country in secret, sometimes on amorous adventures and sometimes with the aim of dispensing justice to wrongdoers. James allegedly issued another death threat before the battle, to his master gunner, Robert Borthwick, when the latter stated he wanted to open fire on the enemy as they crossed the Bridge of Till, which went against the king's chivalric sensibilities.[48] Another sign of his refusal by this stage to accept any advice to reconsider battle was the accusation of cowardice against the Earl of Angus, who urgently tried to dissuade the king from a pitched battle. The king scornfully accused Angus of being too old and not having the stomach for a fight, which led to the shattered nobleman withdrawing from the army, leaving his eldest son and a large detachment of Douglases to perish in the battle.[49]

These episodes of obsessive refusal to tolerate dissent during the last few weeks of his life led to the sense that the king could only be reached through supernatural intervention. His repeated determination to ignore pleas for reticence gives a picture of a hell-bent individual who deserved what was coming to him. The king's cruel single-mindedness stripped down his character to a dogmatic level. We hear that he scornfully rejected the advice of the saintly bishop William Elphinstone of Aberdeen not to go to war. The once compassionate king is accused of calling Elphinstone a senile old man.[50] As the hours ticked away towards extinction there is one well verified glimpse of him surrendering to the severe psychological stress which he must have faced before the engagement. It is contained in the contemporary English document known as The Trewe Encountre,[51] and relates how, in response to the Earl of Surrey's shrewd attempt to shift the Scottish force from a commanding position (a play perhaps on James's sense of fairness) on the day before the battle, the king rose to the implicit goading and rebuked the earl for daring to treat him as an equal. Furthermore, he accused the English commander of having recourse to 'some wichecrafte or sawcery' because of his insistence the two sides should meet only at Milfield or Flodden.[52] There is no explanation why he threw this bizarre accusation at the English herald Ruge Cross to carry back to his master, but it must have been received by his enemy as gratifying proof that the Scots king was in a disordered state of mind.[53]

The theme of portents among the Scottish army is strikingly evident in the Italian poem *La Rotta de Scocesi*, 'The Rout of the Scots'. This work is peppered with a huge array of prophetic warnings. Prior to the battle the setting sun appeared more red than had ever been before, and many soldiers saw in front of it a vision of three crowns above a cross. Again, it was said that an ominous wild hare ran madly through the crowded Scottish camp and could not be caught by chasing hounds; nor was it injured by any weapon flung at it. The hare was found by the king's pavilion, 'self slain'. A massive gathering of crows was witnessed in Scotland, causing terror in the cities with their noise. (No chronicler in Scotland noticed this phenomenon.) Also in Scotland, dogs howled at the doors for their missing masters. The Italian says there was a fiery comet seen in the heavens a few days before the battle, and astrologers warned the Scottish king beware. For good measure, the poem gives us a visionary dream the king had the night before the battle. He dreamed of a fight between a hedgehog and a leopard, and the latter beast tore his own flesh. It was so vivid that the pain awoke him. Then he mounted his horse, but was confronted by a weasel, an animal associated with doom.[54]

The anonymous Italian author is avowedly anti-Scottish and

based his work on distorted second hand English propaganda about the battle. Some of the omens, such as the incident with the hare, later used by Holinshed, appear to be a genuine folklore, but much else in the poem is strained invention. False reports about the king and the outcome of the battle were soon circulating in Italy, and these also fed into the composition of the poem. But the theory that geographical distance alone gave rise to tall tales is belied by some of the strange things which were soon being believed in Scotland about the king.

With this weight of legendary material heaped upon the king in his last few days his actions and motives are hard to untangle. Even historians in supposedly more sober times have been tempted to employ supernatural doom. The Victorian writer Cadwallader J. Bates, for instance, saw in the Scottish battle formation the shape of the nine of diamonds, a card notoriously known as the 'Curse of Scotland'.[55] One elusive story about this curse says that the king was playing cards before the battle and wasted so much time searching for a missing card, the nine of diamonds, that he overlooked important military preparations. Whatever the truth in the sequence of events that led up to the battle of Flodden, the ferocity of its conclusion and aftermath, the unexpectedness of its result ensured that the king who died lived on in more ways than one.

Chapter 3

A Diversity of Death

On 11 August 1513 an officer of the Scottish Crown prepared himself for one of the most onerous duties ever performed by a public servant at home or abroad. Sir William Cumyng of Inverallochy was the highest heraldic officer of the realm, Lord Lyon King of Arms, and had journeyed from Scotland to the camp of the English army who had been besieging the town of Thérouanne in north-east France for the past week. His mission was to deliver an ultimatum from King James IV to King Henry VIII. Cumyng had left Scotland on 26 July 1513 with the ill-fated Scottish fleet commanded by the Earl of Arran, and his arrival in the English camp coincided with foul weather which must have dampened his spirits and besmirched his splendid heraldic uniform.[1]

The letter he carried contained a list of grievances that King James had against Henry VIII and a threat to invade England. Sir William's duty obliged him to remain resolute and unshrinking under the fierce eye of Henry VIII, then at the supreme height of his physical powers at the age of twenty-two. Cumyng was led into the magnificent royal tent by his English equivalent, Lord Garter King of Arms, Thomas Wriothesley, and informed the king about his mission. The English king was formally chastised for molesting the territories of Scotland's allies, the Duke of Guelders and the King of France. He had besieged the town of Thérouanne for two months without success, though he had caused the French king to withdraw his forces from Milan.

One source portrays King Henry, barely containing his rage, listening to the Scot with his hand twitching on his sword, enough to make any mortal quake.[2] With his hand still on his weapon, King Henry asked, after the Lord Lyon's first few sentences, 'Have ye now your tale at an end?'

'Nay,' said the Lord Lyon.

'Say forth then,' said the king.

'Sir,' said Cumyng, 'he summoneth your Grace to be at home in your realm in the defence of his ally.'

The king said that he had delivered his message well, but it did not become a king of Scots to dare summon a king of England. He had well prepared for the possible invasion of King James and his army. Then he wished that King James would have remembered his family ties with himself rather than the alliance with France, and hinted darkly that his sister had been mistreated in Scotland, which Cumyng refuted.[3]

Further charges against Henry in the letter included grievances closer to home. He had withheld the inheritance due to his sister Margaret from their father Henry VII. Another complaint was the death of the Scottish sea captain Andrew Barton, whom the English regarded as a pirate, slain by English sailors in 1511. Most grievously, according to the Scots, was the murder of one of their Wardens of the Marches, Andrew Kerr, by three men, led by the lawless English borderer, John Heron, known as the Bastard Heron, in 1508. One clause in the Scottish-English treaty of 1502 stipulated that the murderer of any Scot in the borders had to be sought by the English Warden and handed over to the Scots, if found guilty.[4] The unpunished assassination of the Scottish official was regarded as a serious diplomatic incident.

English and Scottish commissioners had been due to meet on the border in June 1513 to discuss Scottish grievances. But the English ambassador Dr West had infuriated the Scots by postponing the meeting until 25 October. King James considered he had no alternative than to address his concerns directly to the English king. The English considered that the Scottish complaints were mere pretexts to support the French and treacherously invade while their king and army were overseas.

Cumyng reportedly performed his duty well, though with

few words, subdued by the presence of the potent monarch,[5] and perhaps his background as a douce Aberdeenshire nobleman helped to keep him resolute. In fact, the few details we know about Cumyng suggest that he was a stout defender of his office who suffered more than his fair share in the line of duty. While on a mission to France to persuade the Duke of Albany to come to Scotland and assume the role of governor during James V's infancy, he was shipwrecked, much to the delight of English officials.[6] Later in his tenure as Lord Lyon he was caught up in the tumult of a country without an adult king. Some time after the battle of Flodden, when he was on his way to deliver important information to the English authorities, he was captured at Coldstream on the Scottish border by the renegade Lord Home and held as a hostage until the Duke of Albany agreed to release Home's mother who was imprisoned in Dunbar Castle.[7] Another notorious diplomatic incident involved him being physically assaulted by the aged Lord Drummond, in the presence of Drummond's grandson the Earl of Angus and his wife, Queen Margaret Tudor.[8] The Lord Lyon was in this instance on official business of the governor, the Duke of Albany, summoning Angus to appear before the Council, and the assault was properly considered treason, albeit that Drummond was acting in defence of Margaret whom Cumyng pointedly referred to as 'My Lady the King's Mother' instead of her previous, more superior royal designation of 'the Queen's Grace'. Drummond was imprisoned, stripped of his estates, and was lucky not to lose his life. If official dignitaries sought a role model for fortitude they could do worse than adopt Cumyng, who stands as one of Scotland's unsung heroes.

However angered the king of England was by the audacity of James IV's letter, he may well have welcomed the break from the mundane life of his campaign in France. Since landing at Calais at the end of June the English army had not covered itself in glory. The town of Thérouanne held out against the English and even when it eventually surrendered it was hardly a glittering prize. Still, King Henry angrily refuted the charges the Lord Lyon brought before him. He was the very owner of Scotland and King James held it only by homage to him. The herald declared that he could not take back the furious message to his master as he had received it and Henry bellowed at him the question of what he was doing there if he would not carry back a response? The herald had to digest the monarch's 'sour and proud wordes', according to the Scottish historian John Lesley.[9] Henry lambasted James for his audacity of daring to challenge the conduct of an English monarch and trying to summon him home out of France.[10] But the king may have been impressed by the messenger's ability to withstand his wrath. While he was composing the written response he asked Garter to entertain the Scottish herald well, for Cumyng was understandably 'sore appalled' after his ordeal.[11] King Henry's bluster may have been exaggerated to impress the Holy Roman Emperor Maximilian I who met the king the same day and was doubtless keenly following the proceedings. Maximilian and his retinue were sombrely dressed in black, in mourning for the recently deceased empress. He was soon, symbolically and somewhat bizarrely, dressed in the cross of St George to show that he was a soldier serving under the campaigning English king.[12]

Cumyng departed the following day, with a reward of a hundred angels for representing his king well.[13] He hurried to the coast of Flanders, but could find no ship to take him back to Scotland, and he was not to return home for some time.[14] The absence of the English monarch and key figures in his court from England undoubtedly contributed to the confusion which has filtered down to us about the battle of Flodden and its aftermath. The uncertainty was evident in the English camp. When Henry wrote to the Duke of Milan, Massimiliano Sforza, on 16 September, he gave him news of the overwhelming English victory at Flodden, but said there was no news as yet about the fate of the Scottish king. On that day the Italian Paulo da Laude heard from the English ambassador at Tournai that the English had indeed defeated the Scots in battle, but the Scottish king could not be found alive or dead.[15] But fresh news arrived in the English camp that day (probably from Catherine of Aragon's messenger John Glynn).[16] A further messenger from England arrived on the 21 September to confirm events.[17] Henry's letter to the Duke of Milan has a postscript stating that the body of James had now been found and taken to the nearest church, which would have been in the village of Branxton.[18]

Rumours about the outcome of the battle were already spreading throughout Europe, transmitted by opposing partisans of the French (and Scots) and the English. Henry himself was spreading word by 19 September that his queen had told him that King James's body was found among the dead, still wearing its iron gauntlets, and these had been sent on to him.[19] Even before the battle had been fought, word reached the French court at Amiens, purportedly from a Scottish messenger, that the English had been crushed in battle and that the Earl of Surrey and fifteen of his chief men had been captured.[20] Some of the English on the continent, ignorant of the fact that the Scottish king was dead, were loudly promising to disinherit James IV for his 'bad behaviour'.[21] The person who reported this quickly bored of the subject, as if it was an inconsequential matter from a far off place he was already sick of hearing about. He heard that the adventure of the Scots against England was dissipating like smoke, and he was glad of it.[22]

But the propaganda war was generating outlandish, feverish rumours. One of the most remarkable whispers is infuriatingly brief. Two Milanese ambassadors wrote from Rome to the Duke of Milan on 16 October that the English army was still at Tournai (where they had moved on to from Thérouanne), and that a Scottish merchant newly arrived in France had reported that the king of Scots was still alive and he had actually spoken to him.[23]

The identity of this itinerant Scot is unknown, nor can anyone say whether he encountered the true king, a fake, or none at all. In Rome the English Cardinal Bainbridge and Alberto de Carpi, the Imperial ambassador, with the Spanish ambassador and four other cardinals, sang high mass in the Augustinian church of Santa Maria del Popolo and let off guns to celebrate the English victory, but the pope insisted there was no reliable news.[24] Cardinal Bainbridge was irritated by the grandiosity of enemy claims. The French ambassador at Rome was boasting that 100,000 Scots had invaded England; Surrey and fifteen lords had been captured and a full 30,000 Englishmen slain. French and Scots in the city were sought out for news, but when letters from Henry arrived their joy was turned to shame.[25] Yet the continuing rumours of English defeat seem to have affected the Cardinal, since the Englishman Brian Tuke accused his countryman Richard Pace and his employer, Cardinal Bainbridge, of casting doubt on the English success. He blamed Pace for listening to the version of events being peddled by the French and their associates.[26] False reports of a Scottish victory continued for some time, but when the truth was reasonably certain Bainbridge and four other cardinals, together with the ambassadors of Spain, Milan and the Emperor Maximilian lit celebratory bonfires in Rome.[27]

After Catherine wrote to Henry he considered the fate of his enemy's physical remains. A lukewarm attempt was made by the English king to have the body of James IV properly interred, but though permission was granted by the pope the burial probably never happened. Henry lost interest in the matter and the corpse languished in a monastery in Surrey.[28] While the body of the defeated monarch was being moved, then temporarily laid aside and finally forgotten, rumours about him and the battle of Flodden still circulated around Europe. The most interesting class of tale about James is that which said he had not perished on the field of Flodden. Perhaps the genesis of the more elaborate, later tales that James survived for a considerable time after 9 September, the initial scraps of story insist that he was taken prisoner. This story was certainly being traded among the English and their allies at the siege of Tournai, for on 20 September the Imperial agent James Bannisius wrote to Lord Albert of Carpi stating that King James had been captured alive, but died of his wounds one hour later.[29]

There was continued doubt about the Scottish king in the English camp in France. A prominent member probably among that contingent in France was the poet John Skelton, who immediately composed a biting, celebratory ballad on the death of England's enemy, *A ballade of the scottysshe Kynge*.[30] This poem, of course, must have been composed after news of the battle filtered across the English Channel, but before definite news of the outcome and James's fate became definitely known, possibly around 16 September. It was definitely written before 22 September when Skelton's significantly different Latin verse *Choris de Dys contra Scottos* was performed during ceremonies celebrating the seige of Thérouanne.[31] On that date the singers of the Chapel Royal sang in a cloth-of-gold tent to celebrate the English victory. There was, besides Skelton's savage poetry, a Te Deum and a sermon by John Fisher, Bishop of Rochester, thanking God for his righteous judgement. The red lion of Scotland had been vanquished by the white lion of the Earl of Surrey.[32]

Skelton's original poem included the rumour that King James had been taken prisoner and transported to Norham:

> For to the castell of Norham
> I understode to soone ye cam,
> For a prysoner there now ye be
> Eyther to the devyll or the trinite.[33]

Skelton later revised his poem as 'Against the Scottes', and shows that he now knew more information like the name of Branxton Moor and details about the fate of James and his body.[34] Skelton also railed against those who were spreading rumours that England had been defeated at Flodden, and sought to cover up his own earlier error about the possibly survival and imprisonment of King James by launching a vituperative tirade against the Scots who claimed to have won the day and the current falsehood that the king was alive:

They say they had
And wan the felde
With spere and shelde!
That is as trew
As blacke is blew
And grene is gray.
What euer they say,
Jemmy is ded
And closed in led,
That was theyr owne kynge.
Fy on that wynnynge![35]

At the French court the concern about the fate of King James was exacerbated by the effect a defeat would have on France's position against England and its allies. In Amiens on 4 October, the gout ridden and anxious King Louis XII wrote a letter to an unknown person, displaying disquiet about conflicting news. He decided to send an agent, who had previously travelled to Scotland for the king's famous tournaments and been a guest at the king's wedding, to discover the truth. This man was the renowned *Chevalier Blanc*, the 'White Knight', so-called from his flamboyant armour or his white clothing. His real name was Antoine d'Arces, lord of la Bastie-sur-Melan in Dauphiné. No stranger to diplomacy, he had acted as James's envoy to the French king in 1508.[36] But though he did not find the lost king in Scotland he remained in the country and became a deputy of the Duke of Albany, and eventually met his death there. With the 'White Knight' the French king sent the Lord Lyon King of Arms. Cumyng, having failed to find a ship back home, made his way to the French court at Amiens, some 81 km (nearly 50 miles) distant from Thérouanne. The French authorities had heard from some source that King James was not dead, but that he had certainly escaped the battle.[37]

Another letter from King Louis displays either genuine mourning about the likely death of his ally, or a carefully constructed conceit disguised as an expression of regret. He expresses fulsome sorrow about the death of James IV, whom he loved deeply, and he will never forget the fact that he physically fought for him against the English. Furthermore, because he has no certain news and it is being said the king is still alive, he is sending to the Queen and the Great Council and Estates to find out the condition of the country and king. The admission of uncertainty may have been designed to delay offering real aid to a stricken Scotland.[38] But later in that month James IV's fate was still not confirmed; it was gravely noted that the truth about the fate of the Scottish king was unknown. News had been received at court that the Scottish king was dead, but an unnamed ambassador from Scotland (who must have been Bishop Andrew Forman), insisted that he was still alive, despite contrary evidence.[39] But the mission of the *Chevalier Blanc* was also more pragmatic. The 'White Knight' was carrying letters from John, Duke of Albany, a relative of King James IV, expressing concern about the state of Scotland. And soon afterwards Albany was invited to go to Scotland as governor during the perilous minority of the infant king, James V.[40]

Cumyng and d'Arces sailed back to Scotland with James Hamilton, 1st Earl of Arran. Arran had luckily avoided the carnage of Flodden, though his career at sea had hardly been glorious. On his way with the Scottish fleet to France he had taken a detour to bombard the hapless town of Carrickfergus.

Whether or not this incident was sanctioned by the Scottish king, it was an essentially meaningless military action. There was a story that he was about to be relieved of command just as he was setting off from the west coast of Scotland. His due replacement as admiral was Archibald Douglas, the 5th Earl of Angus, though the furious king and the earl arrived at port just too late to catch the ships before they departed.[41] This anecdote however has been doubted by at least one modern authority.[42]

One wonders about the atmosphere on board the ship which went back from France to Scotland. Whatever uncertainty was admitted about the fate of their king, rumours about the battle of Flodden must have deeply affected the Scots. Cumyng, the Lord Lyon, may still have been smarting from his ordeal in front of King Henry VIII and he was probably anxious to carry the English king's response back to the Scottish authorities. Arran may have been reflecting on his failure as a naval hero, or perhaps thankful that he had avoided a battlefield death in Northumberland. He may also have been wary of the intentions of the French knight, especially if he was aware that D'Arces was carrying messages from the Duke of Albany. Should the son of James IV die, Albany was next in line of succession, and the next in line after him was Arran himself, as a grandson of King James II. Three fine Scottish ships were left behind in France: the *James*, the *Margaret* and the pride of the Scottish fleet, the *Michael*. The French wanted the extra vessels to fight the English navy, though the encounter never took place and the *Great Michael* was sold to France in April 1514.[43] The ordinary Scottish mariners were thankful to be heading home. Lord Dacre heard later that the returning sailors had complained about their ill-treatment from their French allies.[44] The three men landed in the west of Scotland on 3 November, and once he had recovered from the journey, the Frenchman went to Perth to give communications from Albany to the queen and the Scottish authorities.[45] Despite confusion in France, the reality of the king's fate had now set in for the government of Scotland, who had to deal with reality and not wishful thinking. At a meeting of the Lords of Council on 19 September 1513 the discussion included arrangements for the coronation of the new king, James V, *de facto* recognition that the previous king was dead.[46]

As King Henry VIII prepared to end his continental adventure, frustrated in his hope of martial glory by the perfidy of his allies, the stories about his dead rival reached a tipping point and passed from being mere hearsay. The shade of King James entered the realm of legend, where it was destined to stay. Louis XII's consort – herself soon to be dead – heard that it was not actually King James IV who had died at Flodden, but a 'natural brother' of his who wore identical clothing. This fable found its way to Rome, where Venetian Ambassador Lando communicated it back to Venice.[47] This story of a royal bastard being mistaken for the real king is unique, and there is no clue who this alleged son of King James III was. Perhaps it originated in confusion with James IV's own twenty-year-old illegitimate son, James Stewart, Archbishop of St Andrews, who died on the battlefield. But the element of someone else wearing the royal's clothes and being mistaken for him in death re-occurs in some Scottish versions of King James's survival, recorded a generation later, and show that the Scottish historians were using material that was already circulating in the public domain in 1514.

There was little hope that those on the European mainland could have easily gained a true sense of what happened at Flodden, for the events were confused and the result may have gone against expectation. Working back from the later whispers about the outcome of the battle to the actual facts, it is clear that the Scots had all the advantages: superior numbers, up to date artillery, a strong defensible position and a young agile commander fighting in the front ranks, as opposed to 'an old crooked Caril lying in a Chariot', as the Earl of Lindsay memorably dubbed the septuagenarian Earl of Surrey.[48] Despite the later insistence of folklore, the gods of probability were with the invaders up to the point late on the afternoon of 9 September when the two forces met. The Scots were forced to move to the ridge of Branxton Hill when the English manoeuvred around to their north, between James and Scotland. Even then, their position was strong, and it was only when the English artillery began ripping holes in the Scottish ranks, in response to rather more ineffective Scottish cannon fire, that the Scots moved downhill and the pendulum began to swing the other way.

Although the Scots advanced in good order, going downhill in strictly observed and menacing silence, their steady march was also a metaphorical descent into chaos. James was following what he thought was the most advanced method of field warfare, a Swiss and German mercenary technique which had been deployed to devastating effect in continental Europe. But the unwieldy Scottish pikes became deadly encumbrances when the troops reached the muddy terrain at the bottom of the slope and could not cross a shallow brook. The boggy ground conditions conspired with unsuitable weaponry created an instant killing zone for the Scots.[49] James, in the front row of his men, ensured himself immortality by his very presence there, the last Scottish monarch to advance at the head of his army into the thick of battle. Since he and other commanders fought on foot, there was no one to marshal the army when the front ranks were engulfed. But his bravery was lauded even by the English historian Edward Hall: 'O what a noble and triumphant courage was thys for a kynge to fyghte in a battayl as a meane souldier.'[50] Henry in France may have indulged himself with meaningless sieges of unimportant towns, and at home participated in jousts with hollowed lances, but he never personally led any fighting force into action in a real battle.

The killing process of the battle itself was anything but romantic at close quarters; nor did the participants show particular 'deference to the rules of chivalrous combat', as one

Victorian fondly supposed.[51] Some of the contingents from northern England were conspicuously ineffective. Although the expensive and impressive Scottish artillery blustered and roared ineffectively over the heads of the Englishmen below, the men of Cheshire and Lancashire were terrified and ran away.[52] When King Henry read of this conduct in a letter from Sir Edmund Howard, it caused him 'greate harte burning and manye woordes'.[53] The men of Bamboroughshire and Tynemouth also fled, according to the English commander Thomas, 2nd Lord Dacre.[54] The legend-making process, even among the victorious side, would soon rewrite events after the initial confusion had cleared. The English would compose poems of victory, but the distraught Scots would have recourse to darker tales.

Alexander, 3rd Lord Home, Chamberlain of Scotland and Warden of the Marches, was in command (along with the Earl of Huntly) of the only successful Scottish division in action that day. When they overcame, or at least halted their opposite numbers, some including Huntly expected them to go to the aid of the central part of the Scottish army, where King James was in trouble. But a popular and soon widespread slander said that Lord Home flatly refused to go to the aid of his monarch.[55] Another bit of battlefield gossip damned him further by saying that he did precious little to rescue the costly Scottish guns after the fighting.[56] In all though, some borderers on either side are alleged to have done little to put national interests above their own habitual concerns, which may be part of a pattern of blame and recrimination woven by commentators after the encounter.

After Home's men were checked by the English Warden, Lord Dacre, with 1,500 horsemen, some men from the Home-Huntly division apparently left off the business of fighting the enemy for the more enjoyable pursuit of plundering the dead. Later in the battle a group of English troops robbed the Scottish dead, allegedly including that of the major nobles and King James. One party of English borderers raided the Scottish camp after the battle.[57] They cut the throats of the non-combatants they found there and stole their gear.[58] Not to be outdone, another group of English borderers allegedly pillaged their own camp, rifling the tents, stealing horses and oxen, though Bishop Ruthall of Durham found hard facts about the guilty party hard to come by.[59] In his second letter to Wolsey, written on 20 September 1513, Ruthall heartily wished that these borderers were on active duty in France rather than at home, where they were more of a menace than the Scots. He stated that they did not even alight from their horses when the battle began, but immediately started 'ryfelyng and robbyng as welle on our side as of the Scottes' and even gave over English prisoners to the Scots for money.[60]

Some of the beaten Scots became crazed by defeat and are alleged to have murdered the French soldiers who comprised part of their army, blaming them for the heavy loss, though this may have been a malicious English rumour.[61] A fair share of the French troops fighting alongside the Scots died in the disaster, including their ambassador Jehan de la Motte.[62] Recriminations were also quickly meted out by Scots on their own countrymen. Returning Scottish borderers wasted English lands until they found their own realm, where they earned instant hostility for their alleged cowardice at their supposed inaction.[63] Overzealous English troops who pursued Scots into Scotland were taken prisoner.

One cause for the appalling Scottish death toll is that the Scots on their side fought so sternly and unyieldingly that, unlike in most battles, it was reported that many of the English would not take any prisoners when they had the chance, even though great sums of money were offered by stricken individuals.[64] Bishop Ruthall of Durham reported clinical details of swift butchery. King, nobles, bishops, commoners were no sooner killed than plundered and stripped naked, though he estimated that as many as 400 - 500 Scots were captured.[65] Another reason for the fact that no quarter was given was that the Earl of Surrey resented that James's invasion had deprived him of the chance to accompany his king and his army to France.[66] James was intent on provoking his opponent and goaded the earl beyond the limits of his patience by saying that he had long sought his son, Lord Admiral Thomas Howard, by land and sea, as one who had always avoided battle.[67] Surrey was, by the standards of the time, an old man, anxious to prove himself to his king. His animosity was transmitted through the English ranks. As long ago as 1497, during the Scottish campaign in England, the two men had clashed. King James, in a headstrong gesture, had offered to fight Thomas, Earl of Surrey, in single combat, with the victor taking the prize of the town of Berwick, recently lost to the English.[68] There was a personal animosity at play which contributed to the English earl's refusal to take prisoners. He was rankled by insults carefully delivered by the Scottish king.

The uncertainty about the fate of King James, which gave rise to various reports about his fate, was a product of the overwhelming chaos that reigned on the field. Unfortunately, no contemporary Scottish account of the battle survives, but even the English sources contradict each other about the number of enemy soldiers killed. Most figures obviously exaggerate the number of dead Scots, with perhaps the highest number given out by English propaganda as 17,000, on the memorial of the Duke of Norfolk, as Surrey was created on 1st February 1514.[69] Extravagant figures of 20,000 and even more for the Scottish death toll circulated in Italy soon after the battle, going hand in hand with wild rumours.[70] Most English contemporary sources settle for an estimate of enemy mortality of between 10,000 and 15,000, with Henry VIII stating in a letter to Pope Leo X that over 13,000 enemy soldiers had died that day.[71] Naturally, Scottish sources settle for a lower estimate. Buchanan states that the number of Scottish dead was 'above 5000', basing his information interestingly on parish lists, and he claims that nearly an equal number of English died.[72] Bishop John Lesley flies in the face of rationality by asserting that a greater number of Englishmen than Scotsmen died that day.[73] His opinion, recorded over a generation later, was a wishful delusion shared by other Scots, another symptom of a nation in denial of the truth.[74]

Nobody knew the fate of many of the participants, including the king of Scots, nor the numbers of the slain on either side. Even when it became apparent that the English had won decisively and that the top tier of Scottish society had been almost surgically removed in one military sweep, the exact manner and location of the king's death was unclear. The 'official record' of the manner of King James's death, his wounds, the location of the corpse, who found and identified it, and what happened to it immediately, are not as clear cut as has been supposed. The *Trewe Encountre,* interestingly, makes no mention whatever about the death of the king or the finding of his corpse.[75]

King James's final minutes were spent grimly attempting to reach and slaughter the Earl of Surrey, for the contemporary account of the battle, written by Surrey's son, affirms that his body was found within a mere lance's length of Surrey. The only further detail given about the king is that his remains were taken to Berwick.[76] The heroic proximity to his sworn enemy need not be doubted since it is contained in a terse pragmatic document that certainly had no interest in glorifying his actions. But the king's undoubted martial ferocity was elaborated on later. The Italian poem *La Rotta de Scocesi* has James killing five men with his lance before it shattered in his hand. He then fought on recklessly with his sword before he was cut down by the deadly English bills. Among his last victims was supposed to be one Richard Harbottle. But the work is uncharacteristically coy about the exact circumstances of James's demise.[77] Later sentimental Scottish writers had the king being found surrounded, pathetically, by a circle of slain noblemen who had tried at their last to defend his person. The romantic notice of this living circle defending the monarch was popularised in Walter Scott's poem

Marmion, though it was mentioned by earlier writers.[78] In these desperate last moments King James was perhaps mindful that retreat was personally impossible for him. His own father had been advised by his nobles at Sauchieburn to remove himself to safety while they did the fighting for him. The result of his flight was that King James III flew directly to his own destruction at the hands of an unknown assassin.

Returning to more contemporary sources, the Bishop of Durham, who was not present but was well informed about the battle, wrote soon afterwards to Wolsey that the English captured the Scottish king's banner and that the king, with other nobles and commoners, was stripped naked by looting English soldiers, and that he suffered many wounds.[79] The circumstance of pillaging is reiterated by another reliable source which states they were in fact Sir Edward Stanley's brigade, who gave off pursuing fleeing Scots when they came across enemy soldiers slain already by Surrey's troops. This writer says that some stated Stanley's men had killed James, but he refuted it. The looters did not recognise the king, but they despoiled his remains among the others and found a cross belonging to him and certain other things.[80]

One difficulty in recognising the royal corpse was caused by the assertion that he purposely dismounted and discarded some or all of his distinguishing royal apparel. The king's apparently suicidal decision to go into battle on foot in the front ranks has been given various explanations. One story says that when he saw the left wing of his army under Argyll and Lennox being scattered, he dismounted from his horse to continue fighting more effectively on foot. Seeing that the son of the Earl of Angus, George Douglas, Master of Angus, was still mounted, the king taunted him by asking if it was the fashion of his ancestors to fight on horseback when their prince was on foot. Stung by the rebuke, Douglas dismounted, but said that neither was it formerly the fashion for kings to fight in coat armour or on foot.

King James angrily threw off his coat of mail and cognisance and answered, that he would fight on foot as well as Douglas or any other man, and also without his royal armour and badges.[81]

Otherwise the king's decision to fight on foot may have been partly motivated by a challenge given to him by his opponent the Surrey's son, Lord Thomas Howard, who was responding to James's own taunt of cowardice. Howard communicated to the king that he would lead the vanguard of his army on foot so there could be no charge of cowardice against him.[82] Another more prosaic account says that the Scots chose to dismount because this meant they could not avail themselves of their horses if they felt the urge to run away. Not only did they dispense with their horses, but they also cast aside their footwear.[83] An even more banal explanation was that the slope was slippery and they could only safely descend it in bare feet.[84]

The likely fact of the king being naked and disfigured among his other dead countrymen argues against easy identification. According to MS. Batayle, the most prominent injuries noticed on the body were one caused by an arrow and another caused by a bill.[85] Further details of his injuries are given elsewhere: his neck was widely opened with a wound, his left hand almost severed in two places, and the body pierced by many arrows.[86] The suggestion that James was finally dispatched by a fatal arrow through the mouth is a misinterpretation of the heraldic motif which augmented the arms awarded to the Duke of Norfolk, as Surrey was created soon after the victory: the royal arms of Scotland with the lion pierced through the mouth by an arrow.[87] One Italian source went literally to the other extreme and claimed that the king was killed by a wound in his posterior, which is surely the result of a scurrilous joke evolving into a devoutly believed rumour.[88] There were later claims that pieces of the king's surcoat, as well as his riding harness, sword and dagger were recovered, but this does not tally well with the record with the whole scale scavenging of the English troops.

If the common mob did indeed strip James naked, how could prominent individuals later claim to have ghoulish mementoes of him? One of the major Scottish doubts about the English having found the correct body was that the corpse did not have his perennial iron chain wrapped around it. If this iconic item was laid down before the fight it was never again discovered.

The most fluid account of the initial post-mortem fate of King James IV was written later by Edward Hall, utilising contemporary sources.[89] In the immediate aftermath of the fighting, Hall wrote, neither the victors nor the few Scots who had been captured knew the fate of James, but it was thought he had been taken or captured. The reason there was trouble finding the body was that the English and Scottish dead had been stripped by looters. It was not until the next day that Thomas, Lord Dacre – a man who knew James well by sight – discovered and identified him 'by his pryvye tokens'.[90] The claim was based on Dacre's own statement. The Cumbrian Lord Dacre of the North was familiar with the Scottish king and his queen. He was also one of the English entourage who negotiated the marriage of Princess Margaret Tudor to the King of Scots. And he had been one of the honoured guests at the oddly spectral betrothal ceremony of James IV (who was not present) to Princess Margaret Tudor at Richmond (or Sheen) Palace.[91] Later, in 1504, he joined James IV in person during an expedition to punish outlaws on the borders, an event called the 'Raid of Eskdale', while more recently in 1513 he was in Edinburgh with the English ambassador Dr West attempting to forestall war with Scotland.[92] After Flodden he caused mayhem ravaging the Scottish border in repeated raids, and he became a sinister sponsor of his former enemy Lord Home, who was also intimately tied up in the legends surrounding the king. It is claimed that Dacre gave the body over to the victor, the Earl of Surrey.

So far, so plausible, and other pieces of contemporary

information confirm this broad sequence of events. But Lord Dacre was regarded by some Englishmen as being duplicitous. Rumours of his dubious loyalty surfaced very quickly after Flodden. Recognising this as early as September 1513, Dacre wrote a letter to Bishop Ruthall of Durham in which he said that he was averse to divulging his mind to anyone else. He acknowledged that he was being slandered by the lords and gentlemen who had been on the battlefield and blamed this on jealousy, because he had been allowed into the councils of the Earl of Surrey and his son. Another reason for the discontent of others with him was that he was supporting the 'coming up' of the Scottish prisoner Sir John Forman, sergeant porter of the king. Dacre says he was doing so because it would annoy Forman's brother, the Bishop of Moray, and there was obviously some ill family feeling among the Formans that he was keen to exploit.[93] But the fact that Forman was Dacre's man and helped to identify the king's body casts some doubt on that identification.

The other Scottish prisoner to identify the body was the scholarly Sir William Scott of Balwearie, a counsellor to the king.[94] Both men are reported to have recognised the king and made great lamentation.[95] But Scott too was co-operating with the English at this stage by providing them with slanderous information about the unpopular Bishop of Moray.[96] So there is a suspicion that neither of these witnesses could be classified as entirely trustworthy. On the other hand, Bishop Forman's bad reputation among upper class Scots at the time means that his opinion of him as stated to his captors was hardly treacherous. Scott eventually had to sell off some of his lands in Fife to ransom himself. Back home in Scotland he had a distinguished career in public service and died in 1523.

Lord Dacre himself committed an account of his part in the matter in a long defensive letter sent to the Lords of Council dated 17 May 1514.[97] Dacre was still fighting a rearguard action against rumours of treachery and collusion with the Scots. He reminded his readers that he had taken on the onerous burden of Warden of the Middle and East Marches on condition that no one should believe malicious reports of him until he was able to make answer. There had been some talk that he was conspiring with the Scottish Chamberlain, Lord Home, but he said he had met him only once and then on official business. He pointed out that he personally faced the division led by Home and Huntly on the field of Branxton, and named the prominent Scots slain by his men. As further proof that he and his men did indeed fight bravely, he related that his own brother, Philip Dacre, was taken prisoner by the Scots.

It is only after all this careful self-justification that he claims that he found the dead king of Scots on the field. Even if his claim is true, it has to be taken as part of his attempt to raise his reputation above the negative speculation that was circulating about him. He maintained that he fought manfully on 9 September and boasted that he recovered the king's corpse, strangely adding that no other man had been capable of finding it. For that reason he plaintively stated that the Scots 'love me worst of any Inglisheman living, be reason that I fande the body of the King of Scotts, slayne in the felde'. It seems slightly outlandish that a supremely effective and violent pragmatist like Dacre should portray himself as being stung by the ill-feeling of the enemy Scots.

On the day after the battle he had written a letter to Surrey telling him of the discovery, then triumphantly brought the body to him at Berwick. A cynical conspiracist might think his claim to have found the king's body was a useful piece of self-promoting propaganda. The fact that Dacre did indeed soon conspire with Home, albeit for his own country's advantage, and that he had a network of spies in operation in Scotland, counteract the image he portrayed of himself as a plain dealing border lord who spent all his time patrolling the perilous area on horseback.[98] In the letter to the lords he characterises himself as merely a poor baron who was unwilling to pester his political masters with trifles as others had done.[99] Despite such false modesty he was wily enough to operate as a major player in the region for forty years until his death in 1525, and from the Scottish perspective he remained a dangerous sponsor of malcontents. What he says about the king's body in his letter must be considered in relation to other evidence. The fact that he omits much information about finding the king – the condition of the body, and the means of transportation – could be merely because these details were incidental to the urgent purpose of his letter. In the end, it has to be admitted that the confusing carnage of Flodden created the perfect circumstances for those who chose to believe anything. Ill remembered battles create easy rumours, no matter how unlikely the stories are. The English writer Ulpian Fullwell noted, thirty years after the event, that some people said that King James V suffered a fatal wound at the Battle of Solway Moss in 1542 and died from it later, though it was a verified fact that was not present and died in his bed at Falkland Palace when he heard about that defeat.[100]

Chapter 4

Immortal Remains

If the body the English recovered from the cold battlefield mire the day after Flodden was not the king as they claimed, it was definitely some notable Scot butchered in the front rank. According to one story, the supposed royal corpse was found on the small hillock a short distance west of Branxton Church, called Piper's Hill. This place is probably the same as Piperd Hill, where the 16th century historian John Stow says that James IV was slain.[1] The site is now marked by a memorial cross erected in 1910. Another alleged place where the king died was at the nearby King's Stone. Local folklore says this was the burial place of the Scottish king, but the stone is actually a prehistoric monument which only earned its association with King James IV some time after the battle and was otherwise known as 'the Gathering or Standing Stone on Crookham Moor'. As a conspicuous feature of the landscape it was used as a meeting place for locals in time of emergency.[2]

Wherever he exactly died and whoever he was, the corpse was initially taken to St Paul's Church at Branxton.[3] This church is still standing, though it suffered substantial remodelling in the Victorian era. The long, final journey of the royal remains was conducted like a slow, macabre relay event. From the village of Branxton the body was brought by Lord Dacre to the Earl of Surrey at Berwick-upon-Tweed. Here it was shown to two top-ranking Scots prisoners, Sir John Forman and Sir William Scott, who identified it as the king and were overcome by grief.[4] As we have seen, these prisoners had probably provided information or help to their captors and their public act of recognition might be regarded as not beyond suspicion. Forman and Scott were members of the king's immediate retinue and were considered lucky to have survived, having being saved from death only with great difficulty. Another fortunate prisoner was Sir Adam Forman, the king's standard bearer and another brother of Bishop Forman.[5] The English chronicler John Stow says that when King James saw Adam Forman being beaten down by the enemy he realised there was nothing left for himself but death. But if Forman managed to save himself under this onslaught, could the king also have done so? Instead of trying to surrender, and possibly fearing reproach if he survived, he instead flung himself into the thickest part of the enemy front line.[6]

At Berwick the English moved swiftly to preserve the corpse and to shift it away from the border. The body was disembowelled, embalmed and sealed with wax, wrapped in lead, then conveyed to Newcastle with other, unnamed items. Surrey wrote immediately after the battle to Queen Catherine of Aragon to state that the fate of the king was unknown, but the next day he wrote to say that he was dead and sent a part of his 'coate armure'.[7] One Italian writer said that the king was actually buried at Berwick.[8] While this is almost certainly untrue, this rumour may have been prompted by uncertainty among the English commanders about how to dispose of their royal burden. Transporting dead kings, after all, was no part of a soldier's average duties. There is some supporting evidence that the body was initially held up at Berwick while confirmation about its destination was sought. An official memorandum written on the back of a muster roll return from Henry's camp at Thérouanne confirms that Lord Dacre claimed to have found the king's body on the field (along with the bodies of Lord Maxwell, Lord Herries of Terregles and the Earl of Crawford). This source agrees that the body was wrapped in lead and taken to Berwick, but then states that it would be kept in the town until the king's pleasure was known.[9]

One reason why the king could not have been immediately interred at Berwick was that he was still subject to the excommunication imposed upon him by Pope Julius II in 1511. This had been as much a political as a religious penalty, the price of allying with the papal enemy France. There is nothing to suppose James IV was unduly concerned about the excommunication while he lived. The same sanction had been imposed on his illustrious predecessor Robert the Bruce without hindering his long term royal career. He might have believed that he had plenty of time left to redeem himself with the Catholic Church. His excommunicated corpse however proved to be an immediately embarrassing relic and posed a difficult problem for his enemies.

With King Henry VIII in France the immediate responsibility for the royal corpse was with Surrey and, though he was in contact with Queen Catherine of Aragon, she was in the south of England and communication was slow. It was Surrey's decision to transport the royal corpse south, where it would remain while the English king decided what to do with it. From Berwick the body was covertly taken to Newcastle with other cargo, either because there was still some uncertainty about its identity, or because the English feared that the Scots would attempt to recover it. But Bishop Ruthall of Durham, a prominent local figure, soon heard about the grisly prize. He approached Sir William Tylney and tried to persuade him that the king should be given to him and be buried at Durham Cathedral. From the English point of view, a burial at Durham might have killed all speculation about the fate of the king immediately. It also would have provided an honourable and dignified solution for the problem of what to do with the body.

The Scottish monarchy had a long, fluctuating relationship with the church of St Cuthbert at Durham. The saint was the secret weapon against overly ambitious Scottish rulers who made frequent incursions into Northumberland. It was remembered by the adherents of St Cuthbert that King Alexander III of Scotland died on the anniversary of his destructive raids on St

Cuthbert's land.[10] In earlier times the prayers of the northern English to Cuthbert had made the marauding army of Malcolm III turn back homewards quickly.[11] But the Scots royal house also showed a special devotion for this saint over the centuries, a reflection of shared culture from the past when Lothian and much of south-east Scotland was an integral part of the kingdom of Northumbria. When Cuthbert's body was exhumed for reburial in August 1104, the only layperson present at the holy ceremony in Durham was Prince Alexander (afterwards King Alexander I), a son of the pillaging Scottish king Malcolm III.[12] The Scottish attachment to the saint remained deep even after Northumbria as an entity crumbled into dust. In the period of Viking settlement the once mighty state shrank to a small enclave, at times supported by Scotland, and there may have been hope in the northern nation that an annexation could be achieved. But when the resurgent realm of Wessex expanded northwards, Northumbria opted to ally itself with the fledgling English state. Ties and tension between St Cuthbert and the Scottish kings continued in a love-hate relationship for centuries.

Durham would therefore perhaps have been the next best burial place for the king other than somewhere in his own country. Ruthall's request, however, was motivated by more selfish reasons: he was still smarting from the destruction of his castle of Norham. The Scots had smashed down the walls, breaking the bishop's heart, and he lamented that it would takes years and a fortune to repair, though he later found the damage not so extensive as he feared.[13] The bishop wanted the king's body at Durham as a ghoulish trophy, signalling the ultimate triumph of St Cuthbert over his ungodly northern neighbours. But Ruthall had to content himself with claiming the king's banner, sword, and his 'qwyschys', the harness for his thighs, which his men recovered for him, as prizes for display in St Cuthbert's Church.[14] But the items listed seem strange for several reasons: why, for example, would the king have his riding harness with him when he was fighting on foot? The claim to have purloined James IV's royal sword was challenged by the counter-claim of the Stanley family, though the weapon they claimed as the king's probably belongs to a later date (see the Chapter 9). Bishop Ruthall had reported to Wolsey that the men who carried St Cuthbert's banner into the battle had found the Scottish king's banner, lying near the king. It was now, he wrote, standing beside the shrine of St Cuthbert.[15] Yet there is no mention of these supposed royal mementoes in inventories compiled at the end of the 16th century, though Durham proudly displayed other Scottish relics, such as a banner belonging to King David II.[16] Ruthall's evidence is nevertheless important for the battle, even if he was motivated by the outrage the enemy Scots had inflicted on the property of his bishopric. He believed that the foreign incursion aroused the wrath of St Cuthbert and caused 20,000 men to desert the Scottish army and go home, therefore making assisting an English victory in the battle.[17] The saint's banner had been brought to the field by the bishop's men and it had been displayed at the high mass held in Durham Cathedral on 28 August in front of the Earl of Surrey who had recently arrived.[18]

From Newcastle, Surrey conveyed the king's body to York, rather than have it shipped south, and the overland route must have been as laborious as it was expensive.[19] A few months later Surrey reclaimed expenses of £12. 9s. 10d for having the corpse carefully encased in lead and conveying it from Berwick, to Queen Catherine of Aragon:

> Also payed for diverse cosntes charges and expens had and susteyned aswell in seryng ledyng and sawdryng of the dede course of the kyng of Scottes, as also in carrying and conveying of hym to York and so forth to Wyndsore...[20]

There may have been a lack of suitable sea transport at the time, or else bad the weather or another factor which prevented shipping it south. There was certainly no marauding Scottish fleet in the vicinity to harry English vessels. The great warships which James IV had commissioned reached Normandy in September 1513 without encountering any English ships. There is a tale that the body was taken to York as a sort of symbolic post mortem riposte to James's alleged oath that he would capture that town before Michaelmas,[21] but this sounds like another invented rumour doing the rounds at the time. James had no intention of leading his army so far south into England. It is unclear whether Catherine could have personally received the body at Windsor. Advanced notice of the finding of the king had been forwarded to her by Lord Howard. When she wrote to Henry several days later to tell him the news about the battle she was on pilgrimage at Woburn Abbey, Bedfordshire.[22]

Nor is anything known about the particulars of the solemn journey south of the dead monarch. There may well have been delays or difficulties caused by a great storm which is recorded to have affected London on 10 September. As it was, Catherine was exultant at having possession of James's body and wanted to send it to Henry in France. The queen, according to one Italian, jokingly promised to send her husband this dead king as a king of one-upmanship for him sending her a nobleman, the French Duc de Longueville, who had been captured and shipped as a prisoner to England.[23] But the captains of the English army, probably including Surrey, would not countenance such a 'gift'.[24] The reason for their horror was not only a reaction to the bad taste of such a suggestion. Transporting a lead-wrapped corpse from the north to the south of England was difficult enough, but sending it overseas would have been another logistical nightmare. She had to be content with sending her spouse a piece of King James's coat for his banner and possibly his gauntlets. The cloth was been described as a plaid bearing the royal arms, and it is probably reached the king on the 20 September.[25] Other sources say that the material bore a checked pattern and was stained with blood of the dead monarch.[26] Quite possibly it was a piece of primitive tartan. King Henry VIII showed off the garment to the Emperor Maximilian I at the siege of Thérouanne.[27]

Various other items belonging to the king are also said to have been recovered from the battlefield, including a cross, but these items seem to have vanished, maybe swiftly purloined by a looter.[28] But the most famous item possessed by the king, the iron chain or belt, did not come to light. The simplest explanation for its absence was that James put it aside before the battle because it would have been a severe encumbrance beneath his armour. Another point where it could have gone missing was when he allegedly took off most of his fighting gear on the actual field as an act of bravado in front of the young Douglas. But the lack of the iron belt or chain on the recovered corpse was one reason why some Scots refuted that the body was their king's.[29] The discrepancies between the items found, not found, or the state of nakedness or otherwise of the dead king are symptomatic of the horribly confused conditions on that calamitous afternoon in Northumberland.

On Catherine's authority the body of James (or which was supposed to be James) was deposited in the monastery of Sheen in Surrey. This religious house was close to the royal palace of Sheen (which was renamed Richmond after the earldom which King Henry VII possessed). There is a strange symmetry about James's post-mortem presence here, because one of the most important events in his life also occurred nearby, without him. In the Queen's apartments at the palace of Richmond, the absent King James was affancied, or married by proxy, to Princess Margaret Tudor. This event took place on 25 January 1502, St Paul's Day, with Patrick, Earl of Bothwell standing in for the king and ambassadors from Scotland and officials from England witnessing the ceremony. King Henry VII and his queen were also present, as well as young Prince Henry, and twelve year old

Margaret, who had never met her intended husband. After the princess and the king's proxy had affirmed themselves to each other the trumpeters sounded triumphantly and the minstrels played at the commencement of a feast. It was from Richmond Palace also that Princess Margaret departed on 27 June 1503, on the first stage of her journey north to go to Scotland and her new life. One of the prominent Scots who accompanied her north was one of three commissioners who negotiated the wedding, Adam Forman, soon to be Bishop of Moray.[30]

In 1513 the remains of King James lay only a short distance away from that scene of revelry, in the silence of physical as well as spiritual limbo. The late king's excommunication remained a major obstacle to his decent burial and one which the English king attempted to resolve. Henry wrote to Pope Leo X from Tournai on 12 October asking for permission to bury his royal brother-in-law at St Paul's Cathedral, and advising his holiness not to believe the still prevalent rumours that the English had been defeated. The Scottish king had broken his promises and paid the price for his treachery. Though King Henry says he will not fail to take the advantage that the victory in battle has given him, he slightly mitigates the guilt of his brother-in-law by stating that he had been seduced by French gold.[31] The pope wrote back on 29 November, granting permission for the king to be absolved by Cardinal Bainbridge on the dubious basis that it was presumed he had shown repentance in his final moments, and allowed the king to let Richard FitzJames, Bishop of London, or some other prelate, bury him with full honours at St Paul's Cathedral. The communication importantly gives permission for the body to be moved to the capital several months after it had been transported south, confirming its continued presence outside London.[32] The careful piece of ecclesiastic fiction – presumption of repentance on the battlefield – should have allowed King James IV to have a decorous burial in the heart of his enemy's kingdom, but for reasons which have always been unclear this did not happen, although some believe that he was quietly interred in St Paul's Cathedral.[33] If Henry, contrary to other evidence, did secretly inter his brother-in-law in St Paul's, it would also argue for a subtlety of behaviour not frequently noted in the English king. Henry had been back on English soil for over a month when the Pope wrote to him, so there should have been nothing stopping him personally supervising the burial.

A 16th century source says that the king's body was subject to the humiliation of being displayed naked in a journey through the streets of London, in the fashion of King Richard III after the battle of Bosworth in 1485, whose body was paraded through the streets of Leicester.[34] Upton Fullwell's *Flower of Fame* contains prose and poetry celebrating the glorious reign of King Henry VIII. One section gleefully describes the well deserved end of King James IV. After much substandard verse, written in the first person and celebrating the king's shameful demise, there is a description of him being paraded through London:

> My wretched carcas then was brought in sight,
> Through London streats; wherat the Scottes repine:
> The endeles shame of this mishap is myne.
> Like butcher's ware, on horsbacke was I brought;
> The King of kinges for me this end hath wrought.[35]

The prose section of the work preceding the poem describes the monarch's post mortem journey:

> the dead bodye of the King of Scottes was founde among the other carcases in the fielde, and from thence brought to London, and so through London streetes on horsebacke, in such order as you have reade before of King Richarde; and from thence it was carried to Sheene neere unto Brainford, whereas the queene then laye. And theare this perjured carcas lyeth unto this day, unburied: a condign end and a

meete sepulker for such a forsworn prince![36]

But there are reasons for seriously doubting this story. The first is that Fulwell was writing years after the supposed event (his *Flower of Fame* was printed in 1575) and his work was hardly supposed to represent historical fact. More crucially, it was known that the king's body was wrapped in lead and it is unlikely that this would have been removed while the remains were in transit. But even without the lead covering it would have been physically difficult to drape an already embalmed corpse over the back of a horse.

Another poem, supposedly composed in the reign of Elizabeth I, broadly gives a more reasonable summary of the body's treatment, though probably still with inaccuracies:

The carcase of the king himself
Naked was left as it was found,
The Earl could not know it right,
Searching the same upon the ground.
Till the Lord Dacres, at the last,
By certain signs did know the king;
His corps into a cart being placed
They to Newcastle did it bring.

* * *

King James's body was embalmed,
Sweet, like a king, and then was sent
To Shene in Surrey, where intombed,
Some say there is now a monument.[37]

King James IV's body almost certainly remained in the monastery of Sheen or Richmond, close to the royal palace. Confirmation of this is found in John Stow's *Survey of London*, first published in 1598, and his evidence is more compelling than any other claims about its final destination. The decision of King Henry not to accord his relative a funeral, after going to the trouble of delicately negotiating with the pontiff, could be merely because he lost interest in the matter and left the body to moulder away in a forgotten cranny of his kingdom. It may have been convenient in the end to forget that he had the burdensome remains of his enemy on his hands. On the other hand, the Italian historian Polydore Vergil, who was based in England, stated that James was left deliberately unburied at Sheen because he had violated his treaty with England and incurred excommunication, and Edward Hall states that James was brought south to Queen Catherine at Richmond, with no mention of a detour to London.[38] His sentiments echo the attitude of the poet John Skelton, and even King Henry VIII himself, that the Scottish king not only brought his fate upon himself, but incurred the everlasting wrath of God for his actions. Vergil's history was completed around 1513, but not published until 1534. He may have been ignorant of Henry's negotiations with the pope, or a later editor may have updated the circumstance relating to the remains of the Scottish king. If it had been intended to teach King James a lesson, post mortem, the Tudor king would have surely have displayed the remains in public and not merely stuffed him in a monastic attic.

But there are several factors that might mitigate Henry's negligence in the matter. The first is that Flodden was fought when Henry was still in France and might have hoped that his subordinates would quickly and decently lay James to rest with the minimum of fuss. We have already seen that there was an appalling storm in the London area recorded on 10 September, and this may have continued for some time and disrupted the transit of the corpse. More serious was the major outbreak of plague in the capital in September 1514, which surely would have dissuaded any but the most foolhardy of travellers from entering the city.[39] It was estimated by one foreign observer that three to four hundred people were dying in London every day, and this was surely no time to be ritually parading a corpse, royal or otherwise, around the streets.[40] The party carrying the body may have deposited it at Sheen while they waited for the pestilence to abate. By the time the plague did die down, King James IV was all but forgotten, at least by those who were responsible for ensuring he was properly laid to rest.

But even though the body was left among the dusty lumber in one of the buildings by the River Thames it was destined to be subjected to further casual disrespect. John Stow tells us that he visited the former monastery of Sheen during the reign of King Edward VI (1547-1553). The Earl of Hertford had gained ownership of the property, but he was executed in January 1552.[41] When Stow came to Sheen, the property had passed to Henry Grey, Duke of Suffolk, so the date of his visit can be narrowed down to either 1552 or 1553 (Edward VI died in July 1553). Stow reports seeing the body of King James IV, or what he was told was the body of that king. It was still wrapped in lead, as it had been forty years before, which further discredits the tale of it being shown on the back of a horse in the London streets (even though Stow also heard the persistent story that it was brought to Sheen from London). He relates the desecration of the corpse which happened some time after his visit, under his description of St Michael's Church in Wood Street, in Cripplegate Ward, London:

> There is also (but without any outward monument) the head of Iames, the fourth king of Scots of that name, slayne at Flodden field, and buried here by this occasion. After the battell the body of the saide king being founde, was closed in lead, and conueyed from thence to London, and so to the Monastery of Sheyne in Surrey, where it remayned for a time, in what order I am not certaine: but since the dissolution of that house, in the raigne of *Edward* the sixt, *Henry Gray*

> Duke of Suffolke, beeing lodged and keeping house there, I haue beene shewed the same body so lapped in lead, close to the head and body, throwne into a wast roome amongst the olde timber, leade, and other rubble. Since the which time Workmen there for their foolish pleasure hewed off his head: and *Launcelot Young* Maister Glasier to her Maiestie [Queen Elizabeth I], feeling a sweet savour to come from thence, and seeing the same dryed from all moisture, and yet the forme remayning, with the hayre of the heade and bearde redde, brought it to London to his house in Woodstreet, where for a time hee kept it for the sweetenesse, but in the ende caused the Sexton of that Church to bury it amongst other bones, taken out of their Charnell, &c.[42]

Such seems to have been the ignominious fate of the mortal remains of James IV of Scotland – the 'neglect and unseemly Disregard of his Dead Body; which tho' once a King, could not obtain a Monument, no, nor a Place of Burial', as John Stype, Stow's 18th century editor, put it.[43] Sheen was also noted by Ulpian Fulwell as the place where the body was kept in 1575, and an anonymous witness also saw the remains there in 1513.[44] Possibly the monks who lived at Sheen initially treated the royal corpse with more respect, and the fact that they did not bury it may have been due to fear of King Henry. John Stow also summarised the story of seeing the body at Sheen in his *Annales of England*, where he mentions that it was affirmed to him that this was the body of the king, as if he was not wholly certain of that fact himself.[45]

The precarious state of the Scottish nation after Flodden may have prevented too much enquiry about the fate of their slain monarch. Repatriation of royal remains in any case would not have been considered normal practice in this period. There is no surviving evidence that either the widowed Queen Margaret or any representative of the Scottish government asked about the fate of their beloved monarch's body. Towards the end of the 16th century the humanist and historian George Buchanan certainly knew that the noble king's remains had been treated ignominiously, and he railed against the 'inexpiable hatred for the dead' of the English nation for not burying the warrior king. He did not know whether the southern authorities were motivated by barbarism or by foolishness, but whatever the reason, because of the pretence that he had sacrilegiously borne arms against the allies of the pope, the king was kept unburied in a leaden coffin.[46] If Buchanan's judgement was harsh, it was likely representative of those Scots who shared his knowledge about the fate of James IV's body. The English crime of being arrogantly indifferent to their enemies was perhaps more unforgivable than outright hatred.

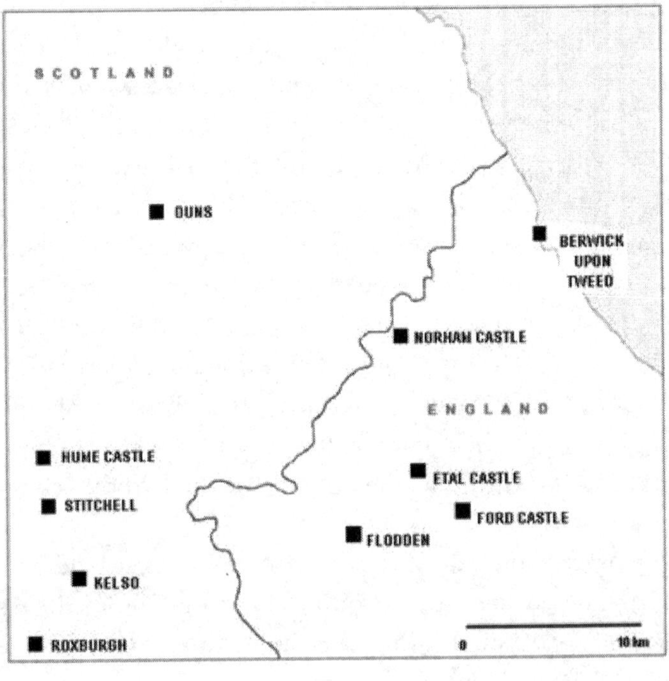

The eastern border and sites associated with King James IV.

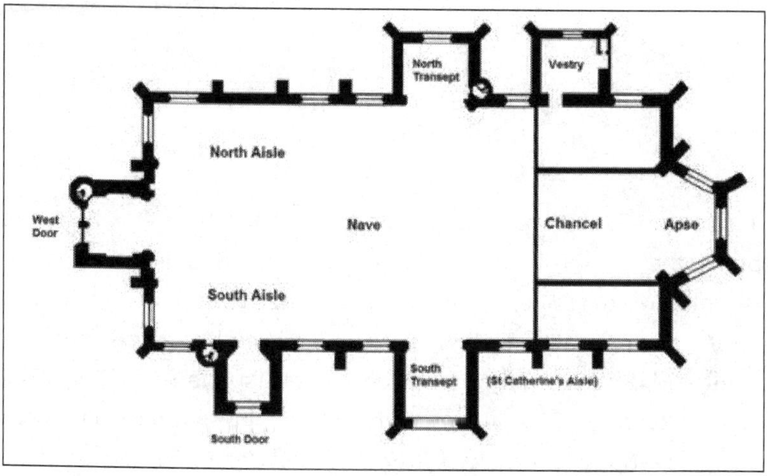

Plan of St Michael's Kirk, Linlithgow. The king saw the mysterious apparition of the man in blue in the South Transept.

St Catherine's Aisle in St Michael's Kirk.

St Michael's Kirk viewed from Linlithgow Palace.

Chapter 5

The Wardens of the Marches

Two noblemen – one Englishman and one Scot – who were both well known to King James IV were crucially involved in the blossoming legends of the dead king. They had faced each other in battle at Flodden, fighting each other's divisions to a standstill, and later they both bore the suspicions of their own countrymen because of their alleged behaviour there. The men also played critical parts in the strained relations between the two nations in the early minority of King James V. Due to their landed interests and official positions these men acted as both territorial and official opponents during James IV's reign and beyond. But soon after Flodden, the Scot was in league with the Englishman, conspiring against the new regime in Edinburgh, which marked him out for death.

Lord Dacre of Gilsland in Cumberland and Lord Home of Home Castle in Berwickshire were respectively the English and Scottish Wardens of the Marches, responsible for keeping law on different sections of the perilous national frontier and for maintaining a military answer to threats from each other's country. But because Home and Dacre were also hereditary barons in the region, they were inevitably closely involved with local issues and personal agendas. Their tenants and followers were frequently engaged in behaviour that centralised government regarded as criminal, such as the notorious practice of 'reiving' or cattle raiding, which was endemic in the region. To survive as an effective authority in this zone involved embracing the duality of poaching and game-keeping, and those born to power here were always treated with suspicion by the rulers in far away Edinburgh and London.

The Scottish Warden of the East and Middle Marches came

from a family deeply rooted in Berwickshire, originally being an offshoot of the Earls of Dunbar.[1] Alexander, 3rd Lord Home (or Hume as the family name was later styled), had taken over the role of warden from his late father in 1506. He was a man of long-standing political and military experience, and he took to the field of Flodden with solid reasons to perform well militarily. The site of the battle was uncomfortably near the eastern border he controlled, and though Home had widely scattered possessions, his heartland was in the Merse, Berwickshire, where a victorious English army easily have crossed the Tweed and caused mayhem.[2] He was also well connected in the realm and held a prominent national role as Chamberlain of Scotland. Buchanan noted that he was a 'great favourite of the king, but of too fierce a disposition'.[3] His inclination towards angry, hasty actions would cost him dear.

In August 1513 Lord Home was also trying to overturn the recent humiliation of being bettered by the English during a cross border sortie which marked the beginning of military hostilities between the two countries. According to the Scots sources this event, which they called the 'Ill Raid', was Home's urgent response to the encroachment of an English force under Sir William Bulmer near Scottish territory. Bulmer had been sent north by Surrey, himself commissioned by Henry VIII to keep a watch on the frontier. The Scottish version of events says that Bulmer broke over the border and set to spoiling and burning the country, then retreated. In answer to this incursion Home, who had been similarly set on a war footing by his king, set off to pursue Bulmer to the further parts of Northumberland.[4] The Scottish Warden went south with several thousand mounted men, but in frustration at not finding Bulmer they started gathering booty.[5] On their way back home on 13 August, burdened with spoils, the Scots were ambushed in a narrow pass at Milfield by Bulmer, whose men lay hidden in a field of broom. A large number of Home's men were killed, and hundreds taken prisoner, including his brother George. To add to his dishonour, Home's own banner was snatched away by the enemy. English retelling of these events unsurprisingly differs from the Scottish account, foreshadowing the confusion which would surround the Battle of Flodden. Edward Hall says that Bulmer had been sent north to counter signs of Scottish aggression and that it was Home who crossed the frontier and was punished for his trouble.[6] There is no mention that Bulmer entered Scotland, and we are left guessing which account is the more plausible. If Bulmer was the aggressor, his plan may have been calculated to draw Home south and escalate events into open warfare. But it was equally likely that the 'Ill Raid' was a speculative incursion on the part of Home, which went dramatically wrong.[7] Either way the incident caused relations between England and Scotland to reach breaking point. The Battle of Flodden, or Branxton, would be fought only a few kilometres away weeks later.

At Flodden, Lord Home commanded the Scottish left wing together with the Earl of Huntly. Their troops performed well initially, forcing back the opposite division, led by Surrey's son Edmund Howard, and perhaps with better luck or more immediate action could have taken the advantage and pressed forward. But the Scots ground to a standstill, the battalion held in check by Lord Dacre. Somehow in this bloody melee Alexander Gordon, 3rd Earl of Huntly, discovered that the king, in the centre of the army, was in mortal danger and begged Home to go to his aid. Lord Home is notoriously reputed to have refused to assist the monarch. According to Pitscottie's testimony, he answered Huntly, 'He does well that does for himself. We have foughten our Vanguards, and have won the same: Therefore let the Lave do their Part, as well as we.'

Huntly responded that, 'He could not suffer his native Prince to be overcome with his Enemies before his Eyes: Therefore he called his Men together by Sluggorn [sluagh-ghairm, war-cry], and sound of Trumpets, to have past to the King: But, ere he came, all was defeat on either Side, that few or none was living, neither on the King's part, nor on the other.'[8] This damning accusation against Lord Home was the central factor in the blackening of his name after the combat.

But it is doubtful whether Huntly could have precisely located the king in the confusion of battle, though the collapse of the king's division may have been visible, and Pitscottie's fondness for inventing colourful speeches casts doubt over Home's vocal treachery. Yet Polydore Vergil, giving the established English version of the matter, suggested that Lord Home did the work of the enemy that day and did not move even an inch to assist the king on the field of battle.[9] But he also admitted that Home was by no means the only person who was unwilling to recklessly throw his life away at this stage of the encounter. Vergil stated that the bulk of the Scottish army who witnessed the horror of their front line being engulfed and decimated would not rally to his assistance because they assumed that he had been slaughtered in the initial charge.[10] So Home's intransigence, if it was based upon a reluctance to rescue the king who was probably already dead, would hardly constitute treason. He made the mistake of voicing the brutally obvious.

After the battle Home was castigated for his failure to rescue his king. Within months of Flodden he was in rebellion against the government of the Duke of Albany and in league with his erstwhile English enemies. His conduct may have encouraged the retrospective invention of treason. Whether true or not, the accusation of not performing his duty on the battlefield was something neither he nor his family ever shook off. One of the reasons it arose was because he was one of the very few high-ranking noblemen to escape the carnage unharmed. Huntly, of course, was another fortunate non-casualty: he fled from the field on a conveniently available horse.[11] It is worth considering whether he or his associates first spread the dark stories about Alexander Home. Although their power base was in the north-east, the Gordons of Huntly had ties with the Homes. Alliances between the two families – sometimes bonding together against King James III – are recorded in the late 1480s and the 1490s.[12] In 1490 Alexander Home was granted the lands of Mar and Garioch for the maintenance and payment of the king's brother the Earl of Mar, territories in the heartland of Huntly country.[13] But there is no record of personal animosity between Alexander Home and Huntly. No serious suspicion of inaction on the field ever attached itself to the latter, and he continued to occupy trusted positions in the country, becoming one of three earls chosen to counsel Queen Margaret in November 1513.[14] In 1517 he was appointed one of the vice-regents and Lieutenants of Scotland.[15] However the English historian Edward Hall historian hinted that Huntly did show the better part of valour by withdrawing from the fray when he saw Sir Edward Stanley overwhelming the earls of Lennox and Argyll.[16] It is also noteworthy that Alexander, Earl of Huntly, was among the beneficiaries after the forfeiture of Lord Home in October 1516. For his 'good service' he gained the lands of the Lordship of Gordon, Berwickshire.[17]

Survivors and others understandably questioned the reasons why the borderers' advance shuddered to a halt. Borderers on both sides were reported to have pillaged the dead and they had long been stigmatised by others as a breed of disreputable thieves, who were frequently more interested in their own acquisitive agenda – the gathering of booty – than in supporting their respective national interests. The major families in this region, English and Scottish, arguably possessed more a focused local than national identity, at least when it suited them to be border men rather than Scot or Englishman.[18] Undoubtedly some Scots and English borderers lost interest in the fray after the initial clash, or may even have tacitly agreed to do each other no injury. For all their interest in feuding with each other in peace time, they habitually colluded with each other when there was war between England and Scotland, to the extent that it was noted they had a secret way of recognising each other in times of conflict.[19] Lord Dacre stated as early as 1524 that intermarriage across the border had blurred racial distinctions between Scots and English in the region.[20] There was even a settlement of 'English Scots' in the Lyne Valley in Cumberland in the late 15th century, whose suspected criminal behaviour meant they were closely watched by the local authority, Sir John Musgrave of Bewcastle.[21]

An Englishman describing the Battle of Pinkie in 1547 said that frontier men from both nations even wore badges so they would recognise and do no harm to each other.[22] This attribution of collusion, with secret signs and a society baffling to outsiders, is tied in with the notion that the border region was a strange place somewhat outside the laws of ordinary civilisation. Mistrust of the region was deep and long-standing among the English and Scottish elite. When King Richard II was levying an army against the Scots in 1385 he stipulated that two-thirds of the force should be strangers to the marches.[23]

Whatever Home said or did not say to Huntly, he and his men (estimated, probably over-generously, at 10,000 strong) are reported by some writers to have stayed on or near the battlefield until the following day.[24] There may have been an attempt to retrieve the expensive ordinance captured by the English, but they were seen off by Home's nemesis, Lord Dacre of the North.[25] Home led his men back northwards, spoiling Northumbrian territory as he went. An evil reputation preceded them:

> At their comming home, euerie man spake euill of them, for that as cowards and naughtie persons, they neither sought to reuenge the death of their noble king, nor yet to succour their fellowes that were beaten downe and slaine before their faces. But namelie Alexander Hume lord chamberlaine was reproued, as cause of all that mischiefe, which behaued himselfe not as a capteine, but as a traitor or enimie to his countrie.[26]

Whatever rumours immediately arose about Home, his standing remained sufficiently buoyant for him to remain one of the major political figures in Scotland. It was not only enemies in Scotland who disparaged Home's suspicious conduct. He was alluded to in a letter which King Henry VIII wrote to Pope Leo X on 12 October 1513, describing the battle. The English king assured the pope that he would certainly take advantage of the victory, even though one nameless Scottish lord (who escaped the battlefield alone) was attempting to crave a truce.[27]

Lord Home managed to retain his influence partly because he was a great feudal baron who commanded extensive loyalty in the borders. Home and the widowed Queen Margaret were uniquely senior figures on the political scene after the battle. There were few survivors from the upper ranks of the previous regime, and many others who were obliged to take up the reins of power were inexperienced. But despite this, the machinery of Scottish government re-established itself quickly after the catastrophe. Home had the foresight to align himself immediately with John, Duke of Albany, the French born son of Alexander, Duke of Albany, a brother of King James III, whose title and estates had been forfeited through treason. Although a servant of the French crown, Albany was seen by many as the only realistic leader of royal blood or rank worthy to lead the nation after Queen Margaret forfeited her right to rule by impetuously marrying the young Earl of Angus (on 14 August 1514). The real mystery of Home in those dark years after the disaster, and the decision which sealed his fate, was his sudden decision to turn against the authority of Albany and ally himself with Queen Margaret and Lord Dacre. His change of behaviour may have been more complex than a simple choice between the two competing parties. It would also be easy but untrue to see Queen Margaret merely as the self-serving head of the English party, and Albany as the weary and increasingly weak vessel of the French. Lord Home remains more of an enigma than either

Margaret or Albany, despite his rough hewn character and blatant treachery. The charge of treason at Flodden may have amounted to no more than a malicious gossip, but his behaviour in the next two years ensured that it was a serious accusation repeated in the works of subsequent historians.

A more sensational slander says that Lord Home or his confederates actually murdered King James IV immediately after the battle, back in Scotland. This accusation of regicide runs counter to the verified reports that Home and his men lingered near Flodden overnight. The obvious illogic in this story did not stop it growing. By the end of the 18th century it had crystallised into a morsel of gothic intrigue. Francis Grose related this commonly held legend about Lord Home's foul deeds in his *Antiquities of Scotland* (1797):

> Some time ago was found at Home Castle the remains of a body, in an Ox hide; it had an iron chain round the loins, and was therefore supposed to have been James IV who was well known to wear an iron chain round his loins, by way of penance, for having been accessory to his father's death; he moreover constantly added a link to this chain every year. His being found in Home Castle is thus accounted for: at the battle of Flodden the Earl of Hume [sic.] with his troops kept aloof; when it is said, the King escaping to him much wounded, threatened to call him to severe account, for being one of the causes of the loss of the battle. The Earl dreading the King's resentment, is said to have murthered him, and buried him privately in Hume Castle.[28]

Following Grose, Sir Walter Scott entered the debate and firmly stated that Alexander Home was not guilty of treason at Flodden.[29] Scott was uniquely placed to tap into the rich reservoirs of border tradition and reported that the skeleton in the bull's hide was found in the well of the castle. But there was no local cohesive legend to back up the tale, though the parish sexton vaguely informed Scott that 'he would not be surprised at such a discovery', adding that that forty years previously some workmen clearing out the draw-well of the ruined castle had found there a skeleton wrapped in a bull's hide, with an iron chain about its middle.[30] There was no hard evidence as proof of this spectacular discovery however, though local rumours may have begun flying around when the ruined castle had its battlements remodelled by the 3rd Earl of Marchmont in 1789.

As time progressed the stories mutated and the body of King James IV, like that of certain saints, was credited with having multiple burial places. One legend says that the skeleton was found in the ruins of Roxburgh Castle, just west of Kelso, during the invasion of Oliver Cromwell in the 1650s. But because of the civil strife in the country no further effort was made to enquire further into the matter and the remains were reburied in a common burial place without any ceremony.[31] But tradition is wide of the mark here, as Roxburgh was not in the hands of the Homes, nor had James IV any particular association with the place. Roxburgh Castle had been demolished by James II's queen Mary of Guelders in the 1460's after her husband was accidently killed by an exploding cannon there, to stop the fortress falling back into English hands.

In the wild and wide range of rumours thrown up in the years following 1513 many people tried to pin down the fate of this one man. But the attempt identify his 'real' burial place merely generated more speculative material. There was a medieval mystique around the resting places of charismatic figures. While the royal and saintly burial sites could bring pilgrims to certain places, there was also a magical allure about not knowing where certain heroes were resting. The Welsh *Englynion y Beddau*, 'Stanzas of the Graves', contained mainly in the 13th century *Black Book of Carmarthen*, is a compilation of verses describing the burial places of famous heroes. A significant number of these were from the old British North, Cumbria and the Scottish Lowlands, who had been relocated in death in the Welsh heartlands where traditions of them continued to be handed down. One verse alluding to the most famous hero of all, Arthur, states it would be a 'world's wonder' if the site of his tomb was discovered. If the grave site was unknown there was no physical evidence that the king had gone the way of other mortal men.[32]

By the Victorian age local traditions about the grave site of King James IV were becoming confused. In 1851 a Kelso man told that in his father's youth in Sprouston, Berwickshire, there was a story about a skeleton being uncovered in the Berry Moss near Kelso. It had around its waist a golden chain, whose links numbered the same as King James's age at death.[33] Someone had told him there was a strange mound in a local kirkyard known as the King's Grave. This was at Hume, whose kirk was in ruins by that date (the parish was conjoined with neighbouring Stichill). Around this mound, 'It was customary, he said, from time immemorial, when a funeral entered the churchyard, to walk in procession round this grave, and return to the spot where the dead was to be buried.' But the strange tradition had since petered out. It was surmised that the grave might be the reburial site of the skeleton found in the Berry Moss, none other than King James IV himself.[34] The mound is probably identical with the 'Pest Knowe', once believed to cover the mass grave of plague victims in the parish. In fact it covers neither a king nor a plague pit, but only the remains of the old kirk. A vague tradition in the area states that the belt on the body in the well was weighed down with stones, suggesting foul play.[35]

After his death, Lord Home was associated with the same kind of intrigue as that of his supposed royal victim. The story of his villainy was firmly established by the latter part of the 16th century at least, in the writings of Buchanan and Lindsay of Pitscottie. These historians, with their own agendas, peddled versions of the supposed survival of King James IV into which the guilty Lord Home was darkly and intricately woven.

It might be expected that the fullest account of Lord Home's alleged dark deeds would be found in Pitscottie, but his account is relatively circumspect. But what he does say is damning, compounding the report of cynical inaction on the field with a refusal to retake the expensive Scottish ordinance next morning. And in Pitscottie there is the first appearance of one of the central and powerfully abiding images in the legend of James's survival:

> Some say, there came four Men upon four Horses riding to the Field, with four Spears, and a Wisp on every Spear-Head, to be a Sign and Witter to them, that every one of them should know other. They rode in the Field, and horsed the King, and brought him forth of the Field on a din Hackney: But some say, they had him into *The Merse*, betwixt *Dunse* and *Kelso*; what they did with him there I cannot tell: But one, ten Years thereafter, convicted of Slaughter, offered to the Duke of *Albany*, for his Life, to let him see the Place where the Prince was yearded; for the Token, he should let him see his Belt of Iron lying beside him in the Grave: But, notwithstanding, this Man got no Audience by them that were about him; the Duke of *Albany* desired not, at that Time, that such Thing should be known.[36]

Importantly, Pitscottie does not directly accuse Lord Home, or any of his followers, with murdering the king after the battle. Once mysteriously escorted back to his homeland in this version of events, this most conspicuous of kings disappears into the ether. Pitscottie possibly only repeated his tale of the mounted escorts as he found it, or on the other hand kept his information deliberately indefinite in order to maintain an air of mystery. Were the figures a mounted bodyguard, at the king's special command? Or were they more ambivalent agents of a less friendly force? Pitscottie does not identify these four sinister and almost supernatural figures, nor say anything about their motives. They come out of the fog of battle, silently spirit the king away, then both riders and rescued king vanish without a trace. But the modern historian Norman Macdougall is surely correct when he equates them with the Four Horsemen from the *Book of Revelation*: Conquest, War, Famine and Death.[37] The subtext must be that the hapless king's shade accompanied these scourges back into Scotland. This unacknowledged parallel elevates the story from one of simple hearsay into a mythic encounter with elemental forces.

The account that the king, or someone much like him, was seen in Scotland on the evening after the battle is echoed in the history of John Lesley, which has him being sighted at Kelso 'hail and sound'.[38] But Lesley says nothing about any alleged rumours of treachery or regicide by Lord Home. Likewise, the Franciscan monk Adam Abell, who was present at Jedburgh at that time, says there was talk of the king being seen alive in that area, but gives no particulars.[39] It is left to George Buchanan to add detail to this story. After admitting that there were different accounts of the fate of the king, he tells how the king was spotted crossing the River Tweed on the evening of 9 September and was slain by some Homes near the town of Kelso. Lord Home may have been directly responsible for the murder, or some of his men might have been acting by themselves. That same night a survivor of the battle and associate of Home's, Andrew Ker of Ferniehurst Castle, burst into Kelso Abbey and expelled the abbot, installing his brother there, which was seen as part of the same orchestrated campaign of violence that included killing the king after the battle.[40] But the fact that Ferniehurst felt free to despoil an abbey argues that he knew fine well that the king was dead.[41] A third possibility is that Ker was acting to secure the strategic site against possible English invasion after the battle.

Some conspiracists favour the theory that Home killed the king after Flodden to avoid being punished for his treasonable procrastination on the battlefield. This rests on the dubious assumption that his military behaviour was really culpable. Even if it was true that this long-standing associate of the king killed him because he feared punishment, surely he would have considered the greater risk of execution he might expect for regicide? The near-contemporary English poem *Scotish Feilde* suggests that James IV was furious about the humiliating defeat of the 'Ill Raid', and accused the Scots involved of being cowards, though this is hardly a trustworthy historical source. It makes the elementary mistake, for example, of stating that the Scottish commander was Lord Maxwell, not Lord Home.[42]

An alternative theory for the Home's regicide is that he feared revenge for his family's role in the overthrown of King James III. This theory is even more implausible because James III had been dead for over twenty years and James IV had not targeted the Homes (or anyone else) for their part in his father's demise. Another suggestion is that it was one of Home's followers or adherents, a man whom Buchanan calls David Garbreth or Galbraith. He is said to have responded to the Duke of Albany's later retaliation against the rebellious Homes with the statement that his allies were sluggish cowards because they had suffered a stranger to rule over and tyrannise them, referring to the Duke of Albany. He then boasted that he was one of six 'private companions' who had checked the insolence of the king at Kelso.[43] There was obviously once a fleshed out story about these six men slaying King James IV, but like the substance of many of the other legends the details have evaporated over time.

Whether this Galbraith was the same person as the unnamed man mentioned by Pitscottie, who tried to give details of the dead king's secret fate in return for his life, is unclear. The condemned man may have been arrested for boastfully linking himself to the common rumour that the Homes had slain the king. Buchanan's main source for his information was the 'honest and learned' Laurence Telfer or Talifer, who informed the historian that he had personally witnessed the king cross the Tweed on 9 September. Telfer was the vicar of Kirkpatrick near Glasgow, and was twenty-four years old at the time of Flodden, and was present at the battle, as a page to the king.[44] He was of sufficient standing to obtain the post of Secretary in 1520.[45] It is interesting that Galbraith is not credited with reporting that Lord Home had instigated the murder. Buchanan himself had heard that the king was killed near Kelso by the vassals of Home, but he did not know whether the deed was done by his orders or by the rashness of his men who hoped to please him.[46]

The claim that Home was personally responsible for the king's murder was advanced by the English writer Nathaniel Spencer, in *The Complete English Traveller* (1772). Spencer says that the king was witnessed crossing the Tweed by Flodden survivors and went to Lord Home's castle, presumably Home Castle. The king was never seen again, and the writer says – based on unnamed sources who 'positively asserted' the story – that James was killed that night by Home himself. The body was buried near the castle and a skeleton with a chain around it was found nearby some time later by a labourer and removed to be re-buried at Holyrood Abbey. Spencer's sources for these scraps are unknown, and he adds the story that Queen Margaret announced that the body would be known by its iron chain, but after the battle a diligent search was made but no body with a chain was found. It was a counterfeit king who was carried off the battlefield by the English and taken to be buried at Windsor.[47]

Returning to the earlier and more reliable writers, it is seems that Buchanan and Pitscottie may have similar shared sources of information for their written versions of the Flodden legends. There must have been competing stories about James's survival flying around at the time. One tale insisted that the cunning king dressed ten men at Flodden in his armour to confound the enemy. Among these were two of his guard, Alexander MacCulloch and the Squire of Cleisch, who resembled the king.[48] Sir Alexander MacCulloch of Myretoun was a member of the royal household and appears in the Treasurer's Accounts as the king's 'familiaris miles'.[49] The Squire of Cleisch was either a Meldrum of Cleish in Kinross-shire, who was active in the navy, or a William Meldrum from a similarly named place, who is the hero of a poem of Sir David Lindsay, the *Historie of Squyer Meldrum*.[50] But Buchanan is equivocal about the identity of the body that the English found: it may have been either the king or Alexander, 1st Lord Elphinstone, who also resembled King James.[51] Bishop Lesley says that it was not King James IV whom the English carted off Branxton Hill, but the laird of Bonhard.[52] This was John Cornwall, who held land at Bonhard midway between Linlithgow and Bo'ness.[53] The identity of the other six royal imposters, if they existed at all, is a complete mystery. But the story of these imitation kings on the field may be more than a mere legend. At the battle of Fuornovo in July 1495, the French king Charles VIII is reputed to have dressed others in similar armour to confound his Italian opponents.[54]

Lord Home was not the only Scottish scapegoat blamed later for the battle and the king's death. Andrew Forman, Bishop of Moray, career cleric and diplomat, travelled widely in Europe on behalf of King James IV and he was held accountable for stirring up trouble between England and Scotland. An interesting and talented man, it was remarked that Forman might have achieved as much as his contemporary Cardinal Wolsey if Scotland was a larger nation.[55] Pitscottie's gives a comedic anecdote about him being so grossly ignorant of Latin at a papal dinner that he was forced to give a coarse Scots blessing in the presence of the pontiff and assorted cardinals, damning them all to the devil.[56] This image goes against the known facts about him; he was employed by France as well as Scotland in negotiations with Rome, eventually gaining the abbacy of Bourges, along with other benefices. A powerful lord like him, clerical or temporal, who did not perish at Flodden and remained involved in the maelstrom of Scottish politics afterwards was open to accusations of treachery, as if survival was a punishable offence. In fact Bishop Forman, like the hapless Earl of Arran, was abroad when Flodden was fought, having gone to France several months before the battle.[57] Otherwise he may have died there, as did other notable clerics, the Archbishop of St Andrews, the Bishop of the Isles and the abbots of Kilwinning and Inchaffray.[58] The blackening of Forman's name was fuelled by his pro-French stance, and he hardly helped his case when he wrote to his master and said that if he did not move to support France his royal honour would be lost.[59] Back in Scotland after Flodden he managed to successfully manoeuvre his way through the political minefield, in contrast to Lord Home.

In England, Forman was cast as someone who had principally contributed to the conflict, being the architect of the Franco-Scottish alliance. Immediately after the battle Dacre and Bishop Thomas Ruthall named him as a chief cause of the battle. Ruthall had this confirmed by Sir William Scott, a prisoner after Flodden (and one of those who identified the king's body at Berwick), who blamed Forman's 'sensual mind' influencing the king again the wishes of most of the nobility.[60] The Scottish authorities also denounced him as a traitor in the aftermath of the defeat. A letter sent in the name of King James V to Pope Leo X on 4 March 1514 stated that Forman had been charged with treason for his actions in the previous reign.[61] Although he quickly regained most of his status under the governorship of the Duke of Albany, his reputation continued to suffer in the following decade. The cleric and historian Adam Abell wrote of Forman in the 1530s that Flodden was instigated by French men and also by Forman.[62] The next generation of historians, generally Protestant, remembered Forman as a scheming, evil Catholic mandarin lurking behind the throne and infecting Scotland with poison drawn from papist Europe.[63] As James IV's image was manipulated after his death, so was Forman's, but in a far more negative fashion and for a shorter period before memory of him entirely faded.

Bishop Forman was originally a Berwickshire man, related through marriage to the Homes, which was one reason why he appealed to Lord Home in the dispute for the archbishopric of St Andrews, to which he had been appointed over another claimant, John Hepburn, who was already Prior of St Andrews.[64] The position of Archbishop of St Andrews was the highest domestic office a Scottish cleric could aim for, but it was a controversial one, having recently been annexed by the monarchy, with James IV granting it to his brother and his bastard son in succession. But even before this the office had been occupied by contentious figures, like Patrick Graham, who was deposed for being corrupt and insane and his successor, the astrologer William Scheves.

Forman's rival Hepburn also had ties of kinship with Home, being the grandson of the first Lord Home.[65] But the 3rd Lord Home opted to support the claims of Forman, who eventually became archbishop. This decision earned him the abiding hatred of Hepburn, who inveigled his way into the confidence of the new governor John Stewart, Duke of Albany, and poisoned his mind against both the bishop and the border lord. Appealing to the Scottish lords to support his ecclesiastic rights, Hepburn alleged that Forman was entirely to blame for the debacle of Flodden and was motivated by greed.[66] In doing this he was in part tapping into a seam of public prejudice against the alleged regicide and the late king's evil counsellor. Among other allegations he dredged up for Albany is that Home behaved dishonourably on the battlefield at Flodden.[67]

Hepburn's campaign of slander was thorough, blackening the clan of Home throughout history, from Bannockburn to Flodden, and he insinuated that the Homes had benefitted from the disgrace of the duke's own royal father. The secular power held by the Bishop of Moray and his supposed misuse of benefices for his own kith and kindred were also brought to the governor's attention.[68] The newly arrived Franco-Scot Albany, who had never been to Scotland and could not speak his ancestral language, may have given credence to Prior Hepburn's accusations.[69] Hepburn blamed Home and Forman for the death of the king and causing the battle. In the aftermath of Flodden, Lord Home had agitated for the invitation of Albany to Scotland to take over the governorship of the country in place of Queen Margaret, who had made herself unacceptable by allying herself with the pro-English Earl of Angus, whom she married at the earliest opportunity.

When Albany arrived in Dumbarton in May 1515, Home was there to meet him, and the account of their initial encounter is coloured with folkloric elements. The great feudal border baron arrived, according to one report, with a retinue of 10,000 supporters dressed in his livery of Kendal green, with the effect of threatening rather than impressing Albany, who was entirely ignorant of Scots customs and manners. Although the duke had been a soldier and statesman of France, serving in Italy and further afield, it is unlikely that he had ever witnessed anything like this. Another version of the meeting states that Lord Home's retinue only numbered 24 men. But either way the display did nothing to counteract the clash of cultures. Albany was unimpressed and muttered a Latin phrase to one of his men – *Minuit præsentia famam* – which was evidently a remark about Lord Home's low stature or his startling retinue.[70] Another report said that one of Albany's companions, who was familiar with Scottish politics, Antoine d'Arces De La Bastie, the 'White Knight', commented that Home was held to have been responsible for the king's death, to which Albany made a diplomatic response in Latin. Whatever was said, and whatever it meant, it was repeated to Lord Home and sparked the animosity between the two men.[71]

It is questionable whether it was this misunderstanding at Dumbarton or the poisonous whispers of Prior Hepburn which turned the new governor against Lord Home. One English source says that the enmity between Home and Albany was rooted in the fact that the duke was invited into Scotland not by Home, but at the behest of Archbishop James Beaton of Glasgow, specifically to counter the domestic power of Lord Home and his kindred. Albany learnt about Home's opposition to his appointment and that Home was spreading lies about him to the queen and others regarding his supposed intention of usurping the throne.[72] But this tale is contradicted by others which insist that Home was prominent in bringing Albany to Scotland. Home, like others, may well have resented the over zealous exercise of authority that Albany exercised soon after his landing, the nobility by this stage becoming used to governing their own affairs. A competent governor intent on interfering with the powers freely enjoyed by the lords of the land could quickly have been branded a despot.[73]

It was soon evident that the behaviour of the warden, whatever its cause, began to try the patience of Albany, who was also having trouble from Margaret Tudor and Angus. Another factor was the uncomfortable overlap of interests between Home and Albany in the eastern borders. One of Albany's titles, inherited from his father, was Earl of March, and the attendant lands and power base were situated near Home's territory. Home's kin benefitted materially from the removal of the first Albany from their territorial homeland through forfeiture in 1483.[74] This was despite the fact that Home's own father Alexander, second Lord Home, had been closely involved with Albany in 1482-3.[75] It may have struck the governor how many similarities there were between his own father and Lord Home. The most important common factor is that both were Wardens of the March and therefore occupied an invidious position straddling two competing national powers, having to mollify both, and being open to the charge of collusion or treachery when not being visibly aggressive enough to a powerful neighbour.

Alexander, Duke of Albany, had attracted the suspicion and jealousy of his brother, King James III. As in the case of Lord

Home, the actual evidence of treachery came some time after the accusation was first made – as if the very suspicion helped to make the actual high treason a fact. John Duke of Albany did become a traitor through his plotting with England, aspiring to the throne of James III when he returned from exile in France, with his self-styled (though over-reaching) title of Alexander IV. The senior Albany's personal popularity made him a focus of dissent for those opposed to the king, which Home certainly could not rival on the national scale. But Home, like John Duke of Albany, was a charismatic and impulsive character, to the extent that, on one occasion, he talked his way out of prison in Edinburgh Castle and persuaded his gaoler to go on the run with him.[76] This event must have stirred uncomfortable echoes in the governor's mind of the story of his own father's escape from the same place; albeit his father had escaped by murdering his guards and using a rope to flee the fortress.[77]

The younger Albany's deteriorating relationship with Home, and the involvement of James IV as a factor in their antagonism, cannot wholly be understood, since there is no consistently reliable account of their disagreement in the period between Flodden and Home's death. One possible reason for Lord Home's swift disenchantment was that Albany displayed a dismaying even-handedness initially and that there was no question of Home being rewarded for being the principal instigator in bringing him to the country.[78] It may have been a shock to the surviving members of the Scottish establishment that the new power in the land was so strident in enforcing his authority. But whatever motivation he had, Home reacted swiftly and switched his allegiance to the ousted Queen Margaret and her husband, the Earl of Angus. The latter had been blamed not only for his pro-English stance, but also along with Home and others of supporting criminality in their own territories, as Albany learnt when he made a tour of some areas of Scotland soon after his arrival.[79] Lord Home swiftly pursued a course of rebellion, wasting the country and burning towns. The Earls of Arran and Lennox were sent into Berwickshire to crush him and capture his strongholds, after which he fled into England.[80]

Home's opposite number, the alleged finder of James's body and confounder of Lord Home on the battlefield, was similarly vilified. Thomas, Lord Dacre, warden of all three sections of the English marches from 1511 to 1525, had long been suspected by his overlords of treachery with the Scots.[81] His family had been a power in Cumberland since the 13th century[82] and he was adept at manipulating the labyrinthine and ever-changing politics of the marches for his own ends, which sometimes aroused suspicion in far-off Westminster. As already mentioned, Dacre fortuitously stumbled across the badly mutilated body of the Scottish king and claimed to recognise it, despite its many disfiguring wounds. But Dacre had known the king well and the inner circles of Scottish high society. Suspicions against him mounted until he was charged with conspiring with the Scots in 1522 and lost his official position soon afterwards.[83] He was summoned before Cardinal Wolsey and incarcerated in the Fleet prison before being released in September 1525. But his knowledge of the debateable lands made him too valuable to dispense with.[84] One countryman who knew him well in the north claimed no other Englishman knew more of the Scots' secrets.[85] The complicated nature of the region's politics, involving blurred national allegiances and involvement in the local criminal culture as part of the warden's duty, meant that his son William, 4th Lord Dacre, was also accused of treason in 1534, though he was acquitted.[86] According to the historian Edward Hall, Lord Dacre of the North was also oddly passive on the actual field of Flodden: 'The Lorde Dacre wyth hys company stode styl all daye unfoughten with all.'[87] But the reigning powers in Holyrood and Westminster continued to mistrust the native overlords of the marches, especially a man like Lord Dacre, who could easily call on 4,000 wild fighting men to do his bidding.[88]

Dacre's part in the disorder which occurred when Home turned against the rule of Albany was to thankfully accept his former enemy's fall from grace, for it was part of his remit from the English government to foment chaos in the region, hoping that this would force Albany to retire to France and make the Scots sue for peace. By the middle of 1515 Dacre was secretly supplying Lord Home with men and gunpowder.[89] Despite troops being despatched against him and the lack of support for him among the peerage, Home's actions became ever more unrestrained, and there is no doubt that he was firmly in the pocket of the English Warden. He conspired to help Margaret spirit the young king south into England. Another time he made plans to capture the Duke of Albany.[90] He afterwards kidnapped the Lord Lyon King of Arms at Coldstream as he was on his way to the English government on official state business; he was exchanged after a lengthy period of captivity for Lord Home's mother who was held under guard in Dunbar Castle.[91] Even Home's imprisonment in Edinburgh Castle, as noted above, did not stop his campaign of outlawry, for he escaped prison in October 1515 and persuaded the Earl of Arran to rebel against Albany also.

Home did became temporarily reconciled with Albany and was restored to his position as Chamberlain of Scotland in April 1516.[92] But several months later he failed to answer a summons to appear before the authorities and had his estates confiscated.[93] One of the charges levelled against him on this occasion was that he was conspiring to kidnap young King James V from Stirling Castle and deliver him to the English. Albany went on the offensive against the rebel and had a large force invade Home's territory and his lieutenants demanded that Lord Home deliver possession of his strongholds.[94] Some castles were delivered up to the authorities but Home was unwilling as yet to surrender his person. He managed to recapture Home Castle at the end of August, and he demolished some walls and filled in the well 'for ever more' so it should not fall into the hands of enemies again – or, some might say, to cover up the remains of the notable man killed and buried there.[95]

But time was clearly running out for Alexander Home. There is uncertainty about the details of his final days and no extant record of his trial, if there was an actual trial. Pitscottie says that he was lured to Edinburgh on the pretext of attending a conference. But Home was still cautious, as was his brother William, who would not come to the meeting at the Abbey of Holyrood without being sent the ring of Lord Home as a token he would be safe. By false promises Alexander Home was assured of his safety. His brother came and both men were imprisoned. One version of events states that William Home was dispatched to prison on the island of Inchgarvie in the Forth while Alexander Home's trial began immediately.[96]

No details of the swift condemnation and executions are given by Pitscottie, and there is the suspicion that if he had known any salacious details relating to charges against Home connecting him with treason against James IV he would have written about them. He merely states that both men were summoned on the pretext of providing expert information against the English. Albany tricked Lord Home into sending for his brother and the next day they were both found guilty of treason and beheaded.[97] The reports of Lord Home's ill behaviour on the battlefield were probably lifted from common circulation, and the fact that he knew nothing about the trial may indicate either there was nothing extraordinary to report, or that details were suppressed by Albany's authority.

Bishop Lesley's account of the event is not much more detailed. He says that Lord Home, William Home and their associate, Andrew Ker of Ferniehurst (alias Dand Ker, who had raided Kelso Abbey on the evening of the Battle of Flodden), were charged with treason, plausibly stating that there were many complaints made against them. But the conviction rested on the charges that the Homes had sustained in their houses thieves and traitors, and complaints made to Albany that Home's kindred were the chief source of theft, robbery and raids in the borders. But there were also unspecified 'fouller crymes' among the charges, and we are left guessing what these might be.[98] The anonymous *Diurnal of Occurrents*, based on near contemporary information, states that on 8 October Home was beheaded, allegedly for the sole stated crime of allowing Norham to be rebuilt, and that William Home was beheaded next day in the presence of the governor.[99] Norham Castle, damaged in the Scottish invasion, was seen as being a formidable bastion of English strength on the frontier. The *Diurnal* states that Home and his kinsman, the Prior of Coldstream, had treasonably allowed this castle to be rebuilt.[100] This particular charge seems makeshift and impossible to verify, even from English accounts. Bishop Ruthall himself bewailed the likely cost and length of time it would take to repair the Scottish damage to his beloved home, though he later found the damage not as bad as he had initially feared.[101] Andrew Ker was given a day's grace to prepare his soul before execution, but instead of using it as a period of prayer he wisely bribed one of his French guards to gain his freedom, according to one story.[102] Given the sketchiness of the whole proceeding, Ker may more simply have been found not guilty.[103] Ker was one of the most vibrant border figures of his day, as we have seen, raiding Kelso Abbey and slipping out of the executioner's grasp. For all his supposed treachery, Ker reverted to a native antagonism against the English. He survived a siege of Fernihurst Castle by his 'mortal enemy' Lord Dacre in 1523, but was taken prisoner.[104] Surprisingly he lived to relatively old age, and died in 1545.

The most sensational relation of the Lord Home's trial comes from George Buchanan, though his version of events is not as full as we could wish. He begins by saying that no new crimes were levelled against Home at the trial. The principal charges, those which were proven, were his 'private crimes' and 'many former rebellions'. Allegations were raised about Home's behaviour on the field of Flodden, but these charges were not substantiated. During the proceedings there was a furious outburst by a spectator. James Stewart, Earl of Moray, was a natural son of King James IV, and he angrily accused Lord Home of causing his father's death, 'who came alive off the field, as many witnesses did prove.'[105] No source is given by Buchanan for this extraordinary piece of melodrama, so it remains open to doubt. If it did occur, it could be wondered whether the allegation was commonly believed at the time. Moray was the king's son by his mistress Janet Kennedy, and he had probably recently returned from education abroad. Some have doubted that James Stewart was present, suggesting that he only returned to Scotland from France in 1519, but he may have returned at the same time as the Archbishop of St Andrews in 1510 and left again at some point after the trial of Lord Home. John Pinkerton suggested that the person who accused Lord Home of regicide was not the Earl of Moray, but the bishop of Moray, James Hepburn.[106] But there is no reason to suppose that Buchanan confused the two men.

Can Moray's outburst have been the impulsive guilt and fury of a young immature man who had been far from the place where his father was slaughtered? One of the next historians to weave intrigue out of the scanty web of facts was William Drummond of Hawthornden, writing in the early 17th century. He repeats the statement that no new charges were laid against Home at the show trial, and includes Buchanan's vignette about Moray. Then he relates that Lord Home had been charged with causing dissent, supporting criminals on the border, and being dishonest and dishonourable at Flodden, 'performing neither the duty of a soldier nor commander'. The charge of allowing the rebuilding of Norham Castle is again mentioned. Home was unable to counter any of these accusations effectively. The judges were prepared by Albany to find him guilty, but in case there was not proof enough of his manifold guilt, Albany gave those judges 'information of a heinous crime committed by the chamberlain and his brother, for the odiousness of it not to be revealed to the people'.[107] Having hinted at a dramatic and dreadful crime, Drummond follows the other historians by revealing nothing further.

Even among the scanty accounts of the major chroniclers, the details of Home's treachery at the battle of Flodden and his supposed removal of King James IV after the battle, are not treated as fact. Home's initial success on the field, the fact that he could not or would not press that advantage, or that he allegedly refused to rescue the costly Scottish artillery next morning, were marks against him. But as a man of high rank he had much to lose by betraying the king, who was a personal friend. As Buchanan remarked, 'He a great favourite of the king, but of too fierce a disposition...'[108] His impulsiveness and pride were elements he had in common with the king, but his quick temper ultimately led him astray. After Flodden his course of action in rejecting Albany was unwise, to say the least. As Warden of the East and Middle Marches he had a solemn duty to guard his country's frontiers. He not only went against the administration of Albany and resorted to banditry, he became the agent of his opponent Lord Dacre and seriously damaged national security. Dacre employed an extensive network of spies in Scotland, including useful men like the Abbot of Kelso, as well as maintaining close contact with Queen Margaret Tudor,[109] but none was in the trusted position that Home occupied. Besides which, Home had been warned when he was reprieved in March 1516 that he would not be pardoned again; and though the precise details of his collusion with his enemy have not survived, there is no doubt that he was guilty. Despite a few murmurs about his demise, there were few outside the kindred or followers of the Home family who protested about his execution. Thomas Howard, Earl of Surrey (son of the victor of Flodden) later attempted to characterise Home as one of the truest subjects of his prince who ever lived, which was the reason why Albany brutally butchered him. But there were few in either realm who could have believed he was innocent.[110]

As for the association of Home with the murder the king after Flodden, he was perhaps drawn in to locally circulating stories because he was a man of note whose tarnished reputation attracted allegations. The feverish vision of the Four Horsemen was symbolic of the desolation inflicted on Scotland on 9 September 1513. It is conceivable that the ten men dressed in the king's armour were real enough, and perhaps it was one of those lookalikes who escaped the carnage and was seen in the dull evening light near Kelso, something recognised in the 18th century by George Ridpath.[111]

Lord Home had no reason to kill the king, no matter what deeds he did later, or what boasts were made by men like Galbraith. The severity of Home's crimes can be gauged by the fact that he was the only high-ranking Scot to suffer capital punishment during the entire troubled rule of the Duke of Albany.[112] As well as the slander of regicide, his actual treason was long remembered in Scotland. In 1522, when the Duke of Albany led a reluctant army over the border once more, the shades of the butchered Flodden legions accompanied them, and the reluctance of the Scottish army to take the field against England again was evident. Albany exhorted them that they should not be discouraged by the memory of Flodden, which had not been lost through the fault of the Scots, but through the treachery of the Chamberlain, Lord Home. He asked them not to remember the 'grene wound of that defeat' but harken to the souls of their parents crying out for help. They should waken up to revenge the slaughter.[113]

Two years before this date, while Lord Albany was away in France, the impaled heads of Lord Home and his brother had been taken down from display outside the Tolbooth in Edinburgh by his brother George Home and David Home of

Wedderburn, and were given decent burial in the Blackfriars.[114] Albany had appointed his close associate, Antoine d'Arces (the 'White Knight'), as Warden of the East March. But the Homes did not let the execution of their leader go un-avenged. David Home of Wedderburn made complaint that Lord Home had been slain by Albany 'under trust', another hint of treachery against Albany.[115] Border honour was avenged in a particularly grisly fashion in September 1517 when the Homes apparently lured the Frenchman into attacking Langton Tower. They laid in wait and tried to ambush the 'White Knight', who fled on his horse and tried to reach the stronghold of Dunbar Castle. But his poor knowledge of the terrain led him to founder in a marsh, where his pursuers finally caught him. He was slain on the place (near the present farm of Swallowdean) – later known as 'Batty's Bog' – and one of the Homes, either David or George cut off his head and fixed it in Celtic pagan fashion to his saddle by its long flowing hair, and afterwards the head was displayed in the town of Duns.[116] Despite the power of the Homes in the area, many locals pitied the death of the unfortunate Frenchman. A sympathetic ballad about the murder was made up and it was said that an apparition warned him on his way to the encounter that if he crossed the Corney ford he would certainly die.[117]

Alexander Home's reputation never recovered, despite the resurgence of his kindred. But his great enemy and subsequent paymaster Lord Dacre proved more able to balance the competing concerns of national interests and frontier reality. Despite the best efforts of the London authorities to destroy him with a charge of treason, he survived and appropriately died in the saddle, or rather after falling from his horse. Lord Home, on the other hand, was ultimately unable to master his own recklessness and relentlessly charted his own course towards destruction, much like his own king. One of the side effects of his remarkably duplicitous career has been to blur the lines of history and legend concerning the fate of his king, James IV.

The result, as the Duke of Albany's biographer Marie W. Stuart commented, are that, 'The records of the intrigues before and after Flodden are so amazing that one cannot be astonished at anything, not even the kidnapping of a king.'[118]

Chapter 6

The Widows of Scotland

In the period which bookended the battle of Flodden the two nation states of Britain found themselves, for the first time and temporarily, governed by two queens. Both women were foreigners in their respective realms. In England, before the war, Catherine of Aragon had been given the authority (though not the sole authority) to raise an army to counter the Scottish threat when King Henry VIII left for his war with France. During August 1513 Catherine chivvied local authorities into providing men and equipment for the campaign. She ordered battle banners and rounded up a force which she intended to lead north to York and rendezvous with the Earl of Surrey.[1] In the event Catherine's army, like that of Sir Thomas Lovell's at Nottingham, was kept in reserve as a safeguard in case the Scots either defeated or eluded Surrey's army in Northumberland and came south. The fact that there were two further armies available to meet the Scots shows that England had more than adequate resources to defeat them. Resigned to remaining in the south, Catherine was still keen to show her credentials as a strident English leader in the absence of her husband. Her exultancy at the victory, when she wanted to export the corpse of the king as a trophy to France, struck English commanders as excessive. A few weeks after writing to Henry and sending him the Scot's bloody coat for a trophy she wrote to her bereaved sister-in-law. The letter was dated at Windsor, 18 October 1513, and Queen Margaret in her reply thanked Catherine for her sympathy in the misfortune fallen upon her. She also, sadly, hoped her sister queen would 'keep her brother in remembrance of her, that his kindness may be known in this realm...'[2] There was little likelihood that anyone else in Scotland in the autumn of 1513 would have extended similar warm feelings towards King Henry VIII. But the affection between the two queens seems real enough. The women had also been in contact in the lead up to the Anglo-Scottish conflict. Shortly before the battle Margaret had written from Scotland, perhaps sensing sorrow ahead, asking her Spanish sister-in-law to remember her in her good prayers.[3]

The English queen's letter to Margaret in October was written four days after Henry VIII had written to Pope Leo X from France, asking for permission to bury his brother-in-law. Catherine may have known about this apparently sincere intention of her husband and been influenced by his consolatory attitude towards his enemy. She despatched an emissary, Friar Langley, to seek a truce from Queen Margaret and the Scots.[4]

Margaret's request concerning her brother was perhaps more a personal plea than a request from her adopted nation to prevent further bloodshed. Her letter to Queen Catherine contains no mention of her dead husband.[5] Nor is there evidence from historians or documentary sources about any public show of grief from the widowed queen. Judging from the evidence, we can say that Margaret is not known to have shown any sorrow for her husband. Funeral obsequies for the late monarch were only arranged by John, Duke of Albany in July 1515, after Margaret was ousted from power.[6] The only wisp of legend about her being affected by her loss is the romantic fable of her sitting pining in the turret room – afterwards called 'Queen Margaret's Bower' – in the north west tower of Linlithgow Palace overlooking the loch in a lonely vigil for the king.[7] This sentimental legend does not accord well with Margaret's character as it is revealed by her actions in the succeeding years. A similar romantic distortion occurs in a letter written by Paulo de Laude, Milanese Ambassador to the Emperor, to Massimiliano Sforza, Duke of Milan, on 11 October 1513, who states he had heard that Queen Margaret was planning to go to war against her brother to revenge her dead husband, though he prudently dismisses the rumour as doubtful.[8]

The lives of Catherine and Margaret may give an insight into royal women in the Tudor age, but direct comparisons between the two women have to be treated carefully. In Margaret's case, her turbulent life has given rise to a number of full-length studies, far more than have been devoted to King James IV, and most of which have taken a sympathetic view of her.[9] But analysis of her actions in widowhood show that rash opportunism was often behind her actions, albeit she must also have been motivated at times by her extremely uncertain situation in Scotland. Surviving evidence of Queen Margaret's reaction to her loss is admittedly patchy and analysis of her motives is difficult. The contrast between the would-be warrior queen Catherine and the passive, stricken figure of Margaret is compelling. The death of her husband was a defining moment for Margaret and it led to a dramatic change in her public persona.

Immediately after Flodden, Margaret, with her vulnerable young family, was in a difficult position, though she had been given the full powers of regency by her late husband. Her son, the future James V, was just seventeen month old. She bore another son by the king, Alexander, Earl of Ross, in April 1514, who must have been conceived only a few weeks before Flodden. Prince Alexander was the last of six children she had by James.[10] Her primary duty as a royal wife had been honourably fulfilled, even though the stark mortality rate of the age meant that only James V reached adulthood.

Twenty-three years old, alone and yet again pregnant, she became romantically involved with the young 6th Earl of Angus, Archibald, whose father, George the Master of Angus, had perished at Flodden with 200 Douglases.[11] Their plans to marry were arranged in the summer of 1514, and Margaret was so caught up with her intentions that she informed neither the government of Scotland nor her royal brother.[12] They married in secret on 6 August 1514.[13] Her new husband's grandfather, the

5th Earl of Angus, was another Archibald, famously nicknamed 'Bell-The-Cat' for his part in bringing down the dangerous cronies of King James III.[14] He had a long, fluctuating relationship with James IV, which included competing with him for the favours of Janet Kennedy. They finally, tragically, fell out just before the Battle of Flodden, when Angus failed to persuade the king not to go ahead with the battle.[15] After being falsely accused of cowardice, Angus had withdrawn from the fatal field and retired to the king's favourite place of pilgrimage, Whithorn Abbey in Galloway, and when he died in November 1513, his grandson succeeded him, inheriting all the complicated ambition, charisma and ruthlessness of his kindred. The impulsive marriage can be seen as being a combination of personal choice and a strategic alliance with the head of the most notably pro-English families of the Lowlands. It also immediately set most of the nobility against Margaret and led them to invite James IV's exiled cousin John, Duke of Albany to govern the country.

Queen Margaret's behaviour in the years after James IV's death was so markedly different from what we know of her while he was alive, suggesting that she was freed of the constraints her role and his influence had imposed on her. She was also released in the physical sense from the toll of being constantly pregnant, though she did have another child with her new husband. One of the striking things about her after Flodden was the ongoing ineptness of her political manoeuvrings. She failed to appreciate that her choice to marry anyone, least of all Angus, would lead to the immediate loss of her political power and control over young James V and his brother Alexander. The widowed queen also showed that she was prepared to use rumour and slander against her opponents, and even traded in the dubious currency of legend to get her own way. She was certainly able to frame her beliefs around the expectations of her audience, promising at one moment, like a recalcitrant child, to 'be a good Scotswoman,' then stating to someone else that she would 'liever be dead than live among the Scots'.[16] Small wonder that that English ambassador to Scotland, Magnus, reluctantly admitted to Cardinal Wolsey that Margaret never acted agreeable except when she was trying to wheedle money from someone.[17]

Soon after John, Duke of Albany, came to Scotland in 1515, Margaret was obliged to give up the regency and afterwards give up the custody of her two young sons. When she fled with Angus to England in late 1515 she was pregnant with a daughter, Margaret Douglas, who was born in Lord Dacre's castle at Harbottle in November. In many ways her relationship with Albany was the most crucial to herself and the country in the years after Flodden. He was most successful during his first period of regency in Scotland (May 1515 - September1517), which saw him overcome the threat of Angus and Margaret controlling the young king and the country. His second Scottish visit (one is tempted to say 'term', since he may have come to believe his stays in Scotland were like prison terms) of November 1521 - October 1522 saw him temporarily reconciled with Margaret. By his third spell in Scotland (September 1523 - May 1524), he started suffering from the law of diminishing returns and his own disenchantment with the country of his forefathers. Despite his royal lineage he was half French and obviously most at ease in the country of his birth.

The loss of her children to the control of Albany prompted Margaret to engage in an underhand campaign against him. It was a measure of her desperation that she used disparaging rumours which were circulating in Scotland. Queen Margaret's accusations not only involved whoever she viewed as her principal persecutor at any given time (which usually fluctuated between Albany and her husband Angus) but raked up gossip which involved incidents from the reign of her first husband. The prevalence of malicious rumour mongering might be seen as a measure of the health of any particular regime, and it is noteworthy that the reign of James IV was remarkable for its lack of political scandal, at least after the king gained maturity.

By 1516 the English were busy inventing calumnies about Albany. Lord Dacre, not content with paying spies and wreaking physical havoc on the border, was comparing the duke to the malicious King Richard III, implying that he planned to do away with the young princes and wear the crown himself.[18] The English charges were clearly inspired by the fear or fantasy that Albany's aim was to be king, and the rumours grew after the unfortunate death of the young Prince Alexander, Duke of Ross, at Stirling on 18 December 1516.[19] Slandering the duke's name was a powerful tactic that his enemies repeated for many years. But the suggestion by Polydore Vergil that these suspicions against Albany were first raised by the council of Scotland while they debated inviting him to Scotland after Flodden is suspect.[20]

There were plenty of venomous tongues prepared to trade lies about this French born governor. Lord Dacre wrote to Margaret on 10 July 1519 when she was showing signs of being reconciled Albany and reminded her that she had requested the English government to keep Albany out of Scotland. The treacherous sins of Albany's father Alexander against his own brother King James III were dredged up, plus the suspicions that the current Duke of Albany had caused the death of Prince Alexander, infant brother of King James V.[21]

The scurrilous poet John Skelton got in on the act, alluding to the threat the duke was making to the rightful Scottish king in his poem *Howe the Douty Duke of Albany*:

Howe ye pretende
For to defende
The yonge Scottyshe kyng,
But ye meane a thyng,
And ye coude bryng
The matter about
To putte his eyes out

And put hym downe,
And set hys crowne
On your owne heed
Whan he were deed.[22]

Ostensibly Skelton was satirising Albany's failure to successfully command the Scottish army which invaded northern England in 1523, as he gleefully hammers home in his heading to the poem: 'Howe the Douty Duke of Albany lyke a cowarde knyght, ran awaye shamfully with an hundred thousande tratlande Scottes and faint harted Frenchmen...' The campaign was not a success, and the main reason for failure was the disinclination of the Scots to engage in full scale warfare against the English rather than the personal cowardice of the duke, as Skelton suggested. Albany was a better administrator than a general, in the Scottish context at least, though his military leadership for the French in Europe stands up better.

The damaging English rumours about the duke were sent abroad like bacteriological warfare. They spread through the same diplomatic channels which had swapped gossip about the fate of the late Scottish king. Venetians Andrea Badoer and Sebastian Giustinian reported the upheavals in Scotland in 1515 from a supposedly reliable source. In this strand of slander Albany is given the role of a pantomime villain who had exiled Queen Margaret and left her with only two attendants, then forced her to write letters to the pope and her brother saying she had freely given up her children to this scheming devil.[23] The Italians note that one of the queen's children was dead and if the young king perished the kingdom would fall to Albany. This propaganda was in fact fed to the Venetians directly by Cardinal Wolsey, who stated that some of Margaret's associates had been imprisoned and others put to death.[24] After Margaret was reconciled with Albany in 1521, dark lies concerning him were still being bandied abroad. Dacre wrote to Margaret in

March 1521, stating he was surprised that she had gone back to supporting the idea of Albany coming back to Scotland from France, reminding her (as if she could have forgotten) of the allegation that Albany had killed James V's younger brother.[25]

Lord Dacre seems to have been a prime mover in the promulgation of the murderous tales. By the end of that year he was informing Wolsey that the duke was working hard to obtain Margaret's divorce from Angus so he could marry her himself and claim the throne. Dacre also analysed Albany's official statements and surmised from them that he wanted the crown because of possessive references to the parliament and even the border wardens. On a more personal front, Lord Dacre learnt that the duke had asked his borderers if none of them could do him a favour and get rid of Dacre, which surely must have rankled.[26] Perhaps prompted by this personal threat, he shortly afterwards wrote to Wolsey that aid must be given to rebel Scottish peers, otherwise the young king would be destroyed.[27]

Tales about the sinister nature of Margaret's proposed divorce from Angus were also circulated in Europe, after being given a spin by Wolsey. The bishop of Badajoz wrote to Emperor Charles V from Rome, stating that Albany was attempting to facilitate Margaret's divorce from the earl so that he could get rid of young James, marry Margaret and claim the throne.[28] Back at home, Gavin Douglas, the poet and uncle of Margaret's husband Angus, fled to the English court in December 1521 and carried with him a scurrilous litany of complaints against Albany, including a charge that young King James V was not being properly clothed and that Alexander, Duke of Ross, has died from want of necessities or from poison. Douglas made explicit the supposed identical characters of Albany and Richard III.[29]

With such a long-lived slander passing through so many hands, it may seem that Queen Margaret was almost a bystander in these charges which affected her nearest and dearest. Her reconciliation with Albany in 1521 was a serious blow to the English authorities and, following Dacre and Gavin Douglas's failed meddling, her brother Henry VIII wrote to her, expressing concerns about her being easily led by Albany. Margaret wrote back angrily, dismissing Henry's sharp and unkind communication. She denied that she was contemplating a divorce from the Earl of Angus and planned to marry Albany: that was a rumour given out by Gavin Douglas. She had a better friend in the duke than any other; if he had meant to harm her son, she sensibly said she would have been the first to know about it. She also warned her brother that if he continued to be unkind, people would think that it was he who sought to harm his nephew, a deft threat that she would turn the propaganda tables on him.[30]

But the map of Margaret's political allegiances changed again, and by 1523 when Albany was abroad and Margaret was angling to regain power, she fully endorsed the old smears against him, having allowed herself to be persuaded of his evil intentions by Dacre and others.[31] She wrote in a letter to the Earl of Surrey in November 1523, two months after Albany's return to Scotland, that she feared the lords whom Albany had appointed to look after her only remaining son were planning his 'utar dystrokcyon' at his bidding.[32] Surrey wrote to Wolsey on the 2 December, relaying some of Margaret's fears and adding that he thought Albany would soon retreat back to France, taking the young king with him; otherwise the young monarch might be murdered.[33]

Margaret's letter had also homed in on a malicious tale about the new Chamberlain of Scotland, Lord Fleming (who succeeded Lord Home), who was one of the lords charged by Albany to look after the king. She stated that it was common knowledge in Scotland that Fleming had murdered his wife and her two sisters.[34] For good measure, Margaret added the spicy, semi-incestuous gossip (found nowhere else) that Albany had one of

King James V's illegitimate sisters as a lover.[35] John 2nd Lord Fleming's former wife Euphemia was one of the three daughters of John, first Lord Drummond, who died suddenly together in mysterious circumstances in 1502. The incident was one of the few shady examples of political intrigue recorded in the reign of James IV. The reason for the sensation was that another of the sisters was James's mistress (and mother of his daughter Margaret, born in 1497). James had been attached to Margaret Drummond possibly since 1495, and she soon displaced his former mistress, Marion Boyd.[36] Margaret was set up in her own household in Stirling Castle in 1496, though by the following year her romantic star was on the wane for the king. The three Drummond sisters – Margaret, Euphemia and Sybilla – apparently died at the same time one morning at breakfast at Drummond Castle, Perthshire, and it was believed by some that they had been poisoned to pave the way for the king's marriage to Princess Margaret Tudor. One version of events went so far as to state that he had either clandestinely married Margaret Drummond or was waiting for papal dispensation to do so,[37] and it was commonly thought that his attachment to her stood in the way of the English marriage and alliance, or possibly that it accorded the Drummonds too much influence.[38]

Fleming was not the only one gossips pointed the finger at: another putative poisoner was a member of the Kennedy clan, anxious to see that the king's new mistress Janet Kennedy had no earthly rival for his affections.[39] There was of course no public investigation into the matter. English spies or agents were possibly thought to have been involved. Romantic fable or factual tradition, the story was believed by the Drummond clan and was related in a history of the family written by William Drummond, Viscount Strathallan, written in 1681,[40] where Margaret is described as 'a lady of rare perfections and singular beautie'. The truth of malicious poisoning has been recently doubted,[41] and it seems that Margaret Drummond had for several years before her death been superseded in the king's affections by Janet Kennedy, thus removing the supposed main reason for her murder.[42] On the other hand, Margaret may have had unique access to current early family traditions: her husband Angus was the maternal grandson of John, 1st Lord Drummond, father of the tragic sisters. Angus's mother Elizabeth Drummond was married first to Sir David Fleming, brother of John, 2nd Lord Fleming, and it seems likely that Margaret inherited through her second marriage a stake in an antagonism between the Flemings and Drummonds. The fact that she was using this popular current black rumour for her own ends says much about her mindset.

James IV was allegedly sufficiently enamoured with Margaret Drummond at one point to compose the poem about her. The author, unnamed in the original Bannatyne Manuscript of 1568, compared the remembered beauty of the scene to that of his lover: *Quhen Tayis bank wes blumyt brycht, With blosomes blycht and bred.* James supposedly spent time with Margaret here by the River Tay, at the still beautiful Drummond family castle of Stobbshall in Perthshire:

> This myld, meik, mansuet Mergrit,
> This perle polist most quhyt,
> Dame Natouris deir dochter discreit,
> The dyamant of delyt,
> Neuir formit wes to found on feit
> Ane figour moir perfyte,
> Nor non on mold that did hir meit
> Mycht mend hir wirth a myte.[43]

However precipitant the king was in moving on to his next mistress, Janet Kennedy, he did continue to honour the memory of Margaret Drummond. He paid for priests to sing in Dunblane Cathedral for her soul every quarter from 10 February 1503 for many years.[44] It is a matter of conjecture how widespread the whispers about her death were during his reign, but certainly his queen heard them and was able to drag them into the light years later.

The Duke of Albany must have been aware of the painfully fantastic attempts by Margaret to discredit him, and however effective or otherwise he was at imposing order on the leaderless realm during his three extended visits to Scotland, he has to be given some amount of sympathy for the difficulties he encountered. Not only did he have to contend with the dubious loyalty of people like Margaret Tudor, Lord Home and the Earl of Angus; there was constant hostility from England. The main agent of that enmity, Dacre, gave an amusing anecdote about Albany's impotent anger to Lord Surrey (who passed on the joke to Wolsey). He related that every time the duke became overcome with rage he would 'take his bonnet suddenly off his head, and throw it in the fire, and no man dare take it out, but let it to be brent...at his last being in Scotland he did burn above a dozen bonnets after that manner. And if he be such a man, we shall speed the better with him.'[45] Who can guess how much his milliner's bills were during his sojourns in Edinburgh? In fact, his proclivity towards emotionally outbursts were only one facet of his character, which left him disadvantaged by the more devious spirits around him in Scotland and England, as his biographer points out: 'Reckless speech, hot temper, extravagance and a spirit too anxious to please others, were all qualities that unfitted him for the cunning hide-and-seek, stab-and-run methods of the sixteenth century.'[46]

The far-fetched accusations of poisoning and murder were countered by his supporters fostering a romantic image of the duke that was also remote from reality. His arrival in Scotland in the time of its direst need even inspired a historian based in England to compare the coming of this 'Scot who was a Frenchman' to his ancestral soil as being like that of Ulysses.[47] In the event, Jehan Stewart himself must have become quickly disillusioned by the internecine rivalries and alliances among the Scottish nobility. One major shadow which lay heavily across his regency was his own family background. Accusations of attempted murder were part of the controversy involving his own father, his uncle the Earl of Mar and King James III.

Raising a suspicion of poisoning was a favourite accusation among the upper classes when it came to discrediting enemies and heightening misgivings about sudden deaths. Shamefully, even James IV deployed this tactic when he tried to justify his rebellion against his father to the Danes by stating that his father may have something to do with the death of his spouse, Margaret of Denmark, through poisoning.[48]As far back as 1275, Queen Margaret, wife of King Alexander III, was said to have been despatched by this method.[49] In England, King Edward IV is rumoured to have been poisoned by his wife, Elizabeth Woodville; the latter possibly engineered the death of King Edward's brother George Duke of Clarence through accusations of involvement in spells and magic.[50] The association of poison and upper class intrigue continued past the time of James IV, with Henry IV's illegitimate son, Henry Fitzroy, Duke of Richmond, allegedly poisoned in 1536 at the behest of Anne Boleyn and her brother, Lord Rochford. Queen Margaret Tudor and Angus's daughter, Margaret Douglas, was rumoured to have been poisoned by the Earl of Leicester following her death in 1578.[51] Back in Scotland, the Duke of Atholl was said to have been murdered by the Earl of Morton using this method, the poison being administered at a feast.[52]

Margaret and her associates who used stories about the threat of poisoning to James V were therefore conforming to a malicious upper class tactic, common in her time. The same kind of lies were directed at the Douglas family, in the period 1526-28 when they were accused of attempting to poison James V,[53] and a measure of the banality of all such rumours was the allied tittle-tattle that was circulating in 1521 to the effect that the real King

James V had been kidnapped and conveyed to England, and the child sitting in Stirling supposed to be the king was a plebeian doppelganger.[54]

As mentioned, Margaret's allegiance to the English party was linked to the political inclinations of her husband Angus, and she was by no means unswerving in her adherence to it. Her marriage to the earl showed signs of being in trouble as early as 1517 when Margaret was still in England,[55] where she had been from September 1515. She came back to Scotland in June 1517, but did not mention the possibility of divorcing Angus until early 1519.[56] Marital discord had become painful when she returned from England to find that Angus had impregnated a daughter of the laird of Traquair, and produced a bastard daughter.[57] His relationship with this lady was used in an abortive attempt to gain a papal divorce, when Margaret claimed Angus had a pre-nuptial contract to marry her.[58] A putative reconciliation mooted with Angus in 1518 did not last long.[59] One of the self serving factors which swayed her eventually towards accepting the Duke of Albany's rule was the fact that he was related through marriage to the Medici Pope Leo X and could therefore aid her in getting a divorce[60] But the path towards divorce took several years, during which time there was much financial wrangling with Angus.[61] Albany was in a position to help her most directly during the second period of his direct regency, beginning in late 1521, not only through his family links with Rome but also to help her gain monies due to her in Scotland. English retaliation against this alliance of former enemies came in the form of rumouring that Margaret was guilty of adultery with the duke.[62] This in itself was only a variation of the story, repeated at various times, that Albany and Margaret were planning to marry, despite the fact that Albany already had a wife.[63]

Various tactics were employed by Margaret to gain her divorce, notably including that Angus had a pre contract with the daughter of the laird of Traquair, a fact which he eventually acknowledged.[64] The depth of Margaret's desperation to obtain her wish is detailed in a letter written by the English ambassador Dr Magnus to Wolsey on 23 June 1525. There is nothing compelling about most of the contents of the letter. Magnus writes with concern about the truce between England and Scotland which was due to expire the following month. Sir William Eures had made it known to him that there were two Scottish raids across the border, for which he seeks redress. The Scottish authorities had therefore asked their Warden of the Marches, the Earl of Angus, to look in to the matter. Angus is reported to have taken some of the Armstrongs and other thieves of Liddesdale, but they were not in prison. There are further details about the current state of relations between Angus and the earls of Lennox and Arran.

Then the most extraordinary sentence is inserted without comment or fanfare towards the end of the letter:

> The Quenes Grace contynneth still at Sterling, and seweth faste for the devorce betwene Her said Grace and the said Erle of Anguisshe; surmitting her cause to be that She was maried to the said Erle, the late King of Scottes her husbande being a live, and that the same King was living three yeres after the feilde of Floddon or Brankeston.[65]

Thomas Magnus was a cleric and diplomat who had endured long service in the north under Henry VIII, whose most recent mission to Scotland had been a last ditch and futile attempt to reconcile Margaret with Angus (pointless because she had already become attached to Henry Stewart, soon to become her third husband).[66] Given this reliable source and Margaret's proven tendency to use established innuendo to further her own ends, it seems likely that the story about King James IV living three years after Flodden was a current and plausible story circulating in 1524. Much can be read into the fact that Magnus passed no comment on Margaret's desperate employment of an implausible folktale.

But this tantalising clue unfortunately does not lead to finding a full version of the tale that the king lived for three full years after Flodden. It is like a bookmark stuck between the leaves of a legend, imprinted with some of the words but not enough detail. Where was James supposed to be for those three years – on the road to Jerusalem perhaps, or in the dungeon of Home Castle? And how did he finally die? Did Margaret claim to find out about his survival during the three years after Flodden, or did she consciously commit bigamy by marrying Angus?

Margaret typically strained this fragile fairy tale when she used it for her own advantage. It is a measure of her character that one of the few times she is known to have mentioned him after his death, it was in this cynical attempt to obtain release from her own hastily contrived second marriage. Her loyalty to her royal husband immediately after his death did not stretch to making decent enquiry about his body or asking that his remains be repatriated.[67] In the event, Margaret gained her divorce (arranged and paid for by the Duke of Albany whom she had mercilessly slandered over the years), which was pronounced at Rome on 11 March 1527, though news of it did not reach Scotland until months later.[68] Unsurprisingly the sentence of divorce, pronounced by Cardinal Ancona, does not mention the claim that King James survived the battle.[69] Towards the end of her life (she died in October 1541) Margaret looked back with regret at the way she had behaved towards her second husband, the Earl of Angus, who had treated her at least as badly as she had treated him. There is no record however of any fond remembered sorrow for King James IV.

Chapter 7

Under the Hill

Even before Flodden was fought and lost, Edinburgh was suffering from an undercurrent of unrest caused by the war with England. On 5 September 1513, four days before the battle, the anxious authorities tried to act against the deserters and 'all maner of personis' who had fled from the Scottish army in England and were infiltrating into the burgh. These deserters were some of the 20,000 men who were alleged to have absconded from the Scottish ranks by the Bishop Thomas Ruthall of Durham, though his figure may be an exaggeration. The deserters were ordered to return to the army immediately, though it is doubtful if any of them did so. There were also a noticeable number of other men capable of bearing arms still in the town and these were ordered to present themselves to the Provost. The penalty for not complying was loss of their lands and goods, and possibly death. Able-bodied men found in the town would have their names passed on to the king when he returned, by God's grace, which of course he never did.[1]

The strained atmosphere in the crowded capital had been responsible for strange events before the army departed, as demonstrated by the Summons of Pluto at the Market Cross. In the days that followed that incident the apprehension rose to an uncomfortable level for the inhabitants. Uncertainty about events in England played a major part in the town's tension. On 10 September the burgh records acknowledged there was a 'great rumour' being spread concerning the sovereign lord and his army. The ominous talk caused alarm and all remaining able bodied men were ordered to bring weapons to the presidents for the provost when they heard the ringing of the common bell. Once mustered, the men were ordered to attend to the 'defens of the toun aganis thame that wald invaid the samyn'. The need to manage outbreaks of hysteria is clear in another decree that outlawed clamouring and crying at the city gates by women, especially vagabond women, who were warned they should go about their usual business.[2]

A hastily constructed defence was thrown up to defend the burgh, afterwards known as the Flodden Wall. What its citizens could not have known was that the English army was low on resources and did not have the capability of striking at the capital of its enemy. One of the first survivors to reach Edinburgh, possibly late on Saturday 10 September, was Randolph Murray, captain of the city band, who brought back with him the famous Blue Blanket, the banner of the trades guild, rescued from the battlefield. This standard was given to the guilds of Edinburgh in 1482 by a grateful King James III after the capital's tradesmen rescued him from incarceration in the castle, and it was carried by the Edinburgh contingent into the battle of Flodden. To mark this poignant return of the Blue Blanket, a ceremony is carried out in the capital each year, on the Sunday before the Riding of the Marches. The remains of the ancient defence, the Flodden Wall, are inspected, with a moment of silence at each stop. Earth collected from the actual site of Flodden is used to mark each stop.[3] The drama in post-war Edinburgh was a favourite subject for the melodramatic Victorians. The best known example if perhaps the poem by W. E. Ayton, 'Edinburgh After Flodden'.[4] Several paintings also depict the abject Murray returning to Edinburgh.[5]

The shocked and bitter survivors were unlikely to have offered a cohesive picture of the scale of the disaster. Confusion about the numbers of Scottish dead was complicated by the swarm of Scottish deserters. Different rumours about the fate of the king began to arise before the outcome of the battle of Flodden was known, another manifestation of chaos. News of the encounter spread around the continent not because it had resulted in the death of a popular king or involved carnage on an industrial scale; the battle made news because of its significance in international politics. Flodden was a proxy blow for France and a boost for England's allies. The high death toll and the exotic foreign location must have added spice to prattling tongues in Italy and France. Contemporary perspectives placed emphasis on the upper class casualties and not those nameless thousands who also perished. The peers and other gentry died in abnormally large numbers because of their personal adherence to their king.

The lords and lairds of Scotland went dutifully to their deaths though many must have naturally felt foreboding about the merits of the war. A glance at the names and numbers on that death-roll is sobering. At least nine earls died alongside the monarch,[6] and more than a dozen peers. Around sixteen sons of noblemen are listed as casualties and five high-ranking churchmen (including the king's natural son Alexander Stewart, Archbishop of St Andrews). Add to this the toll more than fifteen other landed gentlemen and we have a picture of substantial mortality among a particular class, if not total decimation.

The English authorities might have countered tales of the enemy king's survival by displaying the royal corpse. This had happened in the past in the case of English monarchs who died in suspicious circumstances. The prime example was Richard II, who was almost certainly killed at Pontefract Castle in 1399. His remains were exhibited for three days in London, but did not completely quash rumours that he lived on. The fact that the English did not display the body of James IV was possibly because they chose not to dignify foreign tittle-tattle about his survival, or else they knew that such a display would not necessarily kill rumours. And the rumours flourished in Scotland. Home's damaged reputation and Queen Margaret's increasingly desperate clutching at the straws of court gossip show that the upper classes as much as anyone were involved in creating legends about Flodden.

The view of the fate of James IV among ordinary Scots is more difficult to glean. Most commentators were inevitably close to court, but one exception was Adam Abell, an Observantine friar and a member of the recently founded priory at Jedburgh at the time of Flodden, and therefore geographically well placed to provide information. Abell wrote a Latin history of the Scots from their mythological beginnings to his own day, which has been lost, but he also completed an abridgement in Scots, *The Roit or Quheill of Tyme,* which survives in manuscript.[7] The chronicle charts events up to the year 1533 (with a continuance to 1537), and Abell was in his thirties or forties at the time of Flodden.[8] Abell's view of the king is strongly positive, not least because the monarch was a benefactor to the Observatine Franciscan order, and he generally supports the establishment in his writing. During the minority of James V he continued to show strong support for the lawful but contentious rule of John, Duke of Albany, who was 'sa prudent in his doings'.[9]

Abell is also the only eyewitness to the reigns of both James IV and V whose work was written before the Reformation.[10] His important statement that the king may have survived the battle of Flodden was sourced from someone within his own religious house, but he juxtaposed it with the more rationalist, competing belief that James had perished. Abell wrote that a fellow monk in the monastery of Jedburgh insisted that the king had not perished in England.[11] It is a pity this writer, the closest historian in terms of time and proximity to the battle, does not elaborate, though further detail about Flodden may have been contained in the lost Latin original of his work.

This conflict between the rational and the hoped-for fate of King James is echoed in the next generation of historians and surely reflects the contemporary living tradition concerning the king. John Lesley, Bishop of Ross, wrote his history in 1571, and even by this date there was considerable ambivalence about the fortune of King James IV. He begins his account prosaically enough, stating that the king's body had been taken the day after the battle to Berwick and then on to Richmond in Surrey. But it was widely believed that this corpse was actually the laird of Bonhard (or Bonehard). Then comes the extraordinary statement concerning the king's survival: the king was seen that night at Kelso, hale and sound. Many people believed that the king afterwards went on pilgrimage abroad, particularly to Jerusalem. The rest of his life was spent devoutly in 'dule and dolour', in exile in the holy places.[12] In the Scots version of his work Lesley adds, whatever his fate, the king was never seen again in Scotland, and links the tale to that of Charles, Duke of Burgundy, who also died in battle, albeit that his people vainly predicted his eventual return to them.[13] This links the survival rumour to a wider European folk tradition, but the tantalising localisation at Kelso is a less substantial belief. It occurs, as we have seen, in the work of Lindsay of Pitscottie, who has the king being removed from the field on a 'dun hackney', and perhaps being seen that evening in the uncertain gloaming shadows between Duns and Kelso. There his story falls apart, as Pitscottie admits that no one knows what these phantom-like figures did with the rescued royal thereafter. But he reposts the rumour that a condemned man ten years later tried to escape his sentence by offering to show the Duke of Albany the king's alleged burial place.[14] George Buchanan has the king being seen re-entering Scotland by crossing the Tweed. He states that the king was murdered near Kelso by Home's vassals. But the stories he heard did not specify whether these men acted alone, hoping to please Lord Home, who feared he would be called to account for his battlefield inactivity.[15]

Early in the 17th century, William Drummond of Hawthornden summarised a range of stories about the king. He repeated the arcane tale of the four horsemen with streamers of straw on their lances mounting the king on a sorrel hackney and being seen between Kelso and Duns. Again, the majority of suspicion was directed at Home:

> Many hold, he was killed in the castle of Hume, either by intelligence between the English and the lord Hume's kindred, or out of fear (for they were at the slaughter of the king's father, and the most violent in that fight) or of hopes of great fortunes, which would follow innovations, and the confusion of the state, being men who lived best in a troubled commonwealth and upon the borders.[16]

The burgh of Kelso looms largely in these traditions, being the closest Scottish town to the battlefield, less than 18 km (11.2 miles) west of Flodden. Survivors from the battle would have been able to reach Kelso by the evening of 9 September. In terms of the geography of the various legends, the main occurrence of sightings of the king and other incidents seems to fall roughly in a triangle, with the points at Flodden, Roxburgh and Duns. The stories attached to places like Stitchell and Home Castle, discussed below, occur within or just outside this area.

Drummond also notes that the most commonly believed survival tale was that James had escaped to the Holy Land:

> The common people, ever more addicted to superstition than verity, believed he was living, and had passed over the seas, and, according to his promise, visited the holy sepulchre in Palestine: and that there, for his other offences, and the bearing or arms against his father, in prayers and penance, he spent the remainder of his tedious days. That he would return again when he found opportunity, and the necessity of Europe required him. This report was of as great truth, as that which the Britains have of the return of their king Arthur, and the Burgundians not long before conceived of their duke Charles after the battle of Nancy, most of them believing he

escaped from the conflict.[17]

The comparison with the rumoured survival of other dead rulers, also found in Lesley, was first made in print by John Major, whose *History of Greater Britain* was published in Paris in 1521, demonstrating that accounts of James's IV's strange fate were widespread within a decade of his death:

> Wherefore the Britons had the expectation that Arthur after a long time would return. So that this came to be a proverb when one who shall never come back was yet looked for – 'You are waiting for such an one, as the Britons for their Arthur'. This is but the blind affection of a people for their king, whom, all dead though he be, their unreason leads them to think of as still among the living. Just the same has been said of Charles of Burgundy; and of our own James, the fourth of the name, a like invention has found favour.[18]

As the writers themselves observed, there were plenty of precedents for beloved rulers who were supposed to have somehow survived their final catastrophe and resumed life elsewhere, albeit in a more circumspect fashion. The most recent European example, as noted by Major (and later by Lesley and Polydore Vergil), was Charles the Bold, Duke of Burgundy, who perished at the battle of Nancy against the forces of the Duke of Lorraine on 5 January 1477, and whose fatality was not credited by the Flemings.[19] Charles died fighting before the walls of the town and his naked body, like that of James IV, was subject to multiple wounds, which made identification difficult. When he was eventually discovered several days later, his head was found to be cut in two and the corpse had been partially eaten by wolves.

Central ingredients in the legend of an undying hero include a violent death in dramatic circumstances and confusion about the fate of an individual's mortal remains. But even without a supposed supernatural element, the death of a charismatic ruler in battle frequently engendered legendary confusion, as in the death of King Charles XII of Sweden in 1718, rumoured to have been killed not by the enemy Danes in battle but by one of his own troops. The occurrence of a major national disaster seems to fuel legends and magnify the death tales of leaders involved in disaster. Such a case was the final fall of Constantinople, which was captured by the Turks in 1453. The last Byzantine emperor, Constantine XI Palaiologos, ensured himself hard won immortality when he died fighting in the city, instead of accepting the Ottoman offer to flee. Constantine only ruled the constricted rump of the Byzantine Empire for a few years, yet his lack of military prowess and leadership qualities did not prevent him from becoming an enduring figurehead after his death for a vanished civilisation. Most sources agree that he died at the Gate of St Romanos in the millennium-old citadel, either crushed in the panicked crowd or cut down by enemy soldiers. Although there was doubts about his death and difficulty identifying the corpse, the most trustworthy version of events state that his head was cut off and presented to the sultan.[20] One factor in the confusion, and another element which raised his death to martyrdom, was the story that he cast off his royal raiment and fought as a common soldier.[21] There were three separate stories that the emperor had somehow escaped from the devastated city, but none of them gained widespread support.[22]

Like King James IV, Emperor Constantine was vouchsafed an uncanny vision. Guarding the walls of the city with his nobles, a heavenly queen approached the nearby church of the Virgin. She spoke to the emperor, telling him the city was dedicated to her and many times she had saved it from the anger of God. But this time it could not be saved because of the sins of its inhabitants. She took his crown and sceptre from him and said she would keep them safe until God would allow another to come and claim them. Constantine gave her the care of his soul with the crown and sceptre and the lady vanished. The legend sought to explain why the imperial jewels were never found.[23] Constantine was also said by some to be sleeping and would return one day to drive the foreigners from Constantinople, though some sources claim this heroic act would be accomplished one day by someone known as the 'poor man' and not the last emperor.[24] A more remarkable fable said that when Constantine was about to be killed by Turks an angel carried him away and turned him to marble, then hid him in a cave near the city's Golden Gate. He was destined to stay there until the time came when the angel would awaken him. The new masters of the city knew about the miracle and made frantic efforts to find the marble emperor, but they could not locate him. To prevent his returning through the Golden Gate one day the Turks walled it up. But it was prophesied that God would send the angel down to awaken the king and he would drive the Turks out of the city.[25] The afterlife legends surrounding Constantine seem devoid of any element of personal magnetism in the man himself.

The next king after James IV to be propelled into a similar world of legend became even more influential in his afterlife, and the Scottish king's fate seems like a template written more than half a century before his death. On 4 August 1578 thirty-three year old King Sebastian I (Sebastião) of Portugal perished at the battle of Al-Ksar al-Kabir (also known as Alcácer Quibir and the battle of the Three Kings) in Morocco, a national disaster which led to the fall of the Aviz dynasty and paved the way for 60 years of Spanish rule in Portugal. The circumstances of his defeat has many of the same elements as Flodden. Sebastian was a dazzling young monarch (known as the 'Desired') and he was keen to launch a crusade against non-believers. Like James IV, Sebastian was spurred on to ill-advised adventure in foreign territory by outside influences, in his case a faction of the ruling class of Morocco. The campaign culminated in a crushing defeat with a huge loss of life which decimated the Portuguese nobility, and the event was blamed for the waning of Portuguese influence in South America and the Far East. King Sebastian, like James, forbade any of his nobles to take the offensive against the enemy without his formal orders. After it was obvious the battle was lost and thousands of his troops slaughtered, Sebastian led a futile but brave personal charge into the enemy's ranks. He had been offered an honourable escape when his Moorish enemy Maulá Ahmed offered to escort him to Tangier, but his pride prevented the indignity of surrender. A mutilated body said to be his was shown to some survivors of his army, who identified it. The remains were first kept in a palace in Morocco, then reburied in the enclave of Ceuta, before finally being interred in the Hieronymites Monastery in Lisbon.[26] Despite this physical evidence many people disputed the death of the royal hero and there were persistent rumours that he escaped his fate, adventuring on to Ethiopia or the East Indies. Some people at the end of the century still believed he was alive and this fervent hope inspired at least four pretenders to materialise and claim to be Sebastian. Several of these fake 'hidden kings' were executed and one fraud who surfaced in Venice was put in prison. He was later released, imprisoned again in Naples, then sent to the galleys, and probably ended his life in San Lucar in Spain.[27]

But the cult of Sebastian did not end with the deaths of those imposters. The dead king would return when his country called him, and some believed to a late date that he was still alive. King John IV of Portugal had to promise to abdicate in 1640 if King Sebastian were to return (in which case he would have been 86 years old). Sebastian was destined to become a hero of the mist, embedded in national consciousness. His survival or hoped for return became both a political and spiritual cult which endured for centuries, and was even powerfully present in post-colonial Brazil in the late 19th century.[28] The king became *O Príncipe Encuberto,* the Hidden Prince, who would one day return to reestablish the Fifth Empire of Portugal. Sebastianism remained a vital part of the national intellectual character of the country into modern times, and its mystical symbolism inspired modern intellectuals, who incorporated Sebastianism into their modern Portuguese Renaissance.

But mystical writings foretelling the encoberto, a nameless national hero who would lead the nation in the future, in fact first surfaced in the 1530s, popularised by a man named Gonçalo Anes, and only later became attached to the lamented Sebastian.[29]

The reason why the legends of King James IV did not achieve such long lasting resonance or intensity may be due to the twin cultural fault lines caused by the reformation and the relocation of the Stuart monarchy to England. It is clear that James, like Sebastian, earned his place in this category of legend due to the catastrophic manner of his death in combination with the resonance of his personality. Constantine XI, on the other hand, enjoyed an afterlife legacy which was inherited from centuries of apocalyptic tradition related to the end of days and a legendary 'Last Roman Emperor' rather than any personal achievements.[30]

Given these parallels, the legends of James IV fall into an established pattern of European folklore. The religious aspects of 'Hidden King' cult fits in well with medieval Catholic belief. The Reformation in Scotland diverted the legends of James IV away from religion and into folklore and secular legend. The tale of the journey to Jerusalem may have been attached to James IV because of his repeated pledges to go on pilgrimage or to join a crusade. Whether this was the most widespread belief about him at the time, or shortly after, as Drummond appears to suggest, is uncertain. The legend of the voyage to Jerusalem appears in a ballad which is credited with being contemporary:

An about the mids o' the night
He crap to the field o' the bluid:
Laigh he bowit an dour he lookit,

But never a worde he spak.
He turned the dead knight round about,
Till the moon shon on his bree;
But his soth was tined wit a bluidy gash,
Drumbelee grew his ee.
Up and awa my lither foot page,
An Scotland and I maun part:
But sweere by the deed in ilk bluidy shrowd,
That thou layn my lare i' thy hart.
Giffe I were a King, as now I'm nane,
Ille battell wold I prove,
My birde ladie in Halyroode;
Wae worth the wyt o' luve.
Sanct Giles sall ring ilk larum belle,
Wauk up the craimes and bowse,
Earl Angus has taen hime to Floudenne

* * *

He cut the crosse on his right shoulder
O' claith o' the bluidy redde,
An hes taen his ways to the haly land
Wheras Christe was quick and dead.[31]

But the provenance of this ballad is doubtful. The writer Daniel Wilson claims to have found the incomplete poem stuck in the pages of an old book, a copy of Sir David Dalrymple's *Remarks On The History of Scotland* (1773), with a note in the same hand: 'This I got from an old man, James Spence, gardener at Earlsha'; it had been on the fly leaf of a Psalm-book in the family as long as he remembered.' The place meant may be either Earl's Town or Earl's Hall, Erceldoune, in the Borders, or Earlshall in Fife. But whatever the origin of the verse, the motif of the injured or defeated hero retiring to the Holy Land was a venerable one with a long history. The king would certainly have guaranteed himself fame or notoriety and would likely have been the first king from the north of Britain to have journeyed to Jersusalem.[32]

James IV's intended pilgrimage to the Holy Land was a well-known and abiding obsession. This objective, or its allied plan of leading a new Crusade, is frequently cited as evidence of the king's unrealistic romanticism. The inspiration for his schemes may have lain in the deaths of one or other of his children or out of atonement for his father's death.[33] But the plan was certainly serious enough for him to send an envoy named Marco Alvise to Venice to enquire, on 21 December 1506, about the possibility of procuring ships to take him and his men to the Middle East.[34] Four years later he was corresponding with the French king Louis XII and entering into great detail about his proposed mission to the Middle East. He wanted to know how many men could be provided and how many ships and cannon could be acquired. He queried the timescales involved in procuring everything required, and wondered which town would make the best military target, Alexandria or Constantinople.[35] James envisaged himself as the military leader in an expedition against the aggressive Ottoman Empire, and throughout 1510 and 1511 he was trying to solicit help from European leaders, some of whom cynically encouraged his forlorn ambition for their own reasons.[36] This personal ambition may have been vainglorious, but the threat from the expansive Turks was real enough, and thirteen years after James's death they defeated the Hungarians in the battle of Mohács and were threatening further conquest in central Europe. As late as the spring of 1513, King James IV was repeating his intentions to travel east and explicitly informed the English ambassador, Dr Nicholas West, that one reason he needed continued French alliance was to ensure that his forces could travel across their territory and on to Palestine.[37] This pact with France led to the rupture with England and ultimately the disaster of Flodden. James's dogmatic pursuit of a personal mission to the Holy Land was one element in his downfall. The appraisal of Islamic threat to Europe was correct, but his continued attempts to physically put himself at the head of an avenging Christian army demonstrated poor judgement. On one level, his self-promotion as a crusading avenger may have been an attempt to elevate himself in the ranks of piety among Western Europe's leaders. The King of France was traditionally designated the 'Most Christian King' and Henry VIII was still the 'Defender of the Faith'. James IV had to be satisfied with the papal gifts of a sword of state and hat gifted to him by Pope Julius II in 1507,[38] but a sense of competition may have spurred him on to seek further glory in the Middle East. Whether he knew it or not, the King of Scots was pursuing an idealistic ambition which was in fact hideously corrupted by events two centuries before his time. King Philip IV of France, called the Fair, combined an excessive religious certainty with a megalomaniac conviction that he was destined to be the chosen overlord of all Christianity, ruling all God's kingdoms from a throne in Jerusalem. He envisaged himself as the head of a combined army of all the religious military orders, Templars, Teutonic Knights and others, as the *Bellator Rex,* the Warrior King, and the refusal of the Knights Templars to countenance his delusions led to their annihilation, directly instigated by Phillip the Fair.[39] Those in France who had access their own dark history may well have smiled cynically when they heard about the Holy Land ambitions of the upstart Scottish king.

James's desire to lead an army against the Ottomans was common knowledge in Scotland and England. It was enthusiastically celebrated by the Franciscan priest Alexander Barclay, who was educated in England but was probably born in Scotland. His ancestry perhaps helps explain why he inserted laudatory verses to James IV in his translation of Sebastian Brandt's *Ship of Fools* (1509). But his praise is so extraordinary that it deserves to be quoted at some length. Barclay's stanzas on James IV follow a section which extols King Henry VIII, and proposes that King James IV would make an excellent battle leader for forces heading to Palestine. Barclay stated that the leaders of a proposed Christian war on the Turks had only one choice for their bold captain:

Take Iamys of Scotlonde for his audacyte
And proued manhode if ye wyll laude attayne
Let hym haue the forwarde, haue ye no disdayne
Nor indignacion, for neuer kynge was borne
That of ought of warre can shewe the vnycorne
For if that he take onys his spere in hande
Agaynst these Turkes strongly with it to ryde
None shall be abyll his stroke for to withstande
Nor before his face so hardy to abyde
Yet this his manhode increasyth nat his pryde
But euer sheweth he mekenes and humylyte
In worde and dede to hye and lowe degre
In prudence pereles is this moste comely kynge
And as for his strength and magnanymyte
Concernynge his noble dedes in euery thynge
One founde or grounde lyke to hym can nat be
By byrth borne to boldnes and audacyte
Vnder the bolde planet of Mars the champyon
Surely to subdue his ennemyes echone
Mars hath hym chosyn: all other set asyde
To be in practyse of Batayle without pere
Saue ryches lacketh his manfull myght to gyde
He hath nat plentye of all thynge as is here
The cause is that stormes in season of the yere
Destroyeth the corne engendrynge so scarsnes
Whiche thynge moche hurteth this Prynces worthynes
Let hym be formest, than dout ye nought at all
For onely his loke (so bolde is his courage)

The turkes pryde shall make decay and fall
Lyke to a Lyon in dedes he shall rage
Thus he beynge gyde the fury shall asswage
Of the fals Turkes: so that they shall be fayne
Our christen londes to vs to yelde agayne
If the Englysshe Lyon his wysdome and ryches
Conioyne with true loue, peas and fydelyte
With the Scottis vnycornes myght and hardynes
Than is no dout but all hole christente
Shall lyue in peas welth and tranquylyte
And the holy londe come into christen hondes
And many a regyon out of the fendes bondes.[40]

Barclay's vociferous testimonial for the Scottish king might lead one to think he was a marginalised, outspoken figure, who possibly put himself in danger because of his pro-Scottish views. But Barclay's sometime poetic opponent John Skelton spoke up against an unidentified group who viewed his own anti-Scottishness as extreme. It is important to recognise that Barclay was in fact highly regarded by the establishment, being mentioned in a letter concerning the Anglo-French alliance at the Field of the Cloth of Gold in 1520. Barclay was specially called upon to compose stories and histories concerning the fabulous buildings constructed on the Field.[41] He also seemed to be closely in tune with contemporary political poetry in Scotland. The warlike allusion in his verse to the English Lion and Scottish Unicorn joining together in war echoes Dunbar's poetic use of the two heraldic creatures, though the Scottish poet had used them as symbol of peaceful union between James IV and Margaret Tudor. The secret lines of communication between the Scottish regime and southern sympathisers is tantalising, but the details may now be irrecoverable.

In legend, the most famous king from Britain rumoured to have disappeared to Jerusalem was King Harold Godwinsson, after the battle of Hastings (as recorded in the 13th century *Vita Haroldi*). Like James, the brutal disfigurement of his body on the battlefield made identification difficult and fuelled survival rumours. One cherished legend says that after recovering from his wounds he travelled through Europe, trying and failing to gain support to regain his throne. He then spent some time as a wandering pilgrim, journeying to Wales, before returning to England, ending his days as a hermit in Chester.[42] Harold's intended pilgrimage may have been in emulation of the 10th century Viking king Olaf Tryggvason, who died dramatically in a great sea-battle at Svold in 999 or 1000. When he saw at the last minute that escape from his enemies was impossible, Olaf theatrically drowned himself, diving into the ocean from his ship, the 'Long Serpent', bearing his shield above his head to stop his enemies seizing him, with his scarlet cloak billowing out behind.[43] Olaf had spurned the advice of his associates, as James IV did, ignoring those who wanted him to escape when there was a lull in the battle. His followers had told him plainly that they were chiefly in danger because he was there.[44]

The legends of this Norwegian king, as compiled from earlier sources in the 13th century Saga bearing his name, may not all be contemporary with his disappearance, but they contain the hallmarks of being invented by a grieving culture group. The best known story about his survival is that Olaf freed himself of his chain mail underwater and was picked up by a Wendish boat and transported to an anonymous life in a foreign land.[45] But the king's friend, Hallfreðar the Troublesome Poet, was sceptical about Olaf's survival, although the majority of people seemed to believe it:

> There are those who tell me, poet skilled in verse,
> That the King is wounded, and that from the clash of arms
> He to the east escaped away.
> But from the great fight south I have learnt the truth,

The King is dead.[46]

Olaf did much to prefigure his enduring legend during his lifetime. He was renowned in Scandinavia, and his aggressive campaigning ensured fame throughout the Viking world. A popular version of his survival states that he made his way to Rome and met the pope, then he journeyed on to Jerusalem.[47] Five years after the fateful battle some Englishmen encountered a man who claimed to be King Olaf, and he gave them a book to take home as a gift for King Ethelred.[48] Another encounter with the monarch in the Holy Land was supposed to have occurred as late at 1046, when a traveller from Scandinavia met Olaf there. But in this tale the witness is guided by a dream and magically led to an idealised monastery where the exiled king also has the enhanced appearance of a demi-god or immortal. This story has the hallmarks of being an invented literary legend.[49] The Saga writer concluded his retelling of the legends with a sentence which John Lesley unconsciously echoed about James IV centuries later: 'Whichever way it was, King Olaf Tryggwason never afterwards returned to his realm of Norway.'[50] The myth of the penitent king, devoting his last days secretly to religion, whether in Jerusalem (which must have been crowded by a succession of kings in hiding through the centuries) or elsewhere, is inextricably tangled with secular tales of incognito kings turning up in all sorts of unexpected places in different times. This syndrome could be a symptom of medieval wishful thinking and chicanery.

Many people have reported supposedly deceased kings mysteriously alive far from the places where they disappeared. An already cited example is King Richard II of England, who died in 1399. Belief in the survival of Richard was strong, especially in the county of Cheshire where he had enjoyed great support, and a man purporting to be him appeared at the court of King Robert III in Scotland, where he was used as a propaganda tool by the Scottish government.[51] One account says that Richard was discovered in the guise of a kitchen servant in the Hebrides, whence he had wandered after a spell as a vagrant. He ended his days 'in idiocy' at the Scottish court, a fitting judgement by God for one who had once brutally ravaged Scotland with his army.[52] Whoever the poor man was, he was maintained in high style and buried with all due honours at Stirling in 1419.[53] One of the most notorious royal imposters was the hermit who purported to be Baldwin IX, Count of Flanders, who had been made Emperor of Constantinople in 1204. He vanished, and was probably killed, after being captured by Bulgarian forces in 1205. There was huge support for the pseudo-count, who was only finally unveiled as a fraud when King Louis VIII of France closely interviewed him and declared him a liar. He eventually confessed to being a fake and was executed in 1226. In his confession he indicated that he had been the dupe of certain knights who made him follow the pretence.[54] Various other royal pretenders pop up and pepper the chronicles throughout Europe, including Edward II in the 14th century, and in the 15th century, Richard Duke of York. Later examples include a man who showed up in Venice in 1599 and said he was Sebastian of Portugal, who died in the deserts of Africa.[55] In 17th century Russia there was a 'False Dmitri' who claimed he was a son of Ivan the Terrible, or the Polish king Stefan Batory. This man may actually have been a monk named Grigorii; his deception was so successful that he ruled as tsar for ten months until he was killed. One of the immediately preceding rulers, Boris Godunov (who died in 1605) was exhumed by rival factions after his death and reburied. But it was said in Moscow that Boris had actually fled and someone else had been placed in the second tomb. Officials sent messengers far and wide to search for Boris. He was said to have gone to Sweden or else been smuggled out of the country along with his fortune by wily English merchants. As the 'False Dmitri' rose against him, Boris turned to magic and necromancy to combat him and thus made himself a target for rumour in his own afterlife.[56] When mobs ransacked Boris's palace, some witnesses said they had seen the tsar lurking in the cellars. He was said to have gone to Sweden or else been smuggled out of the country along with his fortune by wily English merchants.[57] During the subsequent 'Time of Troubles' many more hopeful pretenders emerged from the underground and even as late as 1864 there was a pretender who claimed to be the long-dead Tsar Alexander I.[58]

It is surprising that no enterprising fraudster appeared on the Scottish scene or abroad in the aftermath of Flodden and pretended to be King James IV. The Scottish king's fame had spread throughout Europe and there was at least as much speculation about his fate as there had been about the Princes in the Tower. The only other recorded fake who claimed to be a Scottish royal seems to have been 'the False Margaret', a young German girl who passed herself off as the daughter of King Eric II of Norway and Margaret of Scotland, and who was burned to death for her audacity in 1309.[59] John Lesley's heartfelt assertion that the king was still thought to be alive in the 1570s leads us to believe that there were plenty of people who would have welcomed the physical reappearance of James IV.[60]

Most fraudulent monarchs understandably first appeared at some distance from their alleged native shores, so that those who remembered the original would not be able to detect the counterfeit. A false James in France may have faced the scrutiny of the significant number of eminent Scots resident there. There was the morsel of a rumour, already mentioned, given by an Italian that a Scot in Tournai claimed he had seen the king alive, but whether this sighting was in Scotland or France, and whether it was true king or imposter, is unknown.[61] But if such a person had appeared in far off Italy, for example, he would have stood a better chance of success. Better still would be the prospects for a fake James IV who set himself up in England. He would have found ready official sponsorship (perhaps even by Wolsey himself) by those who might relish stirring up more trouble for poor beleaguered Scotland. It would have been poetic revenge for the role which the late King James had played in harbouring Perkin Warbeck, the supposed Duke of York, one of those lamented Princes in the Tower. But no candidate for the fake kingship arose: any who did would have had to face the realisation that the wages for pretence to royalty were invariably death.

James IV's own record with the English pretender Perkin Warbeck, allegedly one of the children of King Edward IV, throws some light on the personal credulity of the king and the extent to which such royal actors, some more believable than others, role-played on the international political scene. The Jerusalem rumour may not have developed into a full scale story in Scotland: there were too many whispered rumours, dead end tales and hopeful stories being bandied about for any one legend to be accepted as the definite truth and adorned with fantastic yet believable ornament.

Chapter 8

Dreadful Dead Man

While John Skelton was delighting in the triumph over the treacherous Scots and their king, other contemporary literary productions dealing with the death of King James and the battle of Flodden were more interested in dealing with the behaviour of particular sections of the English army, or painting a wider epic of martial courage. James barely figures in the majority of the poems written in the wake of the conflict and there was little tendency for glorification in the amount or quality of Scottish blood spilled.

Two of the earliest literary efforts concerning the battle are the poems 'Scotish Feilde' and 'Flodden Feild'. Both productions were aimed at glorifying the noble house of Stanley, whose heartland was in Lancashire and Cheshire. As such the poems are scarcely interested in giving an accurate account of Flodden. Surprisingly, the unseemly retreat of the Cheshire men in the battle does get mentioned in the first poem.[1]While the details concerning the battle are interesting, the Scots and their king are blank opponents, a backdrop against which this northern English contingent magnified its brilliance. 'Scotish Feilde' couples the martial achievements of Stanley's men at Flodden with their earlier participation at the Battle of Bosworth, and the only matter of historical interest is the confirmation that King James was felled near the banner of St Cuthbert.[2] The second poem, 'Flodden Feild', likely dates to the Elizabethan age, and King James IV does not even rate a mention.[3]

In contrast to the diatribes issued against James by John Skelton, others at the time were more reflective in their criticism of the late king. The Dutch scholar Erasmus Desiderius had close links with the English royal house and he was, for a while, the tutor of James IV's illegitimate son, Alexander Stewart, later Archbishop of St Andrews, when the young prince was studying in Siena, Tuscany. As one of the most acute intellects of his day, his interaction with the royal house of Stewart merits attention, not least for his characterisations of the royal father and son. His lengthy and emotional remembrance of the slain Scottish prince, published in 1515, offers a unique portrait of a lost royal, whose personality would be otherwise entirely lost to history. And the reflection on and differences with his royal father are also intriguing. Erasmus praises his handsomeness, heroism, dignity, and heroic stature. The boy's quick learning and intelligence are also lauded, along with his sensitivity:

> What gifts he had, in heaven's name! How quick his mind, how fertile, how ready to follow any clue, how capable of grasping many things at once!...Nor was it the case with him, as it is with so many others, that he had a natural gift for learning but was less disposed to good behaviour. He was shy by nature, but it was a shyness in which you could detect remarkable good sense...Sensitive as he was, he often concealed his feelings, nor could he ever be provoked to lose his temper; such was his gentle nature and his fairness of mind.[4]

Erasmus shrewdly noted that Alexander's fatal weakness was an 'excessive filial devotion that misled' him:

> You proved your love for your father with a courage that was too great, and unhappily fell with your father on the field of battle. Those gifts of nature, those high qualities, those splendid hopes, were all sunk in the hurricane of a single fight.[5]

Falling victim to the glamour of James IV was a failing shared by many well born sons of Scotland who followed their leader to their deaths. The death of this pupil deeply affected Erasmus, and he commented about the personal nature of his loss and the efforts he put into educating the lost prince: 'Something of mine was lost there too: the pains I had devoted to teaching you, and so much of you was made by my efforts, I claim in my share in you.'[6] The heartfelt statement contrasts with the forced flattery of people like the Spaniard Dom Pedro, who has left his idealised pen portrait of James IV.

Many years later, Erasmus wrote to his friend, the Scottish scholar Hector Boece at Aberdeen, and revisited his thoughts on James IV. He also eagerly enquired about the fate of Alexander's half-brother, James Earl of Moray:

> I have always entertained a great regard for King James because he strove not so much to extend his rule as to adorn it. We should have had to count him among the most happy of monarchs, if his fortunes had answered to his distinguished personal qualities. I have no doubt that the son follows in the father's footsteps just as he has succeeded to the father's throne. When I was teaching King James son, Alexander, Archbishop of St Andrews, at Siena, the latter had a brother with him, barely in his tenth year, a boy of marvellous ability, and even at that early age, showing high promise. I long to know what has come of him. Did he share the father and the brother's fate? Or does he still survive?[7]

James, Earl of Moray did survive, as we have seen, dramatically demanding answers about his father's death at the trial of Lord Home. Later a prominent supporter of his half brother, King James V, in the north of Scotland, he died childless at the age of 44 or 45, in 1544. Apart from this brief, insubstantial enquiry from Erasmus, this longer lived prince's character is lost in time; thanks to the pen of Erasmus again his life is less defined than his half sibling who fell at Flodden.

Erasmus' initial thoughts on James IV (different than his later impression) and his son were included in an edition of his *Adagia,* a collection of essays on classical proverbs. Under the adage *Spartam nactus es, hanc orna* ('Sparta is your portion, do your best for her'), Erasmus judged that the Scottish king should have been content within his own dominions and not invaded England at the behest of France:

> Prosperity and reputation, both without flaw, were his, if he had confined himself permanently within his own frontiers. He was so handsome that even from afar you could see he was a king; he had great powers of mind, incredible and universal knowledge, and unconquerable spirit, a truly royal nobility of feeling, the most perfect courtesy, the most open-handed generosity...[8]

Beyond the usual standard praise for rulers, nobility of feeling and courtesy, the charisma of the king is emphasised. His spirit was unconquerable, matching his universal knowledge, and his character magnified his poor realm. But the king's fate is used by Erasmus as a means of supporting his own ideas about the futility of warfare:

> If, however, all your desire is to extend the horizon of your glory beyond the bounds of your own realm, see to it that your neighbours learn your greatness from the benefits you confer on them, not from your misdeeds. Do you burn farms and trample crops, demolish cities, drive off flocks and herds and slaughter human beings?'[9]

Erasmus also heaps, probably undeserved, praise on Queen Margaret for unstinting devotion to her husband. He was sadly right in believing that when a king left his kingdom it was never a blessing for his country and rarely one for the king himself.[10]

A contemporary of Erasmus who satirised the dead Scottish king was the Italian Petrus Carmelianus (or Peter Carmeliano), a scribe and lutanist in service with the English monarchy. Like Skelton he was in the entourage of Henry VIII at the siege of Thérouanne, and while there – and perhaps in competition with Skelton – he composed a mocking funeral poem about the death of James IV. The king's Latin secretary Ammonius wrote in a letter to Erasmus in November 1513 that the Italian's poem was 'full of unmanly abuse' and stuffed with womanish curses.[11] Erasmus replied with a criticism of the suspect Latin of the would be poet, saying nothing about the worthiness or otherwise of Carmelianus's target.[12]

But it seems that the English public in general soon lost interest in excoriating the memory of their erstwhile enemy. Even John Skelton's poetry, which voiced an attitude of tribal superiority over the northern neighbours and reinforced national solidarity, appeared overstated. Skelton was impelled to defend his ferocious anti-Scottish sentiments in an addendum tacked onto his poem *Against the Scottes*.[13] The new verses bit back at a body of opinion in England which objected to his crowing over the death of the Scottish king. Far from apologising, Skelton used the opportunity to further trammel the reputation of James IV into the mud. King James is denounced as an unnatural brother of King Henry – Cain against Abel – and those who were angry at the poet's mention of his treachery were told they didn't have true English blood running through them. James was decried for religious unorthodoxy as well as secular infidelity: he was almost a heretic and he died as an excommunicate. As already mentioned, one possible opponent was the Franciscan poet Alexander Barclay, an Anglo-Scottish apologist for James IV, who had previously criticised Skelton's work.[14]

The triumphalism expressed in Skelton resurfaced later in the century in *The Mirror for Magistrates* and *Flowers of Fame*, albeit with less mesmerizing venom. Both these works cast James as only one of a whole cast of fallen leaders, and the primary purpose of the verse is to show the folly of these figures, destroyed because they were enemies of the English establishment. *The Mirror for Magistrates* was first issued in 1555 and then in 1559. But the references to the death of James IV only occur in the edition of 1587.[15] According to the prose section linking the two sections of poetry, they were composed 'euen shortly after the death of the sayd King',[16] which is confirmed by internal evidence, according to C. S. Lewis. Lewis baulks at the atrocious style of the verse ('beneath contempt'), and it may seem ironic that the poetry here falls so far short of the acknowledged high standard which flourished in Scotland during the reign of James IV. The delight taken at the earthbound fate of the king has him declaring that his reward for earthly endeavour was only the shovel and spade which led to him digging his own grave.[17] The first section of verse on James IV – 'The Lamentation of King James the fourth, King of Scots'[18] – concludes with the shade of James standing with mortal wounds caused by a spear and a bill, reminiscent of the detail of the fatal injuries given by Edward Hall.[19]

There is mention too that he was not accorded proper Christian burial. The once great king lies not in a church or graveyard, but in a homely shrine, perhaps with an uneasy awareness perhaps that the uncertainty of his spiritual and physical state in death projected him into an uncertain zone, which may have been heaven or hell, or some other place.[20] The second instalment of verse in the work – *The bataile of Brampton, or Floddon fielde...* – is a straightforward account of the battle, and bears the impression of having originated soon after the encounter. There is a suggestion that the historian Ralph Holinshed brought the two sections of verse into the *Mirror for Magistrates*, but there can be no certainty.[21] The prototypes of both sets of verse are found in Harleian MS. 2252 and were published in the nineteenth century; they display differences from the versions in the Mirror.[22] Here the anonymous narrator encounters the shade of the Scottish king lamenting his folly and misery, crying out for mercy (in a refrain from the Office of the Dead which repeats through the poem): 'I herd a Man crye sore trymblyng for fere/Miserere mei deus et Salva me.'

Ulpian Fulwell's *Flower of Fame*, published in 1575, also reflects a hostile attitude to the late Scottish king, sixty years after his demise. Fulwell was not a prominent figure influenced by prevalent views of the court, but a Somerset cleric (though associated with Edmund Harman, a former groom of the privy chamber to Henry VIII). His work is important for details which it contains: the knowledge that the king's body was deposited at Sheen, and the assertion that it was displayed in the streets of London. In the *Flowers of Fame*, King James is again portrayed as a plaintive spirit giving a sorrowful account of his misdeeds.[23] Fulwell repeats the common English accusation that James broke his oath of allegiance to their own king and therefore merited God's righteous revenge. The shade of James calls on the ghosts of the Flodden dead to give warning to the waywardness inherent in the next generation of Scots:

> Ye noble peeres, whose lives with myne did end,
> Send forth from graves your griesly ghosts eche one,
> To wayle the chaunce that Fortune us did sende:
> That we to hedles haste were apt and prone.[24]

The suggestion that the carcass of the king was dragged around the streets of London has already been discussed, and may be more wishful thinking than actual fact. To some extent Fulwell was drawing on popular current traditions to give a picture of King James IV suitably damning to suit his readers' expectations. English relations with Scotland had ebbed and flowed in the intervening sixty years between Flodden and his time, but the fact that the poet included not only a further fulmination against King James V,[25] but also a celebration of English victories at the siege of Haddington and the Battle of Pinkie in the late 1540s[26] shows there was a well spring of anti-Scottish sentiment available to the writer. Fulwell states outright, through the supposed voice of the king, that his fate is not only known about but celebrated as a part of daily life in England. The king is someone 'Whose fall each tong with dayly talke revyves'. But in the prologue the author admits that he is aping the form of the *Mirror for Magistrates* and allowing James IV 'to utter his complaynt and tell his oune tale', though it is interesting that Ulpian's work appeared before the actual version of the *Mirror* which featured James IV.[27]

Apart from the productions of balladeers, polemical poets and 'legitimate' historians, there was a vein of prophetic material which tapped into occult belief about the king's fate. Memories of this supernatural association of James IV and Flodden survived into the Victorian age. It is found, for example, in a little known short poem of James Hogg's called *The Queen of France and James IV*, which takes the form of a dialogue between an unknown seer and lady, who discuss the forthcoming carnage and who put the blame squarely on the womanly encouragement of Anne of Brittany.[28] But earlier traditions were a good deal more subtle than later literary manifestations. There was some anonymous prophetic material in circulation before, during and after the time of Flodden, utilised as an arcane, underground weapon in the persistent antagonism between England and Scotland. As early as the first War of Independence in Scotland, at the end of the 13th and start of the 14th centuries, political propaganda was manufactured by both sides, framed in the guise of prophecy spoken by famous sages from the past.

Many prophecies must have been invented at the behest of the nobility by educated clerics, who were also busy during this period reconstructing national origin myths. It has been argued that the Scots only started using this form of literary weaponry following the example of the English,[29] and that vernacular Scots prophetic poetry did not exist before the 15th century.[30] But this is contradicted by the existence of manuscripts containing prophecy being produced in Scotland in the 14th century.[31] The poet and seer 'True' Thomas Learmont of Erceldoune, who was intimately associated with the latter part of the reign of King Alexander III of Scotland, is said to have predicted his death in 1286 to the Earl of March.[32] The Scottish tradition of prediction, tied up with matters of state and the fate of kings, was partly inherited from the separate poetic convention of prophecy found in Celtic languages. The most comprehensive work involving the rulers of both Ireland and Scotland was the *Prophecy of Berchán*, which details valuable, if fragmentary, traditions about the early Scottish kings.[33] The early Welsh court poets also actively invoked prophecy to bolster the political claims of their patrons. The 10th century Welsh poem Armes Prydein, 'The Prophecy of Britain', envisaged a military coalition from Wales, Cornwall, Scandinavia, British Strathclyde and Scotland that would defeat an aggressively expansionist English nation.[34] Welsh prophetic poems of the 13th century frequently used the setting of *Y Gogledd*, the old Brittonic North, which later became the Scottish Lowlands; particularly those poems featuring the proto-Merlin character, known as the *Afallenau* and the *Hoianau*.[35] It would be contentious to argue there was a significant continuance of tradition in the border lands from Dark Age Welsh to Medieval Scots, but it would be unwise to rule out a lingering of native traditions in this area which included the use of political prophecy. Prophetic cross fertilisation between different linguistic cultures in Scotland survived through the medieval period, exemplified by the fame of the lowlander Thomas the Rhymer, who was frequently mentioned in Gaelic poetry.[36]

Prophecy, wherever it came from, was alive in 16th century Scotland at every level of society, in the hands of those who told tales to children as well as those using it as a political weapon.

Sir David Lindsay comforted the infant King James V with 'The Prophecies of Rymour, Beid, and Marlyng', as well as more humble native folk tales.[37] And the author of the *Complaynt of Scotland* in 1529 warned the Scottish nation against the English who were spreading prophetic tales ascribed to Merlin and others which foretold England and Scotland would be united under a single ruler. The one prince set to rule both nations would obviously be English. The author of the *Complaynt* believed that such a union would occur within a generation, but under the rule of a Scottish prince.[38] The fragility of the Tudor succession was gleefully used as a football by opposing prognosticators.

Much of the material circulating was culled from earlier, deliberately imprecise prophecies which dealt with warfare between England and Scotland – used because they seldom directly named people or signposted events with a date. An Englishman invading Scotland in 1547, for example, heard the Scots gleefully repeat the prevalent prediction of a major battle near Musselburgh, which the home side would inevitably win: 'Between Seaton and the sea, many a man shall die that day'.[39]

Even the clean technological cutting edge of the printing press could not sweep away all vestiges of predictive superstition, and nor could the purifying advent of Protestantism. The title appropriated for this chapter refers to an unknown character found in a long-running series of prophecies in verse, the central idea of which states that an unnamed but powerful dead king will come back to life and bring back with him the true religion. One mention occurs a ballad from the reign of Henry VIII: 'A ded man shall aryse, and that shal bee greate wondre'.[40] It is almost irrelevant to speculate who this dead king was originally intended to be, so powerful is the metaphor (candidates may include King Richard II and even Perkin Warbeck). The image of the ruler dreadfully transformed by death chimes well with the transformed figure of James IV after his demise, when his image was a living force still haunting his nation. The king's spirit still walked in contemporary prophecy, rumour and poetry, and in the praise of historians writing their books. In enemy English verse the king's ghost is a negative figure, a puppet whose misery speaks to a defeated enemy in this world:

> Now let King James his griesly ghost
> awake from fatall sleepe,
> And shewe his hap and rufull fall,
> that causde all Scotlande weepe.
> Let all the Scottish noble peeres
> bewayle the wofull hower
> When they agreede on Bramston hills
> to meet King Henrye's power.[41]

But prophetic matter was more flexible and subtle. When the Duke of Albany assumed the mantle of power in a nation traumatised by Flodden, one way in which his rightfulness to rule was legitimised was through the dissemination of prophetic verse. Some of this poetry, composed in Scotland during his tenure as governor, lauded the 'French Wife's son', a clear reference to the duke.[42] The so-called 'Prophecy of Bertlington' conjures up the vision of a great hero who will come over the seas and right all wrongs, putting the English in their place:

> A keen man of courage, and bold man of armes,
> A Duke's son doubled, a born man in France,
> That shall our mirths amend, and mend
> all our harmes,
> After the date of our Lord 1513...
> The Saxons shall never recover after.[43]

The allusive nature of prophecy renders it difficult to put a date on its composition. Sir David Dalrymple attempted to pin down the writing of these verses between the death of James IV and the arrival of Albany (between September 1513 and June 1515).[44] The hopeful sentiment of the prophecy certainly points to it being invented before disillusionment with the reality of the Duke of Albany's government. A competent administrator he may have been, but Albany was hardly the conquering martial giant that the rhymes promised. Verses about this hopefully heroic 'son of a French wife' would have been in circulation at the same time as the various survival legends concerning James IV. But the attempt to create a favourable legend for Albany failed. An undercurrent of rumour would soon give rise to blatant black propaganda which stated that Albany planned to murder the young King James V and steal the Scottish throne. The negative English propaganda prevented the encouraging Scottish prophecy from being fulfilled.

The vogue for prophecy, shorn of some of its primal power to influence the credulous, extended into the reign of King James VI, whose accession from the Scottish to the English throne in 1603 was seen by some as the fulfilment of prophesies that a Scot would win England's throne.[45] This was a subversion or recycling of the English prophecy noted in the Complaynt of Scotland, that the two countries would unite under an English prince.[46] The accession of James VI was even supported by the reworked verse mentioning a mighty ruler related to Robert Bruce within the ninth degree.[47] In the year 1603, Robert Waldegrave in Edinburgh published a compilation of Scottish prophecies,[48] bringing together a hotchpotch of popular verse from Scotland, England, France and Denmark, much of it reshaped to suit current political demands.

One section of the work – 'The Prophecie of Thomas Rymour' – seems to have originally arisen after the Battle of Flodden and refers to the fate of the 'Red Lion,' i.e. the Scottish king:

Our Scottish king shal come full keene,
The reade Lyon beareth he,

A feddered arrow sharpe I weene
Shal make him winke and warre to see,
Out of the filde he shal be led
When he is bloodie and woe for blood,
Yet to his men shall he say,
For Gods love you turne againe,
And give those Sutherne folke a fray,
Why should I lose the right is mine.
My date is not to die this day.[49] [italics mine]

A very similar version of the above occurs in an edition of prophecies published by Andro Hart in 1615, and was incorporated by Sir Walter Scott in the second part of his ballad 'Thomas the Rhymer'.[50]

This could be interpreted as another version of a living tradition, or merely a blatant theft from one editor of doggerel to another. What seems more important was that there was an attempt by persons unknown to tie in the fate of King James IV with Thomas the Rhymer, the most famous Scottish oracle. Thomas was also believed not to have died in the normal sense, but have been kidnapped or ruled to the parallel world of *Elfame*, 'Fairyland', from where he sometimes returned.

This quicksilver nature of prophecy is difficult to interpret; the deliberately cryptic nature of the verses tends to defeat anyone who tries to disentangle them. The various stanzas in the 1603 'Prophecie of Thomas Rymour' concerning Flodden were updated to refer to the battle of Pinkie in 1547,[51] and other allied verses referring to the ruler descended from Bruce[52] show there was concerted political propaganda at play in the guise of simple 'folk' belief. It is safe to say that the rumours of James IV surviving continued to mutate among several different channels in Scotland throughout the 16th century. The fragmentary prose prophecy attributed to Sibilla, *Regina Austri*, seems to blatantly refer to the Flodden king, even if it does not delve into the details:

'he shall be drawne to a place of Battel, where he shall get great discomfort, by the which he shall die'.[53]

The king's literary legacy in England followed a different route. From being an example of moral folly in the *Mirror For Magistrates* and the *Flower of Fame*, the king made one final starring role in English literature at the end of the century, appearing in Robert Greene's drama *The Scottish History of James the Fourth*, which appeared in 1598.[54] The play is in fact entirely unhistorical, and King James is a mere stock figure. The whole work borrows wholesale from an earlier Italian drama.[55] Greene was also so regardless of historical accuracy that he set his play in the year 1520. Contemporaries in Scotland complained that dramas like this, something of a vogue in London, were mocking the current political condition of their realm.[56] The English trend satirising Scotland was largely a reaction against the expected Scottish takeover of their nation at a time when the barren Virgin Queen was entering her final days. The subtitle of the play, referring to 'Iames the fourth, slaine at *Flodden*', was recognised as dishonest by one early owner of the printed text, whose copy later resided in the British Museum. He inscribed his own accurate opinion on the cover, that the work was 'rather, fiction of English and Scottish matters comicall'. Greene (who died in 1592) portrayed Scotland as a troubled realm overrun with parasitical nobles. The drama is presented by Oberon, King of the Fairies, whose presence in the play may reflect the playwright's knowledge of arcane rumours circulating about the long dead King James IV in Scotland.

Around the same time when unlucky Elizabethans were witnessing Greene's comedy, a man was put on trial for his life in Aberdeen. On 20 January 1598 a reputed healer and wise man named Andro (Andrew) Man was brought before local authorities, having signed a confession on 21 October 1597 which sealed his fate.[57] The admitted charges and crimes ran the gamut from the mundane to the incredible. Perhaps he was lucky to have survived so long in his profession, which in less judgemental times would have be termed healer or folk medicine practitioner. Andro was a native of Ruthven parish in north Aberdeenshire and had been visited as a child in his mother's house, sixty years before, by the Devil in the shape of a woman, 'quhom thow callis the Quene of Elphen.' This being, whether Satan in disguise or the true Queen of Fairies, promised Andro 'that thow suld knaw all tingis, and suld help and cuir all sort of seikness, except stand deid, and that thow suld be weill interteneit, but wald seik they meat or thow deit, as Thomas Rymour did'.[58] This initiation into the calling of magical healing by the Elphin Queen and the most famous mystical figure in Scottish history linked Andro (and not just in the minds of his persecutors) with an enduring supernatural tradition in Scotland.

The records make it clear that Andro was not a simple charmer or male witch. He cured illness in man and beast and foretold the future. One of his magical skills was identifying areas of land to be set aside for the *genii loci* (or the Devil), to ensure the fertility of the land (plots later known as *Gudeman's Crofts*). No mere parochial charlatan, Andro's respected vocation took him over a wide area of north-east Scotland, and there are records of him working at Buckie, on the Banffshire coast, all the way south to Kinnaird in northern Angus. In the latter place he cured a relative of Lady Carnegie of Kinnaird Castle, near Brechin, showing that his specialised talents were not exclusively patronised by the ignorant peasantry. Thirty-two years before his confession, Andro began sleeping with the Queen of Fairies – just as Thomas the Rhymer is alleged to have done[59] – and begat many children with her. It was perhaps surprising that Andro escaped prosecution for as long as he did. The length of his career and extent of his travels demonstrate the demand for his services, and how much the role of wise man was tied in with the transmission of folk beliefs and the spread of legends. In Andro's beliefs the interplay of the Elvin world and the mortal realm was subtle and all encompassing. But once he was accused of being a witch the authorities would not countenance that his traditional beliefs could be held without diabolic involvement.

Therefore, Andro was obliged to admit that, 'the Quene of Elphen hes a grip of all the craft, bot Christsondy [Satan] is the gudeman, and hes all power vnder God, and that thow kennis sundrie deid men in thair cumpanie, and that *the kyng that deit in Flowdoun and Thomas Rymour is their.*'[60] [italics mine] This startling sentence is in fact the only direct written record that King James IV was accorded the ultimate legendary accolade: not only had he escaped the carnage of battle, he had transcended the realm of the merely mortal and been transported into another dimension, in the company of the Scottish national shaman, Thomas the Rhymer. There is no surviving elaboration of the legend, but the theme of a wounded king being carried off the field of conflict by otherworldly beings obviously echoes the fate of King Arthur. Drummond of Hawthornden states that James IV would return to help *Europe* in its hour of need, emphasising his fame as an undying knight who would be the patron of wider Christendom in his afterlife.[61]

According to Scottish tradition, it seems clear that King James IV had been nominated to join an elect band of Scots who had been kidnapped by the Good People and who survived in their land far beyond the span of other mortals. Thomas the Rhymer's ortherworldly kidnap ordeal was commemorated in literature and folklore. A 19th century folk tale tells of a man named Canonbie Dick who is taken by a nameless man to a cavern below the Eildon Hills in the borders.[62] There he sees a host of knights suspended in magical sleep, awaiting the hour, perhaps, when they are needed again. Thomas the Rhymer was surely the guardian of the underworld intended here (unless it is the wizard Michael Scot), but was the sleeping hero Arthur, or even James IV? He became a nationalistic underworld talisman, ensuring that in times of uncertainty the country had on its side a reserve of deep tradition which would see it endure. The repetition of his hopeful prophecies during the Wars of Independence helped to bolster the beleaguered Scottish nation. In John Barbour's epic poem *The Brus*,William Lamberton, bishop of St Andrews, hears about Bruce's murder of his rival Comyn and takes it as fulfilment of the arrival of the national hero prophesied by True Thomas: 'sekyrly I hop Thomas prophecy off Hersildoune sall veryfyd be'.[63]

Another Scottish historical figure who gained an uncanny reputation in later centuries was Michael Scot (or Scott), a Fife born scientist and scholar who lived in the 12th and 13th centuries and was an advisor to the Holy Roman Emperor, Frederick II. Scot spent most of his life abroad, his fame filtered back to his homeland and he was transformed into a miracle worker and a wizard. Although he had been dead three hundred years by the time of the battle of Flodden he was brought into the supernatural cycle of tales associated with the king and the battle. Allan Cunningham, the Scottish writer (1784-1842) wrote a three-volume novel named after the wizard. It features Scot appearing on the devastated field of Flodden after the battle. Although the fictional story has a large supernatural element it does not have the king as a main character. Nor does it seem to follow any active tradition which connects famous wizard with King James IV, although Scot was amply remembered in the Scottish borders.

The Sleeping Hero motif is powerfully represented across a range of culture and countries.[64] Most famous is King Arthur, who occupies umpteen caverns up and down Britain, and even as far afield as Mount Etna. Some of those rulers supposed to be awaiting return would only appear to herald the forthcoming Apocalypse, ruling for a short period as 'Emperor of the Last Days'.[65] Other famous heroes in suspended animation include the emperor Charlemagne, Frederick Barbarossa, and the Serbian king Marko, and Holger Danske of Denmark.[66] Whether King James IV was regarded by some as the exemplary, martial type of hero who would be awakened in the hour of his country's greatest need, as for example Sir Francis Drake is supposed to do, is debatable. Drummond of Hawthornden envisaged the king in this type of role, but perhaps people would be unwilling to summon up the spirit of an individual who had failed so spectacularly on the battlefield, despite his personal valour.

To see the plight of James IV in that strange dimension more fully we can examine the tradition attached to another, less famous captive. Robert Kirk was the Episcopalian minister of Balquidder, and then Aberfoyle, in southern Perthshire, in the 1690's. Kirk's most well-known extra parochial achievement was translating the psalms into Gaelic and supervising a Gaelic translation of the bible. His secular scholarship resulted in an even-handed and valuable study of the living fairy tradition he found among the Gaels. This latter work, sometimes known as *The Secret Commonwealth of Elves, Fauns and Fairies*, was completed in 1691, but did not go into print until 1815.[67] The shadowy world of Elfame, in strange symmetry with the mortal world, is described in the same terms which Andro Man described to his persecutors over a century previously.

Kirk died on 14 May 1692, meeting his end in the evening as he walked in his nightshirt on Doon Hill, a reputed haunt of the fairies, west of the manse of Aberfoyle. The manner of his death, as well as the subject of his writing, inspired strange rumours soon after he departed. His spirit is said to have appeared to a relative, telling him to go to their mutual kinsman Graham of Duchray and tell him he was not dead. Kirk reported he had been carried into Fairyland while in a swoon and he would appear at the baptism of his (Kirk's) child. If his cousin, Duchray, threw a knife over the head of the apparition of Kirk, 'I will be released, and restored to human's society'. The relative did not go to Duchray, and was visited again by Kirk, who threatened to haunt him if he did not comply. Eventually he did go and tell Duchray, but though the spirit did appear, Duchray did not perform the act which would have freed him.[68] As late as 1943, a visiting officer's wife was told that if, during a baptism at Aberfoyle manse, someone stuck a knife into Kirk's old chair, he would be freed from his long supernatural confinement.[69]

The common thread between True Thomas, King James IV and Robert Kirk, seems to be that they manufactured their own fate by inquiring into arcane subjects. They were taken away in perpetuity because they had attracted the attention of arcane forces. Tales of common people being whisked off by the fairies abound in Scottish folklore. One of the finest examples is the ballad 'Tam Lin', where the protagonist risks being passed on to Satan after a period with the fairies.[70] There seems to be no set term of confinement in the other dimension, with some finding release after a number of years and others held forever. The unfortunate prisoner in 'Tam Lin' was due to be given over to Satan by the fairies. In terms of meddling with the supernatural, it has to be said that James IV was not reputed to be interested in the supernatural as such, though he had a broad intellectual curiosity and was fond of stories and songs. There may have been an element of atonement involved in his supposed otherworldly post-life sentence, punishment for destroying a whole stratum of Scots in a single day.

The association between the dead and the fairies became a complicated element of witchcraft trials as the 16th century 'progressed'. A notable example of this intermingling of traditions was the Fife woman, Alison Pearson, who was condemned and burnt as a witch in 1588. Alison had been involved in more than mere diabolism, since she was accused of 'hanting and repairing with the gude nychtbouris and Quene of Elfame'.[71] She said in her confession that a long dead relative, William Simpson, was also at the Fairy Court, and taught her cures she could administer through magic. Significantly, William gained entry to the land beyond due to his sudden, traumatic death on the battlefield (he died at the Battle of Pinkie in 1547).

There were other notables also in that realm, including the Laird of Buccleuch and Maitland of Lethington, both of whom were prominent figures in mid 16th century Scotland.[72] Fame in public life, mixed together with unnatural death and religious politics, made a potent supernatural concoction and could result in individuals being sentenced to a term in the fairy realm. But satirists also muddied the waters of common belief when they accused their political enemies of consorting with witches. One of those said to have consulted the witch Alison Pearson was the Archbishop of St Andrews, Patrick Adamson (1537-1592), a natural enemy of the Presbyterians. His association with this witch and the whole realm of faerie, with its notable captives, was used as an opportunity for political humour. His enemies were employing a powerful weapon against him.

A contemporary poem called the 'Legend of the Bischop of St Androis', by Robert Sempill, satirised gossip about this supposedly unholy prelate. In the verse the Fairy Queen led an unholy cavalcade across Scotland on Halloween, trailing behind her assorted witches and spirits of the dead, which the readers of Robert Burns would recognise:

> Ane carling of the Queen of Phareis...
> Through all Braid Abane scho hes bene,
> On horsbak on Hallow ewin...
> And names out nyt boris sex or sewin,
> That we belevit had bene in heawin.
> Scho said scho saw thame weill aneugh,
> And speciallie gude auld Balcleuch
> The secretare, and sundrie vther;
> Ane William Symsone, hir mother brother...[73]

The poem may be one of the sources used by Scott when he conjured up a supernatural twilight land full of well-known Scottish faces in 'Wandering Willie's Tale'. Old traditions of political prophecy which complemented folklore and the old religion were replaced to a certain extent at the reformation by a kind of religious invective which used folk belief as a weapon against its enemies. Andro Man doubtless sincerely believed he had magical powers of healing, and as he journeyed back and forth through Banffshire to Aberdeenshire and Angus, the legend of the king in the otherworld was also disseminated. Legends were carried through the realm by men and women such as Andro through the ages.

We can see the contrast between the perception of James IV at the close of the 16th century: in England, after a generation of vilification, he became a character in a low drama; in Scotland the confusion about his fate and a surplus of speculation pushed his shade too far into the realms of uncertainty, and he became the eternal captive, forever confined in the national psyche.

It is easy to dismiss stories of the king's survival as the psychological reaction of a disbelieving, devastated populace to the death of a beloved leader. But external social changes also added to the legends of the period, including stories like the king's fairyland captivity. The wild storm of witch-hunting which was to break over Scotland in the generations after the death of James IV was partly caused by the social convulsion of the reformation, and the impetus for persecution came from a deliberate policy of the gentry rather than a spontaneous mass outbreak of superstition among the peasantry.[74]

The seismic upheaval of the change in religion led to the destruction of much associated with the deposed popery. Suspicious, secular beliefs and stories were also affected and perhaps fuller accounts of James IV's abduction were lost also in this period. But for a single sober line in the trial of Andro Man, the gossamer trace of gossip that the Flodden king was undead in Fairyland would be lost forever. Although the trace of that tradition is so fragile it is connected with a recognisable vein of folklore which set the king apart from most other mortals.

Chapter 9

The King Remade

The truth that King James IV perished at Flodden failed to diminish widespread reports that he had survived, though the crowning of the infant King James V, on 21 September 1513, signalled official recognition in Scotland of that fact. The next, long delayed public ceremony observing the transition in power was a magnificent funeral service for the late king, held in St Giles' Kirk, Edinburgh, organised by his cousin, the Duke of Albany, in July 1515. One hundred and forty painted banners decorated the ancient church as the governor and the high officials of the realm heard the requiem mass.[1] There is no record that Queen Margaret was present, nor any suggestion that she had made any effort to organise such a ceremony in the year following Flodden when she had been the ruler of Scotland. Margaret may well have been too preoccupied clinging to power during that period, proceeding with courtship and marriage to the Earl of Angus, yet it is difficult to avoid the conclusion that Queen Margaret, like her brother King Henry, shared an attitude of indifference to the death of James IV.

While the ceremonies at St Giles were being enacted, the corpse believed to be James IV was settling down to its long neglect in a Surrey monastery which was itself in decline. This Carthusian priory, the Charterhouse of Jesus of Bethlehem at Sheen, was built in 1144, just over a mile north of the site of the royal palace of Sheen (renamed Richmond Palace). In 1538 the prior of the Charterhouse surrendered the monastic property to the crown and the buildings were granted to the Earl of Hertford, then passed to the Duke of Suffolk, though the Carthusians were restored to the property for a short period during the reign of Queen Mary (1553-8).[2] Among later owners was Sir Richard

Sackville, who was held in custody here, and Margaret Countess of Lennox, daughter of Queen Margaret Tudor and the Earl of Angus.[3] Several mansion houses and villas were erected on or near the site in the 17th century, by Sir William Temple and others, and the last substantial surviving monastic building was pulled down in 1749.[4]

There are no standing remains of any later buildings here either; the site is now open ground in Richmond, by the River Thames, close to Kew Observatory. If the body of King James IV remains here, it lies unrecognised in a stratum of archaeological rubble beneath the Royal Mid Surrey Golf Course, or the adjacent Old Deer Park Recreation Ground. It is a peaceful resting place for such a warlike man. Apart from personal associations with his royal English in-laws, King James's final earthly destination enjoyed a coincidental, noteworthy array of associations with Scotland in later centuries, which has led to Richmond occasionally being called Scotland-upon–Thames. Fittingly a plaque was planned to be placed in the golf club in 2013 to mark the ephemeral presence of the king.[5] This connection continues to the present: a few kilometres to the east of the site is the ground of the London Scottish Rugby Football Club.

The church where the king's head was allegedly buried survived longer. St Michael's Church in Wood Street, in the City of London, was destroyed in the Great Fire of London, rebuilt by Sir Christopher Wren, and eventually completely demolished in 1897. When the site was redeveloped early in the 21st century there was some hope that a physical trace of King James IV would be recovered, spurred on by the interest of a Scottish writer, the late David A. Ross. Standard Life, which owned the site, spent in excess of £1million on archaeological excavation, primarily in the hope of uncovering important Roman remains. But the scrupulous Victorian authorities removed all traces of human remains when the church was brought down and ensured that the hope of finding the king was made nearly impossible. Many of the identifiable remains were removed to Brookwood Cemetery in Surrey, and no sign of the king's head was discovered. A spokesman pointed out that it was only conjecture that any part of the king's body was buried on the site anyway.[6] But a commemoration service was conducted on location by a Catholic priest, Father Joe Cairns, from Carntyne in Glasgow, in honour of the Scottish monarch.[7] Perhaps fittingly, a public house which partly covers the precincts of the church is called the Red Herring.

It is unsurprising that any part of the elusive King James IV failed to turn up during these modern investigations. Nor is the mistreatment of his corpse so unique that it should warrant outright horror. Richard III, whose brave battlefield death had similarities to that of James IV at Flodden, and who was paraded as a naked corpse around Leicester, had further indignities heaped upon him, being buried in an unworthy style in a Franciscan convent (later subsumed beneath a car park), but there was a legend that he was dug up and dumped in the River Soar.[8] Extraordinarily, recent excavation has destroyed this legend and found the actual remains of the king in the cemetery of the Greyfriars, which gives hope to those who forlornly seek the remains of other long lost monarchs.

According to one account, the bloated remains of James IV's enemy King Henry VIII also suffered post mortem disrespect. Soon after his huge, corrupt body was carried to the church of Syon, just over the River Thames from where the Scottish king was mouldering away anonymously, a stray dog came in and lapped up the putrefying juices which had leaked from the corpse onto the church floor.[9] The remains of the last direct male descendant of James IV to wear a crown, King James VII (II of England), also suffered mistreatment after his death. The king died in exile in France and was not buried because it was assumed by ardent Jacobites that the Stuarts would imminently regain the British throne and the king's body could be triumphantly interred in Westminster Abbey. The corpse was left above ground in a sarcophagus in a Paris church after James's death in 1701. The king's alleged sanctity immediately attracted ghoulish visitors who took away rags of linen soaked in his holy blood, and in the late 18th century the un-coffined corpse became a visitor attraction to be prodded and mishandled. But the allegation that the corpse was thrown into a sewer during the French Revolution is unsubstantiated.[10]

Religious upheavals during the Reformation and later were periods of minimal respect for the earthly remains of royalty and this was particularly evident in Scotland. In 1559 a group of Calvinist militants rampaged through the Carthusian Abbey in Perth and desecrated royal tombs there. Among the victims was Queen Margaret Tudor, whose skeleton was disinterred, burnt, and the ashes scarred in the abbey precincts.[11] Religious intolerance led to similar, though sporadic, incidents in the 17th century. When rumour spread that King James VII had allowed the recently refurbished chapel of Holyrood Abbey in Edinburgh to be used for a Catholic mass a mob tore down all the chapel fittings and ransacked the vault which housed the royal tombs.[12] The claim, made by a biographer of Margaret Tudor,[13] that James IV's body was deliberately targeted and thrown in among rubbish in a lumber room at Sheen Priory by Protestant extremists during the reign of Edward VI is not supported by any evidence.

Oliver Cromwell's remains were also subject to bizarre mistreatment, spawning legends which bear comparison to tales concerning James IV. On 30 January 1661, following the Restoration, Cromwell and other deceased leaders of the Commonwealth were exhumed and dragged through the London streets. His head was displayed on a spike, but the exact fate of his body was unknown.[14] One story says he was reburied at Naseby, the scene of his great military triumph. Conflicting stories about his body proliferated for many years. In the 18th century it was said that the body of the usurper was taken onto a barge and ceremoniously sunk in the Thames. Less dramatic traditions maintained that he ended up in Newburgh Priory, Yorkshire, or in a paddock near Holburn.[15] In the 18th and 19th centuries Cromwell's head was a valuable, ghoulish commodity which changed ownership several times and was exhibited to the paying public.

While the body of King James IV was forgotten in a lumber room, and rumours about him grew into legends, some articles associated with him were distributed around England and elsewhere. Catherine of Aragon, we know, tore up his coat for King Henry's banner; the bishop of Durham supposedly ornamented his church with his harness and banner. Other keepsakes of the crushing victory were allegedly taken off the field and circulated as souvenirs. One royal item which is supposed to have made their way abroad to Henry VIII in France was the Scottish king's iron gauntlets. The Italian Paolo da Lodi mentioned that the gauntlets were found, still encasing his hands, and given to Catherine of Aragon who sent them (though presumably not including the hands) on to Henry in France as another questionable curiosity.[16] The Emperor Maximilian, a connoisseur of fine armour, may have gained the gauntlets and other items from King Henry. Maximilian had gifted Henry a suit of gilded horse armour in 1509 and another gift of armour followed in 1514.[17] There is no record of the English king giving a keepsake of his enemy to the emperor, but the two men met a few days before Flodden was fought and King Henry made a reciprocal gift to Maximilian at the siege of Thérouanne. Over dinner the rulers discussed rings and jewels and Henry gave Maximilian a magnificent jewelled eagle to wear around his neck, which is supposed to have previously belonged to Duke Charles of Burgundy.[18] Some armour of James IV may have been given to Maximilian soon afterwards. The Italian traveller Don Antonio de Beatis visited Maximilian's palace at Innsbruck in

1517 and found in an old store room beautiful pieces of armour among a heap of other fine and strange metalwork, which he was told had belonged to a king of Scotland who had perished in England.[19] What became of this armour is sadly unknown. Back in England there was talk of James IV's cross and 'certayn thynges of hys' found on the body or close by.[20] There does not seem to be any subsequent mention of these, and they may have been purloined by a looter.

The College of Arms in London houses in its collection a sword, dagger and gold turquoise ring once believed to have been taken from the body of King James at Flodden by the Earl of Surrey. These relics were kept in the Howard family until 1681, when they were given by Henry Duke of Norfolk to the College of Heralds. There is no doubt that these items were passed down in the Howard family, but the muddled tradition concerning them casts doubt on their authenticity. William, Viscount Stafford, wrote to a female relative in 1680 stating that 'I have the sword that was our great ancestors at the battle of Flodden ffeild, with wch wee have a tradition in our ffamily, hee [the Earl of Surrey] killd the King of Scottland.'[21] No historian seriously admits that the septuagenarian Surrey personally lifted a finger against James (or anyone else) at Flodden, and the story may be merely a manifestation of the famous Howard boastfulness and pride in their ancestry. The ring was supposed to be that which Anne of Brittany gave to James IV as a chivalrous incentive to engage in war with England. The sword is described as just over three feet in length, inscribed on one side with 'Maestro Domingo', suggesting that it was forged in one of the renowned armouries of Toledo in Spain. The other side bears the legend *Espoir Conforte le Gueval*, signifying 'Hope Encourages A Leader'.[22] It has been suggested that the sword may have been the one that James IV received from visiting Spanish ambassadors in July 1489.[23] But the College of Arms now believes that the weapons are later than the time of Flodden. A recent analysis suggests that the sword is from the late 16th century, though the blade may be older than the hilt.[24] It may be that the Howard family used these dubious objects to enhance its reputation in the 17th century.

Other relics associated with the Scottish king are transparently false, despite traditions concerning them being relatively old. The National Trust property of Speke Hall, Liverpool, has a false legend literally built into its fabric. The house was not constructed until 1598, but there was story that a member of the Norris family who served under Stanley at the battle of Flodden brought back some books and wainscoting from James IV's palace at Edinburgh.[25] Sadly for this story, no English trooper in 1513 came anywhere near Holyrood Palace. The tale muddles up the facts about some objects of possible Scottish provenance which may have been looted by English troops later in the 16th century. The association with James IV here may be a case of confused dates rather than intended untruth. The fame of the Flodden king made a picturesque hook to hang the story on.

A grisly story of Flodden body parts has come to light in recent years. A newspaper column claimed that one of the king's detached fingers was wrapped in a piece of the Scottish royal standard and found its way into the possession of an anonymous, prominent, Northumbrian upper class family and have been passed down to this day, though it seems the tale was a joke rather than a serious claim.[26] As seen from the post mortem adventures of Oliver Cromwell, there are occasions when bodily relics remain unburied for extended periods. In the Scottish context, another example is the unfortunate De La Bastie, the 'White Knight'. After he was slaughtered by the Homes in revenge for the state execution of Alexander, 3rd Lord Home and his brother, his decapitated head was nailed to the Market Cross of Duns in Berwickshire. It was passed down as a grisly heirloom by a local family and only finally disposed of when a 19th century lady owner decided it was too indelicate an object to retain.[27] The remains of other famous people who suffered violent deaths were occasionally turned into keepsakes. A family in Yorkshire treasured the withered arm of the Marquis of Montrose, along with his sword. It was probably stolen from public display in a Scottish burgh, where it had been set up as a warning to the Scottish populace, and brought south by an English soldier.[28]

The glamour attached to royalty seems to allow greater scope for taller tales when it comes to stories of body parts being kept as heirlooms. In 1826 a skull which seemed to have marks of violence was unearthed near the altar of St Andrews Cathedral during works to remove rubble left over from depredations at the Reformation. Contemporary writers leapt to the conclusion that this must certainly belong to the scholarly, hapless prince, Alexander Stewart, the royal archbishop who died alongside his father at Flodden. Unfortunately there was no evidence whatever to support this and the claim remains extremely doubtful. The urge to connect the remains to the alluring touchstones of Flodden and royalty was strong.[29] Further afield, Dr Robert Bruce Honeyman, a Scottish doctor who emigrated to Virginia in the 18th century, died in 1824 and bequeathed in his will a rib which he stated had belonged to King James V, who died at Falkland Palace in 1542. It would be interesting to know how the rib was initially procured, since this king died of natural causes and was interred in a normal fashion.[30] Such tales are perhaps the remnants of secularised tales of the bodies of royalty having actual powers, much like those of holy people. Even the desecrator Launcelot Young, who kept James IV's head as a keepsake, may have recognised the intrinsic magic of the head, with its sweet smell reminiscent of the 'odour of sanctity' attributed to the remains of some kings and saints.[31] The powerful, totemic image of the Celtic severed head also hovers into mind; particularly the magical head of the hero/god Bran the Blessed which was finally buried at the Tower of London. A more extreme mystical association was summoned up by the artist and author Ithell Colquhoun, who pointed out that the decapitated royal head deposited at St Michael's was reminiscent of Taoist beheading rites performed to liberate the spiritual forms of immortal beings.[32]

Beyond these physical items, Flodden and its manifold repercussions burned itself into the Scottish national consciousness as few other events have managed to do. While the Scots have obsessively examined their own past again and again over the centuries, perhaps because of the loss of political independence, some traumatic events have assumed the rosy glow of cosy sentimentality. Bonnie Prince Charlie, Mary Queen of Scots, and even to an extent the supposed racial progenitors the Picts appear now so barnacled with quaint legends that whatever truth that lies beneath is difficult to see. But there are other points in Scottish history which still burn like embers, arousing controversy and emotion.

King James IV's death at Flodden was disbelieved, used as a political weapon, and finally transmitted through the distorting lenses of legend and literature. In Scotland, in the intervening years between the battle and the generation of historians who lauded King James IV, his reputation remained buoyant. The heroic qualities of the fallen leader are exemplified by Sir David Lindsay, court poet and Lord Lyon King of Arms, who personally knew the monarch. Lindsay's poem, the 'Testament and Complaynt of Our Soverane Lordis Papyngo', gives advice to King James V, satirically delivered by the royal parrot. It is interesting for the view it gives of King James IV, being one of the earliest examples of literature describing him, written around 1530. Lindsay lauded his former master for establishing royal order through the Isles and in the borders and then gave what is the first recorded mention of the legend that the realm was made so peaceable that the king could travel anywhere without attendants:

So for to schaw, that he aferit no fone,
Out throuch his realme he wald ryde hym alone.[33]

King James IV is further praised for his high fame throughout Europe, his noble tournaments making him 'the glore of princelie governyng'. But Lindsay's solemn judgement on the cause of the king's demise would be echoed with minor variation by many subsequent writers. The king, he wrote, was not really destroyed by the blustering English army, but by 'his awin wylfull mysgovernance'.[34] The glowing terms used by Lindsay were doubtless shared by many of his countrymen of all classes; one reason for the high reputation of the king being the ill discipline of those parties who jockeyed for power after his death. At the end of the century, outside of history books, he was either a hidden captive in another dimension, or alternatively a cynically distorted character, a cardboard cut out, in a bad English play. And then he was simply cast out of mind by most.

The Scottish and then British royal Stuarts conveniently forgot about their ancestor. In 1612 James VI and I removed his mother Queen Mary Stuart from Peterborough Cathedral and re-interred her with honour in a lavish tomb within Henry VI's chapel at Westminster Abbey.[35] Neither he nor any other descendant are recorded to have made any enquiry into the remains of King James IV. James V, of course, never knew his father, but they allegedly shared at least one noteworthy habit: wandering incognito through their kingdom. In James IV's case, this was one aspect of his habitual restlessness, a condition partly inspired by psychological impulses.[36] One manifestation of his need to be continually in transit was his many pilgrimages to shrines at the opposite ends of his kingdom: the shrine of St Duthac, at Tain, north of Inverness, and the shrine of St Ninian at Whithorn, in Galloway. Though Tain was usefully near his mistress Janet Kennedy's Castle of Darnaway, there is little doubt of James IV's devotion to the idea of pilgrimage, as example the time when he walked the 191 kilometres (120 miles) from Edinburgh to St Ninian's shrine at Whithorn.[37] Another famous instance of the king's prodigious appetite for travel was in the autumn of 1507, when the king set off alone from Stirling, bound for Tain, and he incredibly accomplished the journey in a single day, riding via Perth and Aberdeen to Elgin, continuing to the shrine next morning.[38] Whether this was an experiment to see if the solitary traveller could venture in safety through the length of the realm, or was merely a symptom of inherent restlessness is unknown.

A unifying link between James IV and James V were stories later told about the 'Gudeman of Ballangeich'. This character took his nickname from land adjoining Stirling Castle, from where the disguised king frequently wandered out to travel among his subjects. Many instances of the Gudeman's adventures were retold in later centuries, and though most state it was James V who went incognito, some tales state that the hero was James IV. Pitscottie states that King James IV frequently journeyed through his kingdom incognito, lodging in poor men's houses, asking them if they knew where the king was and what they thought of him, so he could gain a truthful estimation of his worth to his subjects.[39] James IV was certainly a better loved monarch in his own day than his son, which may make him a better candidate for his role of the King in Disguise, though this assumes a logic in folklore that is often absent.

The Gudeman fits into a recognised international folklore pattern featuring and incognito heroes from many lands.[40] A more telling doubt about the truth of the stories, in the case of James V at least, is that he was perceived as an authoritarian character and not the lovable 'Commons King' portrayed in the stories.[41]Against that, however, it could be argued that James V may have felt the need to portray himself as an ally of his ordinary subjects, rather than of the nobles, some of whom gave him persistent trouble. There is also the possibility that King James V knew about such tales told about other kings, including his father. Whoever was the original of the disguised wanderer, father or son, the truth of the traditions can hardly be deduced now as the tales did not appear in print until several centuries after the yeath of the younger James. What truth there was in the tales was soon muddied by writers, including Walter Scott who first hedged his bets and said that both kings travelled incognito, then later decided that James V was the authentic Gudeman.[42]

But it can probably still be said that King James IV was a 'Commons King' in a more demonstrable sense than his son, and his reputation of the monarch as a staunch upholder of the law is reflected in one tale featuring him, set at Clatto Den, in the parish of Kettle in Fife.[43] According to this, the king was wandering past a cave one day when he was attacked by a young member of the Seaton family, who were prominent in the area. Luckily, King James had a dagger beneath his cloak and swiftly used it, severing the briggand's right hand, which was trying to seize his horse's bridle. He then snatched up the detached hand and rode off. Next day the king went to the home of the Seatons with his full retinue. The family head lined up all of his siblings to meet the king, except one son whom he said had been hurt in an accident and was confined to bed. As a concerned monarch (and medical expert), the king insisted on seeing him and demanded to check his pulse. Young Seaton was summoned and reluctantly held out his left hand, but King James said he wanted to see the other hand also. Despite a barrage of excuses he was forced to admit that he had lost his right hand. The king told him he was lucky, for he had a spare hand about his person, 'which was at his service if it would fit him'. The whole Seaton kindred were seized and immediately executed.

Another Fife story allied to the 'Ballangeich' tradition is set in the Court Cave, at East Wemyss. Wemyss, on the south coast of Fife, has a series of caves, many of them marked with ancient Pictish symbols, which have many legends associated with them. The largest cavern is the Court Cave (also known as the

Piper's Cave), which received its name from the lords of nearby Wemyss Castle holding baronial courts here. Its alternative name comes from the story of a piper who unwisely investigated its otherworldly depths and vanished without trace, an archetypal tale which identifies the location as portal to another realm. King James IV came here with a group of gypsies he fell in with while wandering in disguise through Fife. After a good deal of carousing, a fight broke out and the king, for the sake of his own safety, threw off his rags and revealed his true identity, at which all hostilities ceased and he was treated as the guest of honour before being escorted on his way.[44] The tradition may have been in oral circulation for some time before being recorded, and was certainly elaborated in Victorian times.[45]

One variant of the tale says that the quarrel arose over an accusation of theft. The person accused was a rich named Mary Sibbald who had taken up with the gypsies after falling in love with one of them. She had been accused of theft and died after being whipped by the Baron Bailie of East Wemyss. Her ghost appeared in the cave, leading to widespread panic among the gypsies. The person who had wrongly accused her of theft owned up, and the king identified the 'White Lady' as Mary Sibbald.[46]

Whether or not the story has any basis in fact, it shows the public perception of the adventurous side of King James IV, though there is no knowing how early the tale evolved. It also recognises a link between the king and the Gypsies, who may have first entered Scotland in the 15th century, but who appear first in official records during his reign. The leader of these travellers was Anthony Gavino, who styled himself 'Lord of Little Egypt'. James was so pleased with him that he granted him (on 22 April 1505) the sum of £7 and wrote a letter to his uncle, John, King of Denmark, commending Gavino and the Gypsies – 'an afflicted and miserable race of men' – to him, as they wished to pass over the sea to his kingdom.[47] The Gypsies said that their wandering pilgrimage had been ordered by the Pope himself, which the

Scottish king seems to have believed.[48] Popular tradition paired King James and the travelling people as kindred spirits, whether in fact there was any truth in the emotional connection or the folk tale. The romanticising of the entire Wandering King theme, involving James IV and James V, likely developed in later years when the Stuart dynasty has long since absented itself from its native soil and people fondly looked back at a time when their rulers were present and approachable. Hindsight distorted the truth about the dynasty, but it cannot explain away the widespread nature of the stories or the fondness behind them. James IV made himself known to the Scottish people in a way never seen before, and he gained through constant roving an intimate knowledge of his own nation.[49]

The regard of the nation for King James IV survived the calamity of Flodden in an extraordinary fashion. While the country may have lost its stomach for large scale conflict with England, there was not a tide of opinion which demanded an immediate treaty of peace with the southern nation. Nor was there any hint of opprobrium against the late king expressed by those nobles, clerics or others scrambling for power in the wake of the defeat. Lord Home, Bishop Forman, and others, were blamed for their supposed parts in the calamitous ruin of the nation, but no one did the same to King James IV. The major historians who issued major works in the late 16th century had widely different perspectives, Protestant and Catholic, yet each recognised the qualities of James IV.

George Buchanan, staunch Latin scholar and historian, wrote of James IV in 1582 that the king was 'greatly beloved while alive, so when dead, his memory was cherished with an affection beyond what I have ever read, or heard of being entertained for any other king.'[50] But his praise was tempered with an insightful assessment of his popularity, which he thought was due to comparison with less successful preceding and succeeding rulers. His 'popular vices' as well as his virtues made the populance believe that he was virtuous. Buchanan approved of his openness to his subjects, medical skill, and sufferance of the blows of his enemies. But his largesse was criticised (though, oddly, not his womanising) and Buchanan shrewdly observed that if he had lived longer, the economic cost of his overspending would have meant higher taxation and a corresponding nosedive in reputation.

Lindsay of Pitscottie's assessment of the king denied that his death was due to any superiority of the English, but rather to James disregarding the best advice of his nobility and falling prey to his own sensual pleasures, and his downfall was ultimately a warning to other princes.[51] His fate was ordained by his breaches of morality and by disregarding his peers. John Lesley, the Catholic bishop and ardent supporter of Queen Mary Stuart, lauded James IV as among the best kings that Scotland produced, and praised his practice of justice in the realm.[52]

The form of King James IV's reputation hardly altered until Sir Walter Scott wrote his poem *Marmion*, reworking the anecdotes of Pitscottie, such as the Vision in the Kirk and the Summons of Pluto. Scott's ultimate image of the doomed king has him surrounded in death by a circle of slain acolytes, hapless nobles who had no choice but to revolve around him, even though it led to their own extinction. The 'fey man', fascinating because somehow he has been chosen by fate to wander an irregular, brilliant path but destined to die young, is an important feature of Scottish tradition. Various short-lived heroes, some of them subservient to dubious ideals, have soared gloriously and briefly across the Scottish firmament, as allusive and entrancing as the northern lights. James IV has been compared with one of those heroes, John Graham, Viscount Dundee, who died in the hour of his army's pyrrhic victory at the Battle of Killiecrankie in 1689.[53] A leader with personal magnetism, who could draw men to his banner, his reputation was so strong that, twenty-six years after his death, a despairing Jacobite could plaintively cry on another battlefield, 'Oh, for one hour of Dundee!'[54] Dundee was the lynchpin that held a patchwork force of Highland factions together through his own force of will. He shared this personal charisma with King James IV, and all manner of men were willing to follow him into war and to their deaths. Walter Scott recognised the strange duality of his charisma in 'Wandering Willie's Tale,' as noted in the Introduction.

Other leaders like the Young Pretender, Charles Edward Stuart, seem to have been granted this quality only for a short period in their lives. King James was uniquely able to extend this power over his whole reign. But his personal magnetism was counterbalanced by a suspicion that he was supernaturally charmed. Towards the end of his life he was visibly under the spell of an otherworld sanction. Another Graham, James, 1st Marquis of Montrose, was similarly stamped with this indelible mark of feyness, being reckoned supernaturally doomed after the death of King Charles I in 1649. This strange spiritual transformation of character is captured in a description by John Buchan:

> From this moment there is an uncanniness about him, as of one who spends half his time in another world... all youthful weaknesses seems purged away... his patience becomes unearthly, and his gentleness inhuman. He has the air of a 'fey' man, for whom the barriers between the seen and unseen are breaking down.[55]

This association with romantic doom fits in well with the portrait painted by Pitscottie, the notion that the king was somehow earmarked for a place in the next world before his demise. This was the concept of the king in those last few months of life advanced by Andrew Lang, based on the dreadful tension seen in him by the English envoy Dr. Nicholas West, dean of Windsor, while he was deliberating whether he should honour his treaty with France and break with England.[56] In the case of King James, however, his character did not become more gentle in his last few weeks, but more intolerant, threatening his master gunner and Lord Lindsay, disparaging old friends like the Earl of Angus and Bishop Elphinstone. Foreigners who were unaware of the peculiarly Scottish spell of apprehension and doom would have had their own simpler explanation for the king's hell bent course. Fixated, violent reaction was a perceived racial characteristic of the Scots, according to medieval Europeans: *Scotus est, piper in naso*, 'He is a Scot, pepper in the nose'. A French proverb focused on a second deadly national trait noticeable in James IV: *Fier comme un Ecossais*, 'Proud as a Scot'. Once he had decided to invade England, neither man nor any vision sent by higher forces could move him to act otherwise.

Away from the cruel grip of fate and national stereotypes, James IV was the first Scottish monarch whose complex character emerges from the records, with flaws as well as merits. Misconceptions and strident judgements abounded about him, even in the 19th and 20th centuries. The Scottish Victorian writer Robert Chambers fulminated against him, updating Pitscottie's moralistic view of the king getting what his lustfulness deserved, with indignation at his 'gigantic folly, righteously punished'. The notion of imbecilic inaction in not striking first at Surrey's army when he had the chance, out of a 'sentiment of chivalry', is a common accusation.[57]

The king was even given a retrospective nickname, the 'Chivalric Madman',which summed up his most evident vice.[58] Victorians replaced the indelicate fable of the king's fall through sexual vice (with Lady Ford, as alleged by Pitscottie) with the folly of being overwhelmingly chivalric. This version of his fate carried on well into last century, even allowing his astute biographer to label him as the 'moonstruck romantic' whose concerns strayed to the ends of the earth when they should have stayed closer to home.[59] Countering the myth that Flodden was caused by the leader's folly, it could be argued that the disaster was indeed inevitable, though it was at least partly due to national sentiment rather than supernatural design or political pressure from France. As far back as 1487 King James III bluntly informed English ambassadors that he could not offer them a permanent truce because all his realm, counsellors and commoners, hated the English too much.[60] This national abhorrence, rooted in centuries of warfare and peacetime mistrust, had to come to a head at some point, and it did so disastrously at Flodden Field.

In the 20th century, C. S. Lewis's opinion of James IV was less than fulsome about James IV as a leader. He stated that James could be called a knight but he was only secondarily a king. Attempting to find literary parallels for the tragic ruler, he compared James to the 'mercurial, wilful, restless, and inquisitive' King Arthur as he appears in *Gawain and the Green Knight*. Lewis's second literary analogy is more interesting; he likened the king to the doomed, heroic English hero Byrhtnoth, who perished at the Battle of Maldon against Viking invaders in the year 991.[61] But the comparison between Earl Byrhtnoth and James IV is also debatable, especially as Lewis saw both men being motivated by heroic folly. King James may have been willing to lead from the front, to fight to the last man against a traditional enemy. But the Scottish king was not leading a force against overwhelming numbers, nor facing an enemy who had invaded his sovereign territory. Yet there are some similarities between these men who died four hundred years apart. The English earl, as portrayed in the Anglo-Saxon poem 'The Battle of Maldon', was more courteous to his enemy than was wise. Just as King James allegedly refused to set his artillery against Surrey's men to gain early advantage, so Byrhtnoth allowed the Vikings to cross a causeway from the shore to fight on dry land.[62] But the crucial difference (whether the poem is an elegy or exhortation to the English to fight the pagans) is that there is no evidence whatever that James IV expected to die or be anything else but successful on his final day.

More recent analysis can also miss the mark, such as the bizarre summary of the king's character given by one biographer of Queen Margaret Tudor, who stated that if James IV had lived today he could be dismissed as someone tragically overburdened with testosterone.[63] Other off-kilter comments include Wendy Wood's opinion that James IV became the first Trade Unionist because he worked incognito in the fields for the purposes of gaining insight into working conditions within his kingdom.[64] Yet the image of James IV and his idealised Scottish court, a microcosm of a fondly imagined past, has enduring appeal. The writer Eric Linklater, who stood in a parliamentary by-election for East Fife in 1933 as a National Party of Scotland candidate, incorporated the idealised image of the monarch alone with other archaic elements in his agenda for a reborn, self-supporting Scotland, and he was not alone in reaching for these comforting touchstones.[65]

Yet the humane and intelligent side of the monarch are also remembered. On 17 October 1957 three surgeons from Edinburgh, London and New York founded the James IV Association of Surgeons to foster closer ties between surgeons in the U.K. and U.S.A. The king was instrumental in advancing the medical profession in his time. The Royal College of Surgeons in Edinburgh was constituted by an act of the Town Council on 1 July 1505 and a grant to the body was ratified by King James IV on 13 October 1506.[66] His brother-in-law, Henry VIII, followed his example when he granted three physicians a license to set up a medical college in 1518 (though their college was not established until 1523).[67] The interest in medicine, along with dentistry, was the most conventional manifestation of the king's curiosity, which branched out into various chameleon interests, and his support of the profession is evinced in numerous payments noted in the Treasurer's Accounts to 'leeches' or doctors.[68] He might equally be claimed as one of the pioneering patrons of naval technology or ordinance. The man of many faces, the first 'modern' ruler of the northern kingdom, is curiously difficult to pin down or force into any mould.

Accusations of an excessive 'romantic' nature in his make-up force even the rational analyst to venture into strange territory to counter the spell cast by this particular prince. J. D. Mackie, at the end of his biography of the king, speculated about what would have happened if James and the Scots had won the Battle of Flodden.[69] The effect of this, he argued, would have been a swift retaliatory invasion by King Henry VIII, whose monstrous ego could never have accepted military defeat by the Scots. How severe this onslaught may have been is hard to say. Could the borders have suffered more than they did in reality, under Dacre and his English successors through into the years of the 'Rough Wooing'? Edinburgh might have been utterly wasted. But it is unlikely that the Scottish nobles, yet alone the commons, would have been cowed into long term acceptance of English rule. If Henry VIII had flexed his power to its fullest extent against Scotland, that country's antagonism would have irretrievably set against him, and the union of crowns and nations may never have happened. Mackie's urge to wander into supposition was perhaps an internal check against the glamour of his subject. The same impulse not to be enticed by James IV's dazzling light lies behind Buchanan's sober coda on his positive summary of the monarch's life.

On a more local level, the traumatic event of Flodden still reverberates like seismic event through the culture of the Scottish borders. The battle had the same kind of resonance that the Blitz has for a recent generation of Londoners, even if the distance in years has now blurred the reality of the event. Modern borderers and current day ancestors of Homes/Humes, Scotts, Douglasses and Galbraiths arguably possess a keener sense of Scottish nationality and culture than their pragmatic and hard pressed 16th century ancestors did. At the same time the accepted story that the border counties suffered more deaths proportionately than any other section of Scotland is unlikely, but it is true that the aftershock of the battle is kept alive in a genuine sense there. The battle may understandably remain an open wound for those Scots who live nearest to where it was fought, but the memory of it has not led to the secular beatification of James IV here in the way that the Young Pretender was once cherished by a misty eyed section of Gaeldom.

The tradition in the town of Selkirk states that the Town Clerk, William Brydon (or Brydone), led a contingent of 80 men to the Battle of Flodden, of whom only one man returned, a man named Fletcher, who carried with him a captured English standard, striking evidence of the bravery of the townsfolk. A variant tradition insists it was Brydon himself who returned alone to the town, and that he was later knighted by King James V. True though the story is likely to be, it is echoed in the tradition of the return of the famous Blue Blanket, brought back to Edinburgh the day after the battle.[70] Traditionally the banner brought back to Selkirk was that of the Weaver's Corporation, carried by the Standard Bearer in the Common Riding event each year, in which the bearer dramatically 'casts the Colours' down in the market place. The lone survivor is portrayed in the Flodden Memorial, a statue designed by Thomas J. Clapperton, which was unveiled in June 1913. The Common Ridings of the community here reflect the sense of communities under seige from a looming foreign threat, ever present. Flodden, as remembered in the region, even manages to overshadow the dark days of the reivers, with their attendant threat of robbery and murder.

At the unveiling of the Selkirk memorial a speech was made by Archibald Primrose, 5th Earl of Rosebery and former Prime Minister. He paid tribute to the men of the town who lost their lives in the battle, but also stressed the senselessness of the event and attacked James IV with the old charge of 'almost insane chivalry,' going into battle at the behest of the Queen of France.

The king, he said, had expiated his double crime of waging a pointless war and abdicating command by fighting on foot in the front rank as a common soldier. After repeating these age old charges, he prophetically likened the leadership decisions of 1513 to 1913, when those in power were hurtling the country again into catastrophe. 'At this moment all over Europe,' he chillingly announced, 'you see nations armed to the teeth, which... may find themselves involved in wars compared to which this Battle of Flodden was child's play...'[71]

The most unique manifestation of modern fascination with James IV is the case of the Lancastrian playwright Ada Stewart, who claims to be a reincarnation of the king. Born in 1929, the realisation that she was James IV came during her second, prolonged sojourn in Scotland, and the painful process of recovering her real identity was documented in two books. Her second published autobiographical volume came out in 1978 under the confusing title *Died 1513-Born 1929* (the second edition was re-titled *King's Memory, An Autobiography*).[72] This book is a fascinating account of her childhood and time in the services and struggles as a young playwright. The awakening or unconscious regression into a Scotland of hundreds of years before her birth is striking from a psychological point of view.

But the main part of her life as the king is covered in her first published volume, written in the first person in the royal persona, initially published in 1970.[73] This work attracted wide attention after it was issued, but historians at the time understandably shied away from seriously considering the validity of the work, as if to do so would authorize her story. Norman Macdougall, James IV's latest biographer, tersely discredited her recollections, and any sober examiner must be inclined to agree with his conclusions.[74] Some of the 'facts' represented in her book are borrowed from other works, open to question or plainly dubious. Among the suspect assertions is the claim that King James III was homosexual.[75] Although this king was charged by historians with consorting with 'low born' cronies, early accusations of sexual waywardness against him are exclusively heterosexual. Bishop Lesley states that he put his wife aside and kept a whore called the 'Daisy'.[76] Buchanan mentions that James III seduced the wife of his onetime favourite, William Crichton, who found out and in revenge seduced the king's younger sister, Princess Margaret, with whom the historian hints that the king was also having an incestuous relationship.[77] The claim, made by Stewart, that the warship the *Great Michael* was built with the intention of sailing up the Thames and blasting the palace of Greenwich is entirely unsupported.[78] There are also fundamental factual errors in the narrative which the real king would not have made, such as the statement that Henry VII was Earl of Pembroke before he became king, when in fact it was his uncle Jasper Tudor.[79] It is difficult to remove the knowledge while reading the work that its author was previously a successful playwright. Some of the characterisations of the main players on the historical stage seem unbelievable: for example, who could believe that the highly diligent and pious bishop William Elphinstone was 'exceedingly malicious'?[80] On a more pedantic level, the king's repeated interest in his counsellors' zodiac signs and the repetition of the term 'Celtic' (which in fact George Buchanan revived only late in the 16th century) are anachronistic.

But the author does acknowledge her own reliance on books she used to research the king before she fully reached the conclusion that she was the reincarnation of him. The tone of the work, breezy and readable as it is, may strike the reader as being insubstantial in its portrayal of a real 16th century royal. Neither the man nor the nation come to life with convincing vividness, and there is none of that intuitive insight which is found in the best historical works, fictional and factual.

Ian Wilson devotes a chapter called 'The Woman In The Iron Chain' in his study of reincarnation, *Mind Out of Time, Reincarnation Investigated* (1981).[81] He gives a measured response to her claims, pointing out for instance that the subject was certainly wrong in her opinions of the origins of two contemporary paintings supposed to represent James.[82] But he admits admiring the openness of Stewart to questioning and states that she had the support of at least one popular historian, the late Caroline Bingham, who stated there was nothing in her evidence which could be proven to be inconsistent with the life of the king, and came to believe the incarnation story and befriend the author.[83]

Stewart was also interviewed by Roddy Martine for his book *Supernatural Scotland* (first published in 2003), where she professed herself to be emotionally distanced from the rapidly changing political situation in Scotland, taking a muted apolitical stance in the face of the historic implementation of devolution. One of the more interesting aspects of Stewart's latter day experience as revealed in *Supernatural Scotland* is the legend of James IV's horse. According to the story, the king used to frequent Craigmillar Castle (now on the south-eastern outskirts of Edinburgh) while supervising the building of his ship *The Great Michael* at New Haven. James IV travelled to and from the shipyard on his favourite stallion; and this animal also lost his life at Flodden. Apparently the great black steed, with its scarlet and gold harness, was seen frequently as a rider less apparition in the years between 1514 and 1603. The horse disappeared from sight until the 1920s, when rumours of its appearance again began circulating the locality. Ada Stewart herself heard of the ghost horse when she grew friendly with a family from Craigmillar, which in modern times has become the site of a large housing estate.[84]

It is easy to see why historians were reluctant to accept the reincarnation tale proposed by A. J. Stewart, since her claims sit uneasily alongside conventional studies of the period. It is difficult to reconcile her writings also within the traditional body of folklore and legend associated with the king. One stumbling block for belief in modern Western assertions of reincarnation is that the subject invariably purports to be someone glamorous, attractive or famous, which leads to many people claiming to be the same historical characters.

Another person who may have claimed to be King James IV reincarnated was the English occultist Samuel Liddell (MacGregor) Mathers (1854-1918), head of the Order of the Golden Dawn, a renowned Victorian ritual magic society which attracted the likes of W.B. Yeats and others. One of Mather's obsessions was Scotland and he magnified his supposed regal Gaelic descent. According to his enemy (and an admittedly unreliable source) Aleister Crowley, Mathers said that he was the descendant of a Highland Cateran and a fairy woman. 'Another claim,' said Crowley, 'was that he himself was James IV of Scotland, that he had survived the Battle of Flodden Field, become an adept, and immortal.' Crowley pointed out the incompatibility of these two claims, but said they were 'greedily swallowed' by many of Mathers' followers. A less well-known claim about Mathers, which either backs up his tendency for Scottish past life delusion or supports the evidence that he had many enemies, is the story which says he claimed to be Prince Charles Edward Stuart reborn. According to this tale, which was peddled by the theatrical manager Annie Horniman, Mathers at one time thought he was Bonnie Prince Charlie and a friend of his was his reincarnated son who had been born after a liaison with Flora MacDonald.[85]

Whatever the truth about Crowley's propaganda, Mathers was sincere in his beliefs and admitted an interest in the mystery of James IV's remains. The Golden Dawn had fallen apart in acrimony and many of its former members were willing to tell tales against Mathers, whose eccentricities – such as dressing up in attention provoking 'regalia' in public – brought unwelcome attention to more circumspect occultists. His interest in the supposed tradition of the immortal adept King James IV may have led his enemies in the 1890s to spread the rumour that

Mathers was claiming to be a reincarnation of that king. There are hints, here and there, about his pretensions in this area, but there is no hard evidence to say whether Mathers did really claim this.[86] He also allegedly claimed that the name Mathers came from the Gaelic *Mo athair*, supposedly meaning 'the posthumous one'. But there is no definite proof that he definitely attempted to appropriate the royal persona.[87]

Mathers' views, or a prejudiced snapshot of them, came uncomfortably into view in April 1911 when he was called as a witness in a libel case brought by an occultist named George Cecil Jones who was suing a magazine called the *Looking Glass* for saying he had a close (implicitly sexual) connection with the already notorious occultist Aleister Crowley, which he considered prejudicial to his own character. The evidence given by Mathers was so outlandish that it caught the attention of the national newspapers. Like other witnesses, Mathers was evasive when questioned about supposed Rosicrucian and magical organisations. Crowley had been expelled from the Golden Dawn and had published some of their rituals.

However, Mathers happily admitted that he went by the name of MacGregor and said he had an inherited Franco-Scottish title, the *Comte MacGregor de Glenstrae*. But, after stating that the surname MacGregor was prescribed by Scots law in 1603, the counsel for the plaintiff, Mr Simmons, asked slyly:

'Your name was MacGregor in 1603?'

There was much laughter in court and Mathers answered:

'Yes; if you like to put it that way.'

He was asked about various other MacGregor aliases, but said they were used by Crowley, not by him. It is known that Crowley was prone to adopt full Highland dress on occasion, either in mockery or in emulation of Mathers. The counsel had obviously heard rumours about Mathers and reincarnation. He asked:

'Have you ever suggested to anybody that you had any

connection with King James IV of Scotland?'

'I cannot understand what you mean,' Mathers answered blandly. 'Every Scotsman who dates from an ancient family must have had some connection with King James IV, as well as with the other kings.'

But the lawyer would not be put off.

'Have you ever asserted that King James IV of Scotland never dies?' he asked.

'Yes,' Mathers admitted. 'That is a matter of common tradition among all occult bodies. There is an old tradition of that nature in Scotland.' He mentioned Allan Cunningham's novel *Sir Michael Scott* being based on the tradition.

'Do you assert that James IV of Scotland is in existence today?' the counsel asked.

'All I say is that there was that tradition.'

'Do you assert he is in existence today or not?'

'I refuse to answer that question.'

Then came the killer question: 'And that his existence today is embodied in yourself?'

'Certainly not,' Mathers answered. 'You are confusing me with Crowley's aliases.'

The questioning moved on to other supposedly eternal figures prominent in western occult tradition, such as The Count de Saint Germain and Alessandro di Cagliostro. If the intent was to ridicule Mathers' beliefs, the effect was dissipated when the judge threw in another name, the Flying Dutchman, and the witness humorously chipped in with the Wandering Jew. Finally the judge grew impatient with the proceedings and the arcane nature of the demi-monde that was brought to light. Taking his cue from the title of the magazine involved, Mr Justice Scrutton likened the whole matter to the trial from *Alice in Wonderland*. It was doubtless a view shared by the majority of staid readers of the newspapers.[88]

The trial (which ended in success for the *Looking Glass*)

was reported in the press far afield.[89] Summarised reports in newspapers as distant as Ceylon and New South Wales focused on the reincarnation of King James IV, given in proto tabloid style.[90] Can we believe that the arcane secret societies in Europe had closely guarded traditions about the survival of James IV? The world quickly moved on after that sensational trial in 1911and the trail of information about an actual arcane hidden tradition concerning the Scottish king faded away. Whatever the legitimacy of Mathers' beliefs, the myth of the undying king in this form was associated with a Victorian romanticism that soon appeared outmoded. As Rosebery foresaw, Western Europe was soon engulfed in the Great War and Mathers himself succumbed to the Spanish Influenza epidemic of 1918. Despite revivals and recondite recreations of the rituals, most of the secret knowledge of the Golden Dawn died with its original leaders.

In folklore terms, local whispers about James IV mutated and became ever more distant from the original legends. The wisps became ever harder to believe in the Borders, as can be seen in the stories about the supposed burial places of the Flodden king. But the tradition here and there was grafted onto older traditions. The placing of the king's corpse, wrapped in ox hide, at Roxburgh Castle is reminiscent of the practise of Celtic seers, who were said to have induced mantic visions by wrapping themselves in bulls' hides as part of a ritual. The golden belt wrapped around the remains of the king in one version of the story also has resonance in folklore. Beneath the Neolithic chambered cairn known as the Mittenfu' Stanes, or Meeting Stanes, near Longformacus in Berwickshire, were hidden the hide of an ox filled with gold pieces, and anyone who dug in the right spot would luckily find them.[91] This in turn brings to mind a piece of gossamer like folklore collected by the writer Andrew Lang, who heard it at Flodden itself from an old man named Reidpath. One day a woman – that is, a *fairy* woman – came to Reidpath's brother and told him to go and dig in a particular spot (we are not told whether this was at the actual site of the battle of Flodden). He was told he would unearth a stone, and beneath it there would be a stone pillar, and beneath this pillar there would be a treasure. Reidpath eagerly set to his task, aided by his father. They found the stone, the pillar, and another stone beneath that, but no material treasure at the bottom of it.[92] It could almost be an allegory of the reward awaiting those who seek meaning too eagerly in strange places.

It is doubtful if the legends of the afterlife of James IV would have flourished if they had not been born in the Borders. If the Highlands of Scotland retained the resonance of Gaelic and even more archaic culture into the modern age, then the Borders were firmly imprinted with successive periods of conflict. When Henry VII clawed his way onto the English throne in 1485, the point has been made that there had been waves of warfare in the Borders for almost 150 years.[93] But it would be no exaggeration to say that, by the time of James IV, this geographical zone had been shaped by the effected of over a thousand years of intermittent conflict and tension. Romans faced Britons here, then English fought Britons, then Northumbrians battled Scots, and Scots warred with the English. Not to mention the Viking territorial incursions and later mutual harrying of borders on both side, by locals who were Scots and English only when it suited them.

The pattern of warfare, reiving, bloodshed, did not merely affect the most visible structures of society in this troubled region. Jaime Jennings makes the point that the mortality and morbidity rates in this area were significantly higher than in other areas of medieval Britain.[94] The same writer's point that there was a parallel effect on the mental health of this region's inhabitants can be extended to view the place as an ideal, fertile breeding ground for folklore.[95] Once James IV breathed his last on the battlefield of Northumbria, his shade returned to Scotland and he was immediately resurrected.

Flodden exists as one of the stations of the cross of Scottish consciousness, with other martial markers like Culloden and Bannockburn. But there are other atavistic scars which may have taught King James lessons before the event of Flodden. The route south into England was rarely successful for any northern army, who always travelled with great expectations but seldom with sufficient strength. Nine hundred years before Flodden the British war band of the Gododdin kingdom departed from Din Eidyn (Edinburgh), possibly following the same route as the army of James IV. This army too met with annihilation – a different race who spoke another language and had a different motivation.

It is impossible to pull apart the threads of a legend and fully reveal the underlying enigma. The lives of kings are written over and over again, with divergent conclusions. With James IV, we take our pick from the profusion of truths at our disposal. James IV died at Flodden, his body was brought south and deposited at Sheen (if he was not buried at Berwick). We could imagine his presence fading away to nothing beneath the quiet parkland in Richmond, aware of the sound of the Thames and golfers strolling nearby. Others could choose to believe that he was laid to rest without the ghost of any ceremony at Windsor or in St Paul's Cathedral. His separated head may be buried somewhere under the City of London, in the heartland of his national enemy (like the head of the Celtic god Bran the Blessed under the Tower of London). Alternatively, the captured body was not his, but one of those he cunningly attired in his own armour. The deceived English had the corpse of Lord Elphinstone, the Squire of Cleisch, the Laird of Bonhard, or someone else, perhaps even a bastard brother otherwise unknown to history. In reality he was taken off the apocalyptic field alive by four men and across the Tweed (or was it the River Styx?) and done to death by Lord Home, his men, or persons unknown.

In another world of legend the king lies lost beneath the bare battlements of Home Castle. Alternatively he rests beneath the crushing weight of the King's Stone at Branxton. Or possibly he remains, rather more comfortably, beneath the Berry Moss, occasionally disturbed by the thundering of hooves at Kelso Racecourse. Of course, he could still be at Roxburgh Castle, or his remains may have been scattered by the extremist mob which tore apart the chapel at Holyrood Abbey in the 17th century. But one version insists that he survived the battle, but only for a short while and died of his wounds. But others maintain that he became a pilgrim and finally took the long road to Jerusalem. The queen found out that she was not really a widow but a bigamist, for royal James lived on somewhere for three years after his last battle. Another queen, Anne of Brittany who cynically sent an appeal to James IV to advance into England on her behalf, also spread word after the battle of Flodden that he was not truly dead. Tales about the Scottish king – imprisoned, wounded, dead or alive or in fairyland – ensured he was as talked about more in death than he was in life, despite his attempts to portray himself as a crusader or major player in European politics.

Diplomatic spies, courtiers and monarch had James IV's name on their lips all over the continent in the last few months of 1513. In Scotland, the ordinary person also traded in the currency of his survival. Men like Andro Man, who transmitted the tale through the country as part of their baggage of folk beliefs, ensured the legends constantly regenerated. The bed root of the rumours was that part of the Scottish border nearest the scene of the catastrophe. Even the monks of Jedburgh were not immune to believing the prevalent survival rumours. Nor was it only the religious or otherworldly who gave credence to the legend: it was a man of business, a Scottish merchant who told the story in France that he had seen the king alive and well after the fatal battle, possibly following his old habit of travelling incognito.

The figure of the king in his afterlife flees from the encroachment of the myths which incessantly pursue him. While the real spirit of the king is seen in that gleeful, devil-may-care breakneck horse ride he took once from Stirling to Tain, a dark cloud was following him even then. In the end he journeyed further, solemn and sacred as Arthur going to Avalon, on the back of a dun hackney, over the Tweed and into a parallel dimension. The truth, known by some, is that he peered too far into forbidden knowledge and was taken away to the shadows of Elfame and is there still; though his translation to that dubious place may hardly be reckoned as a rescue from the carnage of battle.

References

Introduction

1. Scott, *Redgauntlet*, 112-130.
2. *Ibid*, 124.
3. Murray, ed., *The Romance and Prophecies of Thomas of Erceldoune*.
4. Bower, *The Scotichronicon*, cited by Michael Brown. *James I*, 3.
5. Connolly, 'The Dethe of the Kynge of Scotis: A New Edition.'
6. Dalyell, *The Darker Superstitions of Scotland*, 489. Stevenson, 'The Dethe of the Kynge of Scotis.'
7. 'The Stuarts and Their Champions,' in *Folklore, Myths and Legends of Britain*, 527-31.
8. Fulwell, *Flower of Fame*, 353, 357.
9. Skene, 'On the Traditionary Accounts of the Death of Alexander the Third.'
10. Chadwick, 'The Story of Macbeth.'

Chapter One

1. Buchanan, *History of Scotland*, vol. 2, 261: 'His genius was quick, but, by the vice of the times, uncultivated.'
2. Lesley, *Historie*, vol. 2, 90.
3. Pitscottie, History of Scotland, 74.
4. Lesley, *Historie*, vol. 2, 94-95. Nicholson, *Scotland, The Later Middle Ages*, 485.
5. Lesley, *Historie*, vol. 2, 93. Holinshed, *Chronicles*, vol. 5, 452. Pitscottie, *History*, 84.
6. Carson, *Richard III, The Maligned King*, 119.
7. Nicholson, *Scotland, The Later Middle Ages*, 484-5.
8. *Ibid.*, 485. *Exchequer Records of Scotland*, vol. 7, lxviii.
9. Buchanan, *History*, vol. 2, 201-2.
10. Herkless and Hannay, *The Archbishops of St Andrews*, vol. 1,

82.

11. Lesley, *Historie*, vol. 2, 97. Pitscottie, *History*, 78.
12. Pitscottie, *History*, 90.
13. Lesley, *Historie*, vol. 2, 106.
14. Hume, *The History of the House and Race of Douglas*, vol. 2, 47.
15. Lindsay, 'The Testament and Complaynt of our Soverane Lordis Papyngo,' *Poetical Works*, vol.1, 81.
16. Pitscottie, *History*, 91.
17. Burns, *The True Law of Kingship*, 4.
18. Macfarlane, *William Elphinstone and the Kingdom of Scotland*, 405.
19. Henryson, *Poems*, 40-49.
20. According to Buchanan, after the king's initial teething troubles with fractious nobles, there was a time of 'jocund peace, and universal tranquillity...and, as if fortune had become handmaid to the king's virtues, a plentiful harvest followed, and a golden season seemed to have arisen after a more than iron age,' *History*, vol. 2, 229.
21. Barr, *Flodden*, 21.
22. Pitscottie, *History*, 94.
23. Lesley, *Historie*, vol. 2,105.
24. *Ibid.*, 107.
25. Pitscottie, *History*, 95. Macdonald,'Princely Culture in Scotland under James III and James IV,' 150.
26. Tytler, *Lives of the Scottish Worthies*, vol. 3, 344.
27. The drawing by Jacques le Boucq, now in the Bibliothèque Municipale, Arras, and the image of the king in the *Seton Armorial* of 1591 (Edinburgh NLS MS Acc. 9309).
28. *Accounts of the Lord High Treasurer of Scotland*, vol. 3, civ.
29. Nicholson, *Scotland, The Later Middle Ages*, 531.
30. Hume Brown, *Early Travellers in Scotland*, 40-41.
31. The first long-term mistress was Marion Boyd, and the third was Janet Kennedy.
32. The king's wife, Margaret Tudor, bore him six children,

of whom only King James V survived into adulthood. The reckoning of the king's bastards is necessarily sketchier. Mackay, 'James IV,' *Dictionary of National Biography*, 152, counted seven illegitimate children of the king. Children by Marion Boyd were Alexander Stewart, James and Catherine. James Stewart, Earl of Moray, was the son of Janet Kennedy, and Margaret was the daughter of Margaret Drummond. Isabel Stewart, a daughter of the Earl of Buchan, bore him Jean; and there was one other possible child, Henry Wemyss, afterwards Bishop of Galloway. Less likely progeny were Patrick Hepburn, 3rd Earl of Bothwell and a Lady Fleming who was one of the French attendants of Queen Mary Stuart of Scotland. A somewhat different list of seven children is given by Waterhouse, *A Genealogical Account of the Royal House of Stuart*, 94-95. See also Smith, *The Days of James IV*, 202.

33. Wroe, *Perkin, A Story of Deception*, 274.
34. *Calendar of State Papers, Spain*, vol. 1, Document 130, April 1496. *Accounts of the Lord High Treasurer*, vol.1, xciii. Smith, *The Days of James IV*, 32-34.
35. Vergil, *Anglica History*, 101.
36. *Calendar of State Papers, Spain*, vol. 1, Document 210.
37. Brewer, *The Reign of Henry VIII*, vol. 1, 8-9.
38. *Accounts of the Lord High Treasurer*, vol. 1, 307. Wedderspoon re-occurs in the accounts, as on 12 December 1502, when he was paid 14 shillings, *Accounts of the Lord High Treasurer*, vol. 2, 351.
39. *Accounts of the Lord High Treasurer*, vol. 1, 180. Tytler, *Lives of the Scottish Worthies*, vol. 3, 343.
40. Pitscottie, *History*, 104.
41. Comrie, *History of Scottish Medicine*, vol. 1, 199, Morton, 'Some Aspects of the Early History of Syphilis in Scotland.' Pinkerton, *History*, vol. 2, 34. The king gave a payment to sufferers of grandgore in Stirling and Glasgow in 1497,

Accounts of the Lord High Treasurer, vol. 1, 378.

42. Herodotus, *Histories*, book 2, chapter 2, 117-8.
43. Tytler, *Lives of the Scottish Worthies*, vol. 3, 338. The king also operated on patients with eye conditions and ulcerated legs, see Comrie, *History of Scottish Medicine*, vol. 1, 149, 152.
44. Pitscottie, *History*, 104.
45. Buchanan, *History*, vol. 2, 261.
46. Guthrie, 'The Medical and Scientific Exploits of King James IV of Scotland.'
47. Tytler, *Lives of the Scottish Worthies*, vol. 3, 338.
48. *Accounts of the Lord High Treasurer*, vol. 2, lxxvi. Comrie, *History of Scottish Medicine*, 1, 153-4. Small, 'Sketches of Early Scottish Alchemists: Michael Scot – King James IV – Sir George Erskine of Innertiel.' Read, 'An Alchemical Airman.'
49. Caldwell was paid 27 shillings wages for tending the furnace on 9 August 1506, *Accounts of the Lord High Treasurer*, vol. 3, 330. The following year he received a payment via John Damian for clothes and here he is described as a *potinger*, or chemist, *Accounts of the Lord High Treasurer*, vol. 4, 90.
50. *Letters and Papers, Foreign and Domestic, of the Reign of Henry VIII*, vol. 1 (1862), s.a.1510, Document 1415. Comrie, *History of Scottish Medicine*, vol. 1, 153. Smith, *The Days of James IV*, 109-110. See also *Letters of James IV*, no. 32, for possible earlier date.
51. Dunbar, *Poems* (1834), vol. 1, 36-44.
52. Read, 'Alchemy and Alchemists', 272.
53. Lesley, *History*, vol. 2, 124.
54. *Accounts of the Lord High Treasurer*, vol. 3, lxxxvii.
55. Lesley, *History*, vol. 2, 125.
56. Small, 'Sketches of Early Scottish Alchemists'.
57. Vergil, *Anglica Historia*, 89.
58. Macdougall, *James IV*, 138. The vessel had been bought by the king from French owners in 1496, *Accounts of the Lord

High Treasurer, vol. 1, 301, 303.
59. Dunbar, *Poems* (1834), vol. 1, 145.
60. *Ibid.*, 146.
61. Macdougall, *James IV*, 295.
62. Lesley, *Historie*, vol. 2, 128.
63. Tytler, *Lives of the Scottish Worthies*, vol. 3, 332.
64. *Ibid.*, 334. Dawson, *Scotland Re-formed*, 81.
65. Dunbar, *Poems* (1834), vol. 1, 123-4.
66. Drummond, *History of Scotland*, 179. Drummond's work first appeared in 1655, six years after his death.
67. Pitscottie, *History*, 103.
68. Dickinson, Donaldson, Milne, *Source Book of Scottish History*, vol. 2, 59-91.
69. Spont, Letters and Papers Relating to the War with France, 27.
70. Lesley, *Historie*, vol. 2, 117-118.
71. Wyntoun, *The Orygynale Cronykil*, vol. 2, 266.
72. Reid, 'Alexander III: The Historiography of a Myth', 181.
73. Aitchison, *Macbeth, Man and Myth*, 11, 109. Marsden, *Alba of the Ravens*, 192-3.

Chapter 2

1. Pitscottie, *History*, 111.
2. Ferguson, *Ecclesia Antiqua*, 30-31.
3. *Ibid.*, 36.
4. Tytler, *The History of Scotland*, vol. 5, 67.
5. Pitscottie, *History*, 112.
6. Drummond, *History*, 192-3.
7. Macdougall, *James IV*, 266.
8. Mentioned by Æneas Mackay, Dunbar, *The Poems* (1893), ccxlvii.
9. Pitscottie, *History*, 103.
10. Macdougall, *James IV*, 295.
11. Fradon-Burg, *City, Marriage, Tournament*, 69-70.

12. Buchanan, *History*, vol. 2, 250-1.
13. Strickland, *Lives of the Queens of Scotland*, vol. 1, 68. It was probably the future Sir David Lindsay who is noted in the records in 1508, 'in the stable of the late prince,' the elder Prince James, though the records merely term him 'one called Lindsay', Edington, *Court and Culture in Renaissance Scotland*, 13.
14. Lindsay, *Poetical Works*, vol. 1, 5.
15. *Ibid.*, 239.
16. Edington, *Court and Culture in Renaissance Scotland*, 17, 21.
17. Herkless and Hannay, *The Archbishops of St Andrews*, vol. 2, 30.
18. The king had a strong link with St James the Greater, the brother of Jesus, as his personal patron and he is (together with his queen) depicted with the saint in an illustration in the *Book of Hours* made for himself and his wife, c. 1503. St James is favoured as the apparition's identity by Eyre-Todd, *Scotland Picturesque and Traditional*, 71. St John was suggested by Scott in *Marmion*, notes to Canto IV, lxxiv, and in *Tales of A Grandfather*, vol. 2, 223, and also favoured by Beveridge and Richardson, *Guide to Linlithgow*, 28; Buchanan, *Margaret Tudor, Queen of Scots*, 70; Ferguson, *Ecclesia Antiqua*, 298; and Strickland, *Lives of the Queens of Scotland*, vol. 1, 78-80. Pinkerton, *History*, vol. 2, 95, favours St Andrew.
19. Pitscottie, *History*, 110.
20. Drummond, *History*, 193.
21. Pitscottie, *History*, 113.
22. Drummond, *History*, 192. Holinshed, *Chronicles*, vol. 5, 477. Sinclair, in *Satan's Invisible World Discovered*, relation 7, 39, is derivative of earlier accounts.
23. Beveridge and Richardson, *Guide to Linlithgow*, 28. Steel and Paterson, *The Parish Church of Linlithgow, St Michael's*, 21.
24. Ferguson, *Ecclesia Antiqua*, 143.

25. Chambers, *Picture of Scotland*, vol. 2, 63.
26. Aubrey, *Miscellanies*, 121.
27. Bower, *Scotichronicon*, vol. 5, 421.
28. Wendover, *Flowers of History*, vol. 1, 445.
29. Hutchison, *The Last Days of Henry VIII*, 229.
30. Pitscottie, *History*, 112.
31. A payment was made to the prophet in the king's chamber, 1 November 1511, *Accounts of the Lord High Treasurer*, vol. 4, 315. Chapman, *The Sisters of Henry VIII*, 57. Green, *Lives of the Princesses of England*, vol. 4, 145. Taylor, *Life of James IV*, 213.
32. Nicholson, *Scotland, the Later Middle Ages*, 601.
33. Noted by Roderick Lyall in Lindsay, *Ane Satyre of The Thrie Estatis*, xv. Lindsay's agent in the purchase was a man named John Wilson.
34. Miller,'The Mercat Cross of Edinburgh.'
35. Marwick, *Extracts from the Records of the Burgh of Edinburgh*, 142.
36. *Ibid.*, 143. The regulation against food sellers is dated 29 August 1513.
37. Drummond, *History*, 192.
38. Sinclair, *Satan's Invisible World Discovered*, 39.
39. Pitscottie, *Historie*, ed. Mackay, vol. 2, 380.
40. *Accounts of the Lord High Treasurer*, vol. 1, ccxiv. Barr, *Flodden*, 66.
41. Dunbar, *Poems* (1834), vol. 1, 15.
42. Pitscottie, *History*, 95-96. Macdougall, *James IV*, 53.
43. Macdonald, 'Princely Culture in Scotland under James III and James IV,' 149-150, where the significant fact is mentioned that the Stirling Observant house was not founded until 1494.
44. Hodgkin, 'The Battle of Flodden', 41-42. Oliver, *Rambles in Northumberland and on the Scottish Border*, 235.
45. Barr, *Flodden*, 96.

46. Holinshed, *Chronicles*, vol. 5, 480.
47. Pitscottie, *History*, 116.
48. *Ibid.*, 116. In reality, the Scottish guns would not have had the range to reach any force crossing the river at this point (Twizel Bridge). Mackenzie, *The Secret of Flodden*, 78. Mackie, 'The English Army at Flodden,' 36.
49. Buchanan, *History*, vol. 2, 253-4.
50. Macdougall, *James IV*, 266.
51. Petrie (ed.), 'A Contemporary Account of the Battle of Flodden, 9 September 1513: Hereafter ensue the Trewe Encountre or Batayle lately don between Englande and Scotlande: In Which Batayle the Scottssh Kynge was slayne'.
52. *Trewe Encountre*, 146.
53. As a comparison with this incident of the king's personal superstition, one could compare an incident related by The Earl of Surrey to Cardinal Wolsey, in a letter written on 27 September 1523, detailing the violent English destruction of Jedburgh, led by Thomas, 2nd Lord Dacre. The English horses became crazed during the night and ran into a fire, something which Dacre credited (and Surrey believed) was due to the actions of 'sprits and ferefull sights', and the fact that the Devil had been in their camp six times that night. Ellis, *Original Letters, Illustrative of English History*, vol. 1, 217.
54. *La Rotta de Scocesi*, translated by John Purves in Mackenzie, *The Secret of Flodden*, 107-9. Weasels were sometimes allegedly regarded as messengers between the mortal and spirit worlds, Illes, *The Element Encyclopedia of Witchcraft*, 61.
55. Bates, 'Flodden Field,' 364. But this suggestion appears anachronistic, as the nine of diamonds was not popularly known as the Curse of Scotland until the latter part of the 17th century at the earliest, through its alleged association with Sir John Dalrymple, who gave orders which

precipitated the Massacre of Glencoe.

Chapter 3

1. For the departure dates, see Lesley, *Historie*, vol. 2, 140. Mackay, 'James IV,' in *The Dictionary of National Biography*, 151. Rain storms damaged the splendid tents erected to welcome the Emperor Maximilian. See Diary of John Taylor, clerk of the Parliament, *Letters and Papers, Henry VIII*, vol. 1 (1862), Document 4284.
2. British Library MS Harley 2252 f.41, in Skelton, *The Complete English Poems*, 421. *Letters and Papers, Henry VIII*, vol. 1 (1920), Document 2157.
3. *Ibid.*
4. Mackie, *King James IV*, 99.
5. Hall, *The Triumphant Reigne of Kyng Henry the VIII*, vol. 1, 75.
6. Stuart, *The Scot Who Was A Frenchman*, 29.
7. Lesley, *Historie*, vol. 2, 160. Pinkerton, *History of Scotland*, vol. 2, 152.
8. Drummond, *History*, 217. Leslie, *Historie*, vol. 2, 157.
9. Hall, *The Triumphant Reigne of Kyng Henry the VIII*, vol. 1, 76. Lesley, *Historie*, vol. 2, 142.
10. Vergil, *Anglica Historia*, 216-217.
11. Hall, *The Triumphant Reigne of Kyng Henry the VIII*, vol. 1, 76.
12. Stow, *Annales*, 824.
13. Hall, *The Triumphant Reigne of Kyng Henry the VIII*, vol. 1, 82.
14. Lesley, *Historie*, vol. 2, 142.
15. Paulo da Laude, writing to Massililiano Sforza, Duke of Milan, *Calendar of State Papers, Milan*, vol. 1, Document 656.
16. Letter of Catherine to Henry VIII, 16 September, *Letters and Papers, Henry VIII*, vol. 1 (1862), Document 4451.
17. Diary of John Taylor, Clerk of Parliaments, *Letters and Papers, Henry VIII*, vol. 1 (1920), Document 4284. Edward Hall wrongly stated that the king received news of the

victory on 25 September, *The Triumphant Reigne of Kynge Henry the VIII*, vol. 1, 113.

18. *Calendar of State Papers, Venice*, vol. 2, Document 309.
19. Reported by Paolo de Laude to the Emperor, *Calendar of State Papers, Milan*, vol. 1, Document 659.
20. Sanuto Diaries, letters from De Turnor, governor of Lyons, to Venice, Monsieur de Luçon to the French ambassador at Rome, writing on 6 and 7 September. *Calendar of State Papers, Venice*, vol. 2, Documents 306 and 307.
21. Paolo da Laude, writing to Massimiliano Sforza, Duke of Milan, from Arras, 4 September 1513, *Calendar of State Papers, Milan*, vol. 1, Document 651.
22. Paolo da Laude, writing to Massimiliano Sforza, Duke of Milan, from Arras, 8 September 1513, *Calendar of State Papers, Milan*, vol. 1, Document 652.
23. The Protonotary Carracciolo and Hieronimo Morono to Massimiliano Sforza, *Calendar of State Papers, Milan*, vol. 1, Document 672.
24. Sanuto Diaries, letters from Ambassador Foscari on 15 and 16 September, *Calendar of State Papers, Venice*, vol. 2, Document 314. Letter of Vetor Lipomano, written at Rome, 16 September, *Calendar of State Papers, Venice*, vol. 2, Document 315.
25. Letter of Cardinal Bainbridge and Silvester, Bishop of Worcester, to Henry VIII, 17 September, *Letters and Papers, Foreign and Domestic, Henry VIII*, vol. 1 (1862), Document 4455.
26. Letter of Brian Tuke, Clerk of the Signet, to Richard Pace, Tournai, 22 September, *Calendar of State Papers, Venice*, vol. 2, Document 316.
27. On 30 September or 1 October. Sanuto Diaries. Francesco Foscari, Venetian Ambassador in Rome, to the State. *Calendar of State Papers, Venice*, vol. 2, Document 325.
28. Stow, *A Survey of London*, vol. 1, 298.

29. Santuto Diaries, 8 October. *Calendar of State Papers, Venice*, vol. 2, Document 332.
30. Pollet, *John Skelton, Poet of Tudor England*, 68.
31. Skelton, Poetical Works, vol, 1, 211. *Complete English Poems*, 69.
32. Pollet, *John Skelton, Poet of Tudor England*, 69.
33. Skelton, *A Ballade of the Scottysshe Kyng*, 11, 93.
34. Skelton, *The Complete English Poems*, 114.
35. Skelton, *Poetical Works*, vol. 1, 202-210.
36. Macdougall, *James IV*, 255.
37. Wood, *Flodden Papers*, Document 19.
38. *Ibid.*, Document 20.
39. Letter written at Corbeil on 24 October. Sanuto Diaries, 14 November. *Calendar of State Papers, Venice*, vol. 2, Document 352. Moray's presence as ambassador at the French court is attested in a letter to the Venetian ambassador Marco Dandolo to the state, 14 July to 19 July, *Calendar of State Papers, Venice*, vol. 2, Document 268.
40. Lesley, *Historie*, vol. 2, 149.
41. Buchanan, *History*, vol. 2, 245. Pitscottie, *History*, 110.
42. Macdougall, James IV, 269.
43. Wood, *Flodden Papers*, 113.
44. Dacre to Henry VIII, 13 November, 1513. *Letters and Papers, Henry VIII*, vol.1 (1862), Document 4556.
45. Lesley, *Historie*, vol. 2, 149.
46. Wood, *Flodden Papers*, lxx.
47. Dated 15 October. Included in the Sanuto Diaries, 22 October. *Calendar of State Papers, Venice*, vol. 2, Document 342.
48. Pitscottie, *History*, 115.
49. Younger, 'Crouching enemy'.
50. Hall, *The Triumphant Reigne of Kyng Henry the VIII*, vol. 1, 109.
51. Bates, 'Flodden Field,' 351 .

52. 'Scotish Ffeilde', in Percy, *Folio MS.*, vol. 1, 199-234, f. 229, and also the account written by the Earl of Surrey's son, Thomas Howard, the Lord Admiral, soon after the battle, *Articles of the Bataille bitwix the Kynge of Scottes and therle of Surrey in Brankstone felde the 9 day of Septembre, in State Papers, Henry the Eighth, Part IV*, 1-2. The cowardice of the Cheshire men is also related by Brian Tuke, Letter of Brian Tuke to Richard Pace, 22 September, *Calendar of State Papers, Venice*, vol. 2, Document 316.
53. Hall, *The Triumphant Reigne of Kyng Henry the VIII*, vol. 1, 113.
54. Letter of Dacre to Henry VIII, 22 October, *Letters and Papers, Foreign and Domestic, Henry VIII*, vol. 1 (1862), Document 4520.
55. Pitscottie, *History*, 117.
56. *Ibid.*,118.
57. *The Triumphant Reigne of Kyng Henry the VIII*, vol. 1, 112.
58. Ruthall to Wolsey, 20 September, *Letters and Papers, Henry VIII*, vol. 1 (1862), Documents 4461, 4462.
59. Dickinson, Donaldson and Milne, *A Source Book of Scottish History*, vol. 1, 62-64. Hall, *The Triumphant Reigne of Kyng Henry the VIII*, vol. 1, 112. Ruthall to Wolsey, *Letters and Papers, Henry VIII*, vol. 1(1862), Document 4461. Ruthall to Wolsey, *Letters and Papers, Henry VIII*, vol. 1 (1862), Document 4462.
60. Dickinson, Donaldson and Milne, *A Source Book of Scottish History*, vol. 2, 64-67.
61. Ambassador Spinelly, writing from Lisle, to the English Cardinal Bainbridge at Rome, September 20 1513, *Letters and Papers Henry VIII*, vol. 1 (1862), Document 4459. Fifty French men at arms and forty captains under their own captain d'Aussi were present in the Scots army, drilling the main Scottish divisions in the continental fashion, Vokes, *The Early Career of Thomas, Lord Howard*, 109.

62. Letter of Brian Tuke to Richard Pace, September 22 1513, *Calendar of State Papers, Milan*, Document 661.
63. Holinshed, *Chronicles*, vol. 5, 482.
64. *The Trewe Encountre*, 150.
65. Ruthall's letter to Wolsey, 20 September 1513, Dickinson, Donaldson and Milne, *A Source Book of Scottish History*, vol. 2, 64-67. *Letters and Papers Henry VIII*, vol. 1 (1862), Document 4461.
66. Hall, *The Triumphant Reigne of Kyng Henry the VIII*, vol. 1, 96.
67. Letter of Brian Tuke to Richard Pace, 22 September 1513, Sforza Archives, Milan, *Calendar of State Papers, Venice*, vol 2, Document 316.
68. Goodwin, *Fatal Rivalry*, 26. Mackie, *King James IV*, 87-88.
69. Elliot, *The Battle of Flodden and the Raids of 1513*, 117.
70. *La Rotta de Scocessi* gives the number as 20,000 men, Mackenzie, *The Secret of Flodden*, 123. The Duke of Ferrara wrote to the Venetian State on 6 October 1513, giving the figure as 20,600 men, Sanuto Diaries, *Calendar of State Papers, Venice*, vol. 2, Document 328. Antonio Bavarin wrote from London on 14 September 1513 that 30,000 Scots had been slain in battle and many thousands more drowned in rivers as they tried to escape. *Calendar of State Papers, Venice*, vol. 2, Document 337.
71. 12 October 1513, *Letters and Papers, Henry VIII*, vol. 1 (1862), Document 4502. Modern historian George Goodwin settles for a cautious death toll of 10,000 Scots, *Fatal Rivalry*, 208.
72. Buchanan, *History*, vol. 2, 256-7. See 'The Flodden Death-roll,' 103. Pitscottie does not give a figure for the Scots dead.
73. Lesley, *Historie*, vol. 2, 146. Mackie, 'The English Army at Flodden,' 36, notes the letter written in the name of James V, 16 January 1514, to Christian II of Denmark, which states more English did in fact die, though they were commoners and presumably therefore not tallied correctly.
74. Holinshed, *Chronicles*, vol. 5, 482.

75. Petrie, notes to *Trewe Encountre*, 141.
76. 'Account of the Battle of Flodden,' *Letters and Papers, Henry VIII*, vol. 1 (1862), Document 4441. Lord Dacre says that he took the corpse to the town, *Letters and Papers, Henry VIII*, vol. 1 (1862), Document 5090. Edward Hall has the body identified by Scottish prisoners in the town, *The Triumphant Reigne of Kyng Henry the VIII*, vol. 1, 112. The English claim to have taken the body first to Berwick is acknowledged by Lesley, *History*, vol. 2, 146.
77. *La Rotta de Scocesi*, translated in Mackenzie, *The Secret of Flodden*, 122.
78. Lambe, *An Exact and Circumstantial History of the Battle of Flodden*, notes, 100. Scott, *Marmion, A Tale of Flodden Field*, canto VI, XXXV, 368.
79. Ruthall to Wolsey, *Letters and Papers, Henry VIII*, vol. 1 (1862), Document 4461.
80. Hall, *The Triumphant Reigne of Kyng Henry the VIII*, vol. 1, 110. *MS. Batayle*, in Smith, *The Days of James IV*, 159.
81. Fraser, *The Douglas Book*, vol. 2, 135-6.
82. Letter of Brian Tuke to Richard Pace, 22 September 1513. Sforza Archives, *Calendar of State Papers, Venice*, vol. 2, Document 316.
83. *Trewe Encountre*, 151. Mackenzie, *The Secret of Flodden*, 57.
84. Hodgkin, 'The Battle of Flodden,' 31.
85. *MS. Batayle*, in Smith, The Days of James IV, 158-9. Hall, *The Triumphant Reigne of Kyng Henry the VIII*, vol. 1, 112.
86. Godwyn, *Annals of England*, 14.
87. Camden, *Remaines Concerning Britain*, 294-5.
88. Letter dated 4 October 1513, Francesco Foscari, Venetian Ambassador in Rome, to the State, Sanuto Diaries, 7 October. *Calendar of State Papers, Venice*, vol. 2, Document 327.
89. Hall, *The Triumphant Reigne of Kyng Henry the VIII*, vol. 1, 112-13. Hall's work was unfinished at his death in 1548.

90. Hall, *The Triumphant Reigne of Kyng Henry the VIII*, vol. 1, 112.
91. Leland, *Antiquarii de Rebus Britannicis Collectanea*, vol. 4, 159.
92. Ellis, *Tudor Frontiers and Noble Power*, 156.
93. *Letters and Papers of Henry VIII*, vol. 1(1862), Document 4482.
94. *In the Trewe Encountre*, 150. Scot is called 'a gentilman well lernyd'.
95. Hall, *The Triumphant Reigne of Kyng Henry the VIII*, vol. 1, 112.
96. Letter of Ruthall to Wolsey, 20 September 1513, *Letters and Papers, Henry VIII*, vol. 1 (1862), Document 4462.
97. *Letters and Papers, Henry VIII*, vol. 1 (1862), Document 5090. Pinkerton, *History*, vol. 2, 459-63.
98. Ellis, *Tudor Frontiers and Noble Power*, 156.
99. *Letters and Papers, Henry VIII*, vol. 1 (1862), Document 5090.
100. Fullwell, *The Flower of Fame*, 356.

Chapter 4

1. Stow, *Annales*, 829. White,'The Battle of Flodden,' 229.
2. Jones, 'The Battle of Flodden Field,' 83.
3. Letter of Henry VIII to Massimiliano Sforza, Duke of Milan, 16 September. *Calendar of State Papers, Venice*, vol. 2, Document 309.
4. Hall, *The Triumphant Reigne of Kyng Henry the VIII*, vol. 1, 112.
5. Sanuto Diaries, 22 October, *Calendar of State Papers, Venice*, vol. 2, Document 341.
6. Stow, *Annales*, 829.
7. Hall, *The Triumphant Reigne of Kyng Henry the VIII*, vol. 1, 113.
8. Letter of 6 October 1515, Lorenzo Pasqualigo, Merchant of Venice in London, to his brothers Alvise and Francesco. Sanuto Diaries, *Calendar of State Papers, Venice*, vol. 2,

Document 661.

9. Galt, *Life of Cardinal Wolsey*, 17.
10. Reported by the *Chronicle of Lanercost*, in Anderson, *Early Sources of Scottish History*, vol. 2, 689.
11. Reported in Symeon of Durham, *De Miraculis et Translationibus S.Cuthberti*, in Anderson, *Scottish Annals from English Chroniclers*, 105-6.
12. Florence of Worcester, *Chronicon*, in Anderson, *Early Sources of Scottish History*, vol. 2, 137.
13. Ruthall to Wolsey, 24 October 1513, *Letters and Papers, Henry VIII*, vol. 1 (1862), Document 4523.
14. Letter of Ruthall to Wolsey, 20 September 1513. *Letters and Papers, Henry VIII*, vol. 1 (1862), Document 4462. Barr, *Flodden*, 127.
15. *Letters and Papers Henry VIII*, vol. 1 (1862), Document 4461.
16. *Rites of Durham*, 6. Durham Cathedral library confirm that there is no record of the relics being at the cathedral, email from Marion Whyte, volunteer Durham Cathedral archives, 29 January 2012.
17. Letter of Ruthall to Wolsey, 20 September 1513. *Letters and Papers, Henry VIII*, vol. 1 (1862), Document 4462.
18. Dolman, 'Ancient Ballads on the Battle of Floddon Field', 156.
19. Letter of Ruthall to Wolsey, 20 September 1513. *Letters and Papers, Henry VIII*, vol. 1 (1862), Document 4462.
20. Exchequer Accounts, 18 February, 1514, *Letters and Papers, Henry VIII*, vol. 1 (1920), Document 2651. Mackie, 'The English Army at Flodden,' 80.
21. Sanuto Diaries, 22 October 1513, based on correspondence from England written on 29 September, *Calendar of State Papers, Venice*, Document 341.
22. Letter of Catherine to Wolsey, 16 September, *Letters and Papers, Henry VIII*, vol. 1 (1862), Document 4451.
23. Letter of the Duke of Ferrera to the State, October 7 1513,

Calendar of State Papers,Venice, vol. 2, no. 328.
24. *Ibid.*
25. Diary of John Taylor, Clerk of Parliaments. *Letters and Papers, Foreign and Domestic, Henry VIII,* vol. 1 (1862), Document 4284. Also noted in a letter from Spinelly to Cardinal Bainbridge, 20 September, written at Lille. *Letters and Papers, Henry VIII,* vol. 1(1862), Document 4459.
26. Letter of Brian Tuke to Richard Pace, 22 September, *Calendar of State Papers, Venice,* vol. 2, Document 316.
27. James Bannisius, Imperial Agent, to Lord Albert of Carpi, written at Tournai, 20 September, *Calendar of State Papers, Venice,* vol. 2, Document 332. Letter of Spinelly to Cardinal Bainbridge, 20 September. *Letters and Papers, Henry VIII,* vol. 1(1862), Document 4459.
28. Hall, *The Triumphant Reigne of Kyng Henry the VIII,* vol. 1, 110. 'MS. Batayle', in Smith, *The Days of James IV,* 159.
29. Pitscottie, *History,* 118.
30. Leland, John, *Antiquarii de Rebus Britannicis Collectanea,* vol. 4, 261, 264, 267.
31. *Letters and Papers, Henry VIII,* vol. 1 (1862), Document 4502.
32. *Letters and Papers, Henry VIII,* vol. 1 (1862), Document 4582. Vergil, *Anglia Historia,* 221.
33. Dawson, *Scotland Re-formed 1488-1587,* 85.
34. Carson, *Richard III, the Maligned King,* 267.
35. Fulwell, *The Flower of Fame,* 354.
36. *Ibid.,* 353.
37. Lambe, *History of the Battle of Flodden in Verse,* 125-6.
38. Vergil, *Anglica Historia,* 221. Hall, *The Triumphant Reigne of Kyng Henry the VIII,* vol. 1, 113.
39. Letter of Lorenzo Pasqualigo to his brothers in Venice, 17 September, written at London. Sanuto Diaries, *Calendar of State Papers, Venice,* vol. 2, Document 340.
40. Letter received by the Pasquilago firm, Venice, October 1513. Sanuto Diaries, *Calendar of State Papers, Venice,* vol. 2,

Document 353, Creighton, *A History of Epidemics in Britain*, vol. 1, 289. John Stow noted that the plague in 1513 was especially prevalent in London, *Annales*, 830.
41. Cloake, *Richmond's Great Monastery*, 15.
42. Stow, *A Survey of London*, vol. 1, 298.
43. Strype, *A Survey of the Cities of London and Westminster*.
44. Reported by Weever, *Antient Funeral Monuments of Great Britain*, 181-2. His source was a manuscript associated with Whalley Abbey in Lancashire.
45. Stow, *Annales*, 829.
46. Buchanan, *History*, vol. 2, 260.

Chapter 5

1. Paul, *The Scots Peerage*, vol. 4, 440.
2. *Ibid*., 455.
3. Buchanan, *History*, vol. 2, 248.
4. Lesley, *Historie*, vol. 2, 143.
5. Hall, *The Triumphant Reigne of Kyng Henry the VIII*, vol. 1, 97, says Home led 7,000 to 8,000 men, but Ridpath, *Border History*, 484, reckons his force at 3,000 horsemen.
6. Hall, *The Triumphant Reigne of Kyng Henry the VIII*, vol. 1, 96-97.
7. Macdougall, *James IV*, 271.
8. Pitscottie, *History*, 117.
9. Vergil, *Anglian History*, ed. Denys Hays, London, 1950, 219-221. Mackenzie, *The Secret of Flodden*, 17-18.
10. Vergil, *Anglica Historia*, 219-221.
11. Hall, *The Triumphant Reigne of Kyng Henry the VIII*, vol. 1, 109.
12. Macdougall, *James IV*, 72.
13. Pinkerton, *History*, vol. 2, 10.
14. Lesley, *Historie*, vol. 2, 148.
15. Paul, *The Scots Peerage*, vol. 4, 532.
16. Hall, *The Triumphant Reigne of Kyng Henry the VIII*, vol. 1,

109.

17. Emond, *The Minority of King James V*, 666.
18. Ellis, *Tudor Frontiers and Noble Power*, 155.
19. Mackenzie, *The Secret of Flodden*, 81.
20. Ellis, *Tudor Frontiers and Noble Power*, 97. Gray, *Lawlessness on the Frontier*, 402, quotes English Warden of the East March, John Carey, complaining to the Privy Council that English and Scottish borderers enjoyed too much association with each other.
21. Etty, *Tudor Revolution?* 191-2.
22. Patten, 'The Expedition into Scotland In 1547', in *Tudor Tracts, 1532-1588*, 135.
23. Bain, *Calendar*, IV, 77.
24. Pitscottie, *History*, 118.
25. In the morning a band of around 800 Scots, possibly led by Home, attempted to snatch the ordinance but were fought off. Barr, Flodden, 167. But Hodgkin, 'The Battle of Flodden,' 33, states Home and his men made no attempt to rescue the ordinance. The same is stated in Mackie, *King James IV*, 267. Pitscottie, *History*, 118, states the same and the contemporary belief that one hundred Scots could have taken back the guns.
26. Holinshed, *Chronicles*, vol. 5, 482.
27. *Letters and Papers of Henry VIII*, vol. 1(1920), Document 4502.
28. Grose, The Antiquities of Scotland, vol. 2, 64.
29. Scott, *Minstrelsy of the Scottish Border*, vol. 3, 330.
30. Scott, *Marmion*, cxxiv, notes to canto 6. Scott repeats the rumour in *Tales of A Grandfather*, vol. 2, 238.
31. De Cardonnel, *Numinismata Scotiae*, 83, where the tradition is ascribed to a M.S. of the Earl of Nithsdale in the Scots College of Douai. See also Haig, *A Topographical and Historical Account of the Town of Kelso*, 27.
32. Bollard and Griffths, Englynion y Beddau, 37, stanza 44. Jones, 'The Black Book of Carmarthen Stanzas of the

Graves,' 127, stanza 44.

33. Berry Moss is now the site of Kelso Racecourse.
34. White, 'The Battle of Flodden,' 228. White was supplied these details by William Brockie of South Shields, who received them from a correspondent to the *Kelso Chronicle.*
35. Communication from James Smith of Hume parish, 9 November 2009. See also Gunn, *The Early History of Stichill,* 52-53.
36. Pitscottie, *History,* 117.
37. Macdougall, *James IV,* 247. *The Book of Revelations,* 6, 1-8.
38. Lesley, *Historie,* vol. 2, 146.
39. Abell, *The roit or quheill of tyme,* 225.
40. Buchanan, History, vol. 2, 258. Haig, *A Topographical and Historical Account of the Town of Kelso,* 27. See also Elliot, *The Battle of Flodden and the Raids of 1513,* 133. Macdougall, *James IV,* 299.
41. Ridpath, *The Border History of England and Scotland,* 494.
42. Percy, *Folio MS.,* 210, 218.
43. Buchanan, *History,* vol. 2, 259.
44. *Ibid.*
45. Macdougall, *James IV,* 299.
46. Buchanan, *History,* vol. 2, 258.
47. Spencer, *The Complete English Traveller,* 575.
48. History, *Pitscottie,* 118.
49. Macdougall, James IV, 299. *Accounts of the Lord High Treasurer,* vol. 3, lxxxix.
50. Macdougall, James IV, 299. Lindsay, *The Historie of Ane Nobil and Wailzeand Squyer, William Meldrum,* 1594.
51. Buchanan, *History,* vol. 2, 258. Paul, *The Scots Peerage,* vol. 3, 530-1. This suggestion, which is implausible but not impossible, was also favoured by Drummond, *History,* 200-1.
52. Lesley, *Historie,* vol. 2, 146. Holinshed, *Chronicles,* vol. 5, 482. Elphinstone had been created a peer in 1510, having

previously held official posts in the king's administration including keeper of Stirling Castle, Hepburn, *The Court of James IV*, 169. He was linked to the royal inner circle by marriage to one of Queen Margaret's ladies, see Beer, *Practices and Performances*, 230-1. The family historian of the Elphinstone family states as a fact that the body identified as King James was Lord Elphinstone, Fraser, *The Elphinstone Family Book*, vol. 1, 50.

53. Hendrie, *Linlithgow, Six Hundred Years A Royal Burgh*, 34-35, states that Alexander Cornwall was the laird at this time.
54. Ridpath, *The Border History of England and Scotland*, 494.
55. Pinkerton, *History*, vol. 2, 86.
56. Pitscottie, *History*, 106-7.
57. Mackie, *King James IV*, 232.
58. Emond, *The Minority of King James V*, 634.
59. Pitscottie, *History*, 110.
60. Ruthall to Wolsey, 20 September 1513, *Letters and Papers, Henry VIII*, vol.1 (1862), Document 4462. Lord Dacre also cited Forman as the 'chief provoker of this business' in a letter to Bishop Ruthall of Durham, *Letters and Papers, Foreign and Domestic, Henry VIII*, vol. 1 (1862), Document 4482. For a recent, sympathetic summary of his skill, see Goodwin, *Fatal Rivalry*, 129-130.
61. Herkless and Hannay, *The Archbishops of St Andrews*, vol. 2, 120-1.
62. Abell, *The Roit or Quheill of Tyme*, 225.
63. Macdougall, *James IV*, 298.
64. Pitscottie, *History*, 123.
65. Pitscottie, *Historie*, vol. 2 (1895), 385.
66. Buchanan, *History*, 269. Pitscottie, *History*, 124-5. Herkless and Hannay, *The Archbishops of St Andrews*, vol. 2, 116.
67. Ridpath, *The Border History of England and Scotland*, 500.
68. Pitscottie, *History*, 125.
69. Buchanan, *History*, vol. 2, 268-9.

70. Hume, *The History of the House and Race of Douglas*, vol. 2, 71. Mackay, 'John Stewart, Duke of Albany,' 317. Ridpath, *The Border History of England and Scotland*, 499.
71. Douglas, *A History of the Border Counties (Roxburgh, Selkirk, Peebles)*, 255. *Sisters to the King*, 167-8. Ridpath, *The Border History of England and Scotland*, 499.
72. Vergil, *Anglica Historia*, 239-41.
73. The view of Albany as a tyrant was endorsed by Pinkerton, *History*, vol. 2, 155.
74. Emond, *The Minority of King James* V, 41.
75. Paul, *The Scots Peerage*, vol. 4, 451.
76. Buchanan, *History*, vol. 2, 272.
77. Pitscottie, *History*, 85.
78. Buchanan, *History*, vol. 2, 270.
79. Pitscottie, *History*, 125.
80. Lesley, *Historie*, vol. 2, 158.
81. Ellis, *Tudor Frontiers and Noble Power*, 157.
82. *Ibid.*, 81.
83. Gwyn, *The King's Cardinal*, 163, 219.
84. Ellis, *Tudor Frontiers and Noble Power*, 163, 165. He died in October that year, following a fall from his horse.
85. The quote is attributed to Lord Darcy in 1512. Ellis, *Tudor Frontiers and Noble Power*, 155.
86. *Ibid.*, 233.
87. Hall, *The Triumphant History of King Henry the VIII*, vol. 1, 112. Dacre had perhaps known of this accusation, for he claimed several times that he was too busy on the battlefield to claim prisoners. Vokes, *The Early Career of Thomas, Lord Howard*, 132.
88. Ellis, *Tudor Frontiers and Noble Power*, 101.
89. *Ibid.*, 158.
90. *Ibid.*, 158.
91. Lesley, *Historie*, vol. 2, 160-1.
92. *A Diurnal of Remarkable Occurrents*, 6.

93. Buchanan, *History*, vol. 2, 272.
94. Emond, *The Minority of King James V*, 85.
95. *Ibid.*, 90.
96. Stuart, *The Scot Who Was A Frenchman*, 54.
97. Pitscottie, *History*, 127.
98. Lesley, *Historie*, vol. 2, 165.
99. *A Diurnal of Remarkable Occurrents*, 7.
100. *Ibid.*, 5.
101. *Letters and Paper of Henry VIII*, vol. 1 (1862), Documents 4460, 4461, 4462, 4523.
102. Buchanan, *History*, vol. 2, 275-6.
103. Lesley, *Historie*, vol. 2, 165.
104. For the siege of 1523, in which he was taken prisoner, see Fraser, *The Steel Bonnets*, 223.
105. Buchanan, *History*, vol. 2, 274.
106. Pinkerton, *History*, vol. 2, 160.
107. Drummond, *History*, 222.
108. Buchanan, *History*, vol. 2, 248.
109. Ellis, *Tudor Frontiers and Noble Power*, 157.
110. Letter of surrey to Queen Margaret, 1523, *State Papers, Henry VIII*, part 4, Letter 3. At the time, Lord Dacre made no attempt to rescue Home. See Brewer, *The Reign of Henry VIII*, vol. 1, 223.
111. Ridpath, *The Border History of England and Scotland*, 494.
112. Emond, *The Minority of James V*, 148.
113. Lesley, *Historie*, vol. 2, 188.
114. Paul, *The Scots Peerage*, vol. 4, 456.
115. Brewer, *The Reign of Henry VIII*, vol. 1, 223.
116. Lesley, *Historie*, vol. 2, 170. Pitscottie, *History*, 130.
117. *Historical Tales of the Wars of Scotland*, vol. 2, 267.
118. Stuart, *The Scot Who Was A Frenchman*, 55.

Chapter 6

1. Luke, *Catherine, the Queen*, 141-2. Mattingly, *Catherine of*

Aragon, 121.

2. Margaret to Catherine, written at Perth, 11 November 1513, *Letters and Papers of Henry VIII*, vol. 1 (1862), Document 4549. Margaret stated she had received Catherine's letter on 6 November, though this letter has not survived. The strength of the two reserve armies is noted by Mackie, 'The English Army at *Flodden*,' *69*.
3. *Letters and Papers of Henry VIII*, vol. 1 (1862), Document 4424.
4. Buchanan, Margaret Tudor, Queen of Scots, 83. Mentioned in a letter of Bishop Ruthall to Wolsey, 24 October 1513, *Letters and Papers, Henry VIII*, vol. 1, (1862), Document 4523.
5. *Letters and Papers of Henry VIII*, vol. 1 (1862), Document 4549.
6. *Accounts of the Lord High Treasurer*, vol. 5, 26. Buchanan, *Margaret Tudor*, 97. Green, *Lives of the Princesses of England*, vol. 4, 206.
7. Chambers, *The Picture of Scotland*, vol. 2, 55-56. Her place of vigil is alluded to in Scott, *Marmion*, 256, canto V, X. 'Queen Margaret's Bower' is a small octagonal cap house sitting above the royal bedrooms which were built during James IV's reign.
8. *Calendar of State Papers, Milan*, Document 669.
9. Harvey's popular study *The Rose and the Thorn*, one of several works which examine Margaret alongside her sister Mary Tudor, takes Margaret Tudor's character flaws into full account.
10. Bingham, *The Stewart Kingdom of Scotland 1371-1603*, 138. Dunbar, *Scottish Kings, A Revised Chronology*, 219.
11. Hume, *The History of the House and Race of Douglas and Angus*, vol. 2, 57. Hume's work was completed c.1625-1630 and first published 1644.
12. Lesley, *Historie*, vol. 2, 151.
13. Emond, *The Minority of James V*, 23.

14. Paul, *The Scots Peerage*, vol. 1, 178.
15. Buchanan, *History*, 253-4.
16. Stone, *Studies from Court and Cloister*, 18.
17. Stuart, *The Scot Who Was A Frenchman*, 199. Typical, perhaps, of her behaviour was letting the Duke of Albany pay for her divorce from Angus, despite mercilessly slandering him; then hoping to pay him back and never doing so.
18. Emond, *The Minority of James V*, 83.
19. *Ibid.*, 114.
20. Vergil, *Anglica Historia*, 238-41.
21. Letter of Dacre to Queen Margaret, 10 July 1519, *Letters and Papers, Henry VIII*, vol. 3, Document 373. Emond, *The Minority of King James V*, 166.
22. Skelton, *Poetical Works*, vol. 2, 324.
23. Letter to the Signory dated 20 September, 1515, Calendar of State Papers, Venice, vol. 2, Document 650. Letter to the same, 26 September, Document 651.
24. Letter of Sebastian Giustinian to the Council of Ten, 2 January 1516, *Calendar of State Papers, Venice*, vol. 2, Document 671. Tytler, *The History of Scotland*, vol. 5, 115.
25. Dated 6 March, 1521, *Letters and Papers of Henry VIII*, vol. 3, part 1, Document 1190. Emond, *The Minority of James V*, 272.
26. Dacre to Wolsey, 19 December 1521, *Letters and Papers, Henry VIII*, vol. 3, part 2, Document 1883.
27. Dacre to Wolsey, 20 December 1521, *Letters and Papers, Henry VIII*, vol. 3, part 2, Document 1886.
28. Letter dated 12 December 1521, *Letters and Papers of Henry VIII*, vol. 3, part 2, Document 1858.
29. *Letters and Papers of Henry VIII*, vol. 3, part 2, Documents 1897, 1898.
30. *Letters and Papers of Henry VIII*, vol. 3, part 2, Document 2038.
31. Dacre to Margaret, 4 August 1523, *Letters and Papers, Henry VIII*, vol. 3, part 2, Document 3224.

32. *State Papers, Henry the Eighth,* Part IV, Correspondence Relating to Scotland and the Borders, Document 31.
33. *Ibid.*, Document 34.
34. *State Papers, Henry the Eighth,* Part IV, Correspondence Relating to Scotland and the Borders, Document 31. Lord Fleming did come to a bad end eventually, though not through the malicious tall tales of Margaret. He was murdered by John Tweedie of Drumelzier on 1 November 1524.
35. Emond, *The Minority of King James V*, 378.
36. Macdougall, *James IV*, 113.
37. Taylor, *Life of James IV*, 81. Tytler, *The History of Scotland*, vol. 4, 358. Green, *Lives of the Princesses of England*, vol. 4, 98
38. There had been two previous queens who were born as Drummonds. The first was Margaret Logie, second wife of David II. The other was Anabella, consort of Robert III. See Bingham, *The Stewart Kingdom of Scotland 1371-1603*, 133.
39. Green, *Lives of the Princesses of England*, vol. 4, 99. Strickland, *Lives of the Queens of Scotland*, vol. 1, 20.
40. Drummond, *The Genealogy of the most noble and ancient House of Drummond*, 138-9.
41. Macdougall, *James IV*, 113-14. Goodwin, *Fatal Rivalry*, 52, also casts doubt on the tradition.
42. Barnes, *Janet Kennedy Royal Mistress*, 13.
43. 'QuhenTayis Bank Wes Blumyt Brycht', *The Bannatyne Manuscript*, vol. 3, 660-663. C. S. Lewis cast some doubt on the supposition that the poem refers to Margaret Drummond, *English Literature in the Sixteenth Century*, 72. A branch of the Drummonds still owns Stobbeshall.
44. *Accounts of the Lord High Treasurer*, vol. 3, 56. Macdougall, *James IV*, 114. Mackie, *King James IV*, 100.
45. *Letters and Papers of Henry VIII*, vol. 3, part1,ccclii. Mackay, 'Stewart, John, Duke of Albany (1481-1536)', 322.
46. Stuart, *The Scot Who Was A Frenchman*, 214.

47. Vergil, *Anglica Historia*, 239. Anonymous poetry in Scotland also praised the coming of this 'chiftane mervellus', see Williams, 'James V as Literary Patron,' 179.
48. Margaret of Denmark died 14 July 1486. Macdougall, *James IV*, 1.
49. *The Chronicle of Lanercost*, 10.
50. Carson, *Richard III, the Maligned King*, 17-18, 22-23.
51. Routh, *Who's Who in Tudor England*, 55. For suspicions of the poisoning of Margaret Douglas, see McGrigor, *The Other Tudor Princess*, 207.
52. Watson, *Bothwell and the Witches*, 31.
53. Emond, *The Minority of King James V*, 586.
54. Tytler, *The History of Scotland*, vol. 5, 143.
55. Emond, *The Minority of King James V*, 155-6.
56. *Ibid.*, 216, 232.
57. Hume, *The History of the House and Race of Douglas*, vol. 2, 83-84.
58. *Ibid.*, 83.
59. Brewer, *The Reign of Henry VIII*, vol. 1, 514.
60. Emond, *The Minority of King James* V, 534. Pope Leo's nephew Lorenzo de Medici, Duke of Urbino, was married to Albany's sister-in-law Madeleine de la Tour d'Auvergne in 1518.
61. *Ibid.*, 471, 492-3.
62. *Ibid.*, 289.
63. Mentioned, for example, in a letter from Dr Magnus to Wolsey, 22 December 1524, *State Papers, Henry the Eighth*, Part 4, Correspondence Relating to Scotland and the Borders, 1513-1534, Letter 103. Mackay, 'Notice of A Portrait Group of Margaret Tudor, the Regent Albany, and a Third Figure'.
64. Ridpath, *The Border History of England and Scotland*, 526.
65. *State Papers, Henry the Eighth*, Part 4, Document 134. Magnus to Wolsey.
66. Ridpath, *Border History*, 526.

67. Perry, *The Sisters of Henry VIII*, 76. Cowan, *The Royal House of Stewart*, Cowan, vol. 1, 318.
68. Emond, *The Minority of King James V*, 534.
69. *State Papers, Henry the Eighth*, Part 4, 490-1, note to Letter 130.

Chapter 7

1. *Extracts from the Records of the Burgh of Edinburgh*, 143.
2. *Ibid.*, 143-4.
3. http://www.edinburghridingthemarches.co.uk/History.html
4. Ayton, 'Edinburgh After Flodden', *Blackwood's Edinburgh Magazine*, vol. 63, 165-176.
5. 'The Return of the Trades' Flag to Edinburgh after Flodden,' William Ward. 'After Flodden.' William Brassey Hole. 'After Defeat at Flodden, Randolph Murray Returns to Edinburgh,' Noel Paton.
6. Possibly ten earls died in the battle. James, 2nd Earl of Morton, died some time between 1511 and 1515. Emond, The Minority of King James V, 633. Anon, 'The Flodden Death-roll,' 101, 104-5, states ten earls died. George, Earl of Rothes, is sometimes mistakenly included among the dead, when it was his brother who died in the battle, see 'The Flodden Death-roll, Supplementary,' 171.
7. National Library of Scotland MS 1746. Abell, *The Roit or Quheill of Tyme.*
8. Stewart, 'Adam Abell's Roit or quheill of tyme', 386.
9. Abell, The Roit or Quheill of Tyme, 232. Emond, *The Minority of King James V*, 578.
10. Stewart, Abell, *The Roit or Quheill of Tyme*, 389.
11. Abell, *The Roit* or Quheill of Tyme, 225.
12. Lesley, *Historie*, vol. 2, 146.
13. *Ibid.*, 146.
14. Pitscottie, *History*, 117.

15. Buchanan, *History*, vol. 2, 258.
16. Drummond, *History*, 201.
17. *Ibid.*, 201.
18. Major, *A History of Greater Britain*, 84-85.
19. Drummond, *History*, 201. Lesley, Historie, vol. 2, 146. Major, *History*, 85. Vergil, Anglica Historia, 220-1.
20. Nicol, *The Immortal Emperor*, 76-81.
21. *Ibid.*, 82.
22. *Ibid.*, 82-83.
23. *Ibid.*, 89-90.
24. *Ibid.*, 101.
25. *Ibid.*, 102.
26. Burton, *Camoens*, vol. 1, 361.
27. Disney, *A History of Portugal*, vol. 1, 204. Salces, 'Death in northern Africa: The Battle of Alcazar and its theatrical representation,'190.
28. Burton, *Camoens*, vol. 1, 363.
29. Disney, *A History of Portugal*, vol. 1, 203.
30. Alexander, *The Byzantine Apocalyptic Tradition*, f. 151-3.
31. Wilson, *Memorials of Edinburgh in the Olden Time*, 32-33.
32. Two earlier kings from north Britain had made it at least as far as Rome in the 10th and 11th centuries respectively: Dyfnwal, king of the Strathclyde Britons, who died as a monk in Rome in 975 A.D., and more famously Macbeth, who scattered largesse in the same city in 1050. Anderson, *Early Sources of Scottish History*, vol. 1, 480, 588.
33. Drummond, *History*, 182. Green, *Lives of the Princesses of England*, vol. 4, 138.
34. Sanuto Diaries, *Calendar of State Papers*, Venice, vol. 1, Document 891. Smith, *The Days of James IV*, 1488-1513, 104-5. Macdougall, James IV, 199.
35. Wood, *Flodden Papers*, Document 3.
36. *Letters and Papers, Henry VIII*, vol. 1 (1862), September 1511, James IV to the Emperor Maximilian, Document 1875. James

IV to the Marquis of Mantua, Document 1877. James IV to the College of Cardinals, Document 1878.

37. Letter of Dr West to Henry VIII, 1 April 1513, *Letters and Papers, Henry VIII*, vol. 1 (1862), Document 3838.
38. Macdougall, *James IV*, 196. He had received the gifts of a golden rose and a silver-gilt sceptre from earlier popes.
39. Cohn, Europe's Inner Demons, 81. Even the French contemporary of James IV, King Charles VIII, considered a crusade to the Holy Land at the end of the 15th century, which allows us to see James IV's ambitions in this area as less anachronistic. See Stuart, *The Scot Who Was A Frenchman*, 11.
40. Brandt and Barclay, *The Ship of Fools*, vol. 2, 208-9. Also noted in Jamieson, *Notice of the Life and Writings of Alexander Barclay*, 6.
41. Gray, Douglas, 'Later Poetry: The Courtly Tradition,' 332.
42. Evans, *The Death of Kings*, 155. A version of the tale also entered Icelandic tradition, where it was recorded in the tale of Heming Ásláksson, also written in the thirteenth century. See Westwood, *Albion, A Guide to Legendary Britain*, 135-7.
43. *The Saga of Olaf Tryggwason*, 430, 433. Evans, *The Death of Kings*, 166. Westwood, *Albion*, 136.
44. *The Saga of Olaf Tryggwason*, 426.
45. *Ibid.*, 449-450. Evans, *The Death of Kings*, 158-9.
46. *The Saga of Olaf Tryggwason*, 434.
47. *Ibid.*, 450.
48. *Ibid.*, 450.
49. *Ibid.*, 465-7.
50. *Ibid.*, 432.
51. *Folklore, Myths and Legends of Britain*, 488. Nicholson, *Scotland, The Later Middle Ages*, 222. Wyntoun, *The Orgynale Chronicle*, vol. 3, 76 .
52. *The Book of Pluscarden*, 247.

53. Nicholson, *Scotland, The Later Middle Ages*, 222.
54. Westwood, *Albion*, 137. Wroe, *Perkin, A Story of Deception*, 49.
55. Salces, 'Death in northern Africa: The Battle of Alcazar and its theatrical representation,' 173.
56. Perrie, *Pretenders and Popular Monarchism*, 75-76.
57. *Ibid.*, 76.
58. Evans, *The Death of Kings*, 148, 155.
59. Maxwell, *Robert the Bruce and the Struggle for Scottish Independence*, 49
60. Lesley, *Historie*, vol. 2, 146.
61. Letter of The Protonotary Carracciolo and Hieronimo Morono, Milanese Ambassadors at Rome, to Massimiliano Sforza, Duke of Milan, 16 October, 1513, *Calendar of State Papers, Milan*, vol. 1, Document 672.

Chapter 8

1. 'Scotish Feilde', Percy, *Folio MS*, vol. 1, 212-234, f. 229.
2. *Ibid.*, 212-234, line 231: 'vnder the banner of a Bishoppe'.
3. 'Fflodden Ffeilde,' Percy, *Folio MS*, vol. 1, 318-40.
4. Erasmus, *The Adages of Erasmus*, 188, 189.
5. *Ibid.*, 189.
6. *Ibid.*, 189. There are a few surviving letters between Alexander Stewart and the king's secretary Patrick Paniter, and between Alexander and his father: *Letters of James IV*, nos. 145, 161, 162, 191, 228.
7. Cited by Herkless and Hannay, *The Archbishops of St Andrews*, vol. 1, 269.
8. Erasmus, *The Adages of Erasmus*, 187.
9. Erasmus, *The Adages of Erasmus*, 190.
10. Erasmus, *The Adages of Erasmus*, 183-91. *Erasmus, Proverbs, chiefly taken from the Adagia of Erasmus*, 23-24.
11. *Letters and Papers, Henry VIII*, vol. 1 (1862), xvi-xvii. *Letters and Papers, Henry VIII*, vol. 1(1920), Document 2457.

12. *Letters and Papers, Henry VIII*, vol. 1(1862), Document 2001.
13. Skelton, *The Complete English Poems*, 120-1.
14. Pollet, *John Skelton, Poet of Tudor England*, 55.
15. Archer, *Unperfect Histories*, 30. The two relevant sections in the Mirror are headed 'The Lamentation of King Iames the fourth' and 'The bataile of Brampton, or Floddon fielde' (Tragedies 21 and 32).
16. *The Mirror for Magistrates*, 488.
17. Lewis, *English Literature in the Sixteenth Century*, 241.
18. *The Mirror for Magistrates*, 483-488.
19. *Ibid.*, 483. Cf. Hall, *The Triumphant Reigne of Kyng Henry the VIII*, vol. 1, 112: 'Thys kynge had diverse deadelye woundes, and in especyall one wyth an Arowe, and another wyth a byll as apered when he was naked.'
20. *The Mirror for Magistrates*, 486: 'Who euer knew Christian King in such a case, As I wretched creature that cannot haue/In Churche or Churchyard any maner place, Emong Christen people to lye in a graue...'
21. *Ibid.*, 486.
22. Dolman, 'Ancient Ballads on the Battle of Floddon Field.'
23. *Supplement to the Harleian Miscellany*, vol. 1, 337-74.
24. *Ibid.*, 354.
25. *Ibid.*, 355- 8: 'The Historie of King Jamie's Sonne; who, after the Death of his Father, was King of Scottes; being but a Chylde'.
26. *Supplement to the Harleian Miscellany*, vol. 1, 368-373: 'The History of the Winning of Hadington in Scotland.'
27. *Supplement to the Harleian Miscellany*, vol. 1, 353.
28. Hogg, 'The Queen of France and James IV.'
29. Taylor, *The Political Prophecy in England*, 78.
30. *Ibid.*, 73.
31. Burnham, 'A Study of Thomas of Erceldoune,' 386.
32. *The Book of Pluscarden*, 82-83. Chambers, *The Popular Rhymes of Scotland*, 212.

33. Hudson, *Prophecy of Berchán: Irish and Scottish High-kings of the Early Middle Ages.*
34. Williams and Bromwich, *Armes Prydein, The Prophecy of Britain.*
35. The *Afallennau* ('Apple Trees') and the *Oianau* ('Greetings'), trans. A.O.H. Jarman in Tolstoy, *The Quest for Merlin*, 252-5.
36. Newton, 'Prophecy and Cultural Conflict in Scottish Gaelic Tradition.'
37. Lindsay, 'The Dreme of Schir David Lyndesay', *Poetical Works*, vol. 1, 5.
38. *The Complaynt of Scotland* , 82, 84-85. Murray, The Romance and Prophecies of Thomas of Erceldoune, xxx.
39. 'Patten's Expedition into Scotland' (written 1547, published 1548), in Pollard, *An English Garner, Tudor Tracts 1532-1588*, 64.
40. Previté-Orton, 'An Elizabethan Prophecy', 210.
41. Fullwell, *The Flower of Fame*, 350. The lines appear in the section 'Of the winning of Turwin and Turnay.'
42. Taylor, *The Political Prophecy in England*, 99.
43. Dalrymple, *Remarks On The History of Scotland*, 97-98, from Andro Hart version of the 'Prophecy of Bertlington', 1615. 'The Prophecie of Bertlington,' in *Collection of Ancient Scottish Prophecies*,17.
44. *Ibid.*, 98.
45. See for example Westwood, *Albion*, 361. There was a prophecy that England would have a Scottish king when the rivers Tweed and Pausayl met at Merlin's Grave, in Tweedale.
46. *The Complaynt of Scotland* , 85.
47. For comment on this segment of the prophecies, see Cowan, 'The Discovery of the Future', 14. After Albany, the verses referring to French family were also attached to Queen Mary Stuart, see Murray, *The Romance and Prophecies of Thomas of Erceldoune*, xxxvii.

48. *The Whole Prophecie of Scotland, England, and some part of France and Denmark*, 1603, reprinted in *Collection of Ancient Scottish Prophecies in Alliterative Verse: reprinted from Waldegrave's Edition, MDCIII.*
49. 'The Prophecie of Thomas Rymour,' *Collection of Ancient Scottish Prophecies in Alliterative Verse: reprinted from Waldegrave's Edition, MDCIII*, 21. See also Taylor, *The Political Prophecy in England*, 77-78.
50. Scott, *Minstrelsy of the Scottish Border*, vol. 4, 153-4.
51. Murray, *The Romance and Prophecies of Thomas of Erceldoune*, xxxvii.
52. Scott, *Minstrelsy of the Scottish Border*, vol. 4, 137.
53. Cowan, 'The Discovery of the Future,' 12.
54. Greene, *The Scottish History of James the Fourth*, ed. Norman Sanders, London, 1970. Greene, *The Scottish History of James the Fourth 1598*, ed. A. E. H. Swaen, 1921. Greene's authorship of the play has been doubted; an alternative candidate for its authorship is Edward de Vere, 17th Earl of Oxford. See *Edward de Vere Newsletter*, No. 11, Kelowna, 1990.
55. Giovanni Battista Giraldi Cintio's *Hecatommithi*, published in1565. Cintio's play Arrenopia was also based on the same story. Greene and Swaen, *The Scottish History of James the Fourth 1598*, vi. Greene and Sanders, *The Scottish History of James the Fourth*, xxv.
56. Greene and Sanders, *The Scottish History of James the Fourth*, xxxiv.
57. Miscellany of the Spalding Club, vol. 1, 123.
58. *Ibid.*, 119.
59. Murray, *The Romance and Prophecies of Thomas of Erceldoune*, 7.
60. *Miscellany of The Spalding Club*, vol. 1, 121.
61. Drummond, *History*, 201.
62. Scott, *Waverley*, 26-28. Westwood, *Albion*, 370-1.

63. Barbour, *The Bruce*, 83.
64. This tale type is classified as number 766 in the Aarne-Thomson index, under the heading 'The Seven Sleepers,' Aarne, The *Types of the Folktale: A Classification and Bibliography*, The Finnish Academy of Science and Letters, Helsinki, 1961. Cited by http://oaks.nvg.org/folktale-types.html.
65. Evans, *The Death of Kings*, 147, 151-3.
66. *Ibid.*, 151. Cohn, *The Pursuit of the Millennium*, 55, 103, 106-7. Westwood, *Albion*, 136.
67. Hunter, *The Occult Laboratory Magic, Science and Second Sight in Late 17th Century Scotland: The Secret Commonwealth and Other Texts*. An edition of The Secret Commonwealth, 77-106.
68. Graham, *Sketches of Perthshire*, 253-255.
69. Westwood, *Albion*, 397. Westwood, 'The Road to the Fairy Knowe,' ix. Westwood and Kingshill, *The Lore of Scotland*, 112-13. .
70. 'The Young Tamlane,' in Child, *English and Scottish Ballads*, vol. 1, 114-125. Cf. the variants 'Tam-a-Line,' 258-266. 'Tom Linn,' 267-270. 'Burd Ellen andYoung Tamlane,' 271-2. 'The Young Tamlane,' in Scott, *Border Minstrelsy*, vol. 2, 337-350.
71. Her trial took place at St Andrews on 28 May 1588, Simpkins, *County Folklore, Fife*, 69-75.
72. Scott, *Minstrelsy of the Scottish Border*, vol. 2, 295-99.
73. Sempill, *The Sempill Ballates*, 210.
74. Larner, *Enemies of God, The Witch Hunt in Scotland*, 1.

Chapter 9

1. *Accounts of the Lord High Treasurer*, vol. 5, 26; a painter named Alexander Chalmer was paid for the banners on 23 July 1515. On the same date Albany was given 14 shillings to offer at the mass for the late king. See also Buchanan, *Margaret Tudor*, 97-98. Green, *Lives of the Princesses of*

England, vol. 4, 206.

2. Cloake, *Richmond's Great Monastery*, 9. Garnett, *Richmond on the Thames*, 25.
3. Cloake, *Richmond's Great Monastery*, 9.
4. *Ibid.*, 23.
5. McEwan, *Scotland-upon-Thames, Scotland's Legacy to Richmond and Kew*. Owen, 'A wee bit of Scotland in the heart of Surrey.' The plaque erected at the golf club reads, 'Dedicated to James IV, King of Scots, who fell at the battle of Flodden, 1513, and whose remains were last seen here in the Carthusian monastery of Sheen.'
6. *The Daily Record*, 'Rex Marks The Spot.' *The Scotsman*, '1m pound dig will look for the head of James IV.' A letter by Graeme Allen, published in *The Glasgow Herald*, 30 February 2013, states that the king's head was transferred to a black deed box in the church of St Botolph's, Bishopgate, though I have found no other source to substantiate this.
7. Stephen Fraser, *Scotland on Sunday*, 'Standard Life paves the way for Scottish king's memorial.'
8. Carson, *Richard III, the Maligned King*, 269.
9. Hutchison, *The Last Days of Henry VIII*, 229.
10. Evans, 'The Romance of the Dead,' 193-5.
11. Perry, *The Sisters of Henry VIII*, 156.
12. Grose, *The Antiquities of Scotland*, vol. 1, 29.
13. Buchanan, *Margaret Tudor, Queen of Scots*, 97.
14. Fitzgibbons, *Cromwell's Head*, 29-30.
15. *Ibid.*, 42-43, 45-46.
16. Paolo da Lodi, writing from Lisle, 19 September. *Calendar of State Papers, Venice*, vol. 2, Document 312.
17. Weir, *Henry VIII, King and Court*, 193.
18. Paolo da Laude, Milanese Ambassador to the Emperor, to Massimiliano Sforza, Duke of Milan, 4 September 1513. *Calendar of State Papers, Milan*, Document 651.
19. De Beatis, *Voyage de Cardinal d'Aragon*, Paris, 1913, cited by

D.B.S., 'Armour Worn by James IV at Flodden'.

20. Hall, *The Triumphant Reign of Henry VIII*, vol. 1, London, 110. One artefact recovered from Flodden, but probably not belonging to the king, was an episcopal sapphire ring which ended up in the British Museum. See Lang and Lang, *Highways and Byways in the Border*, 54. A plain gold ring in twisted rope style was found on the battlefield in the 19th century. See 'Archaeological Intelligence,' *The Archaeological Journal*, 269.
21. Young, 'Remarks on the Sword, Dagger, and Ring of King James the Fourth of Scotland, preserved in the College of Arms, London,' 337.
22. *Ibid.*, 335.
23. Mackay, 'James IV,' 146.
24. Moffat, 'Sword and Dagger in the College of Arms, London', www.college-of-arms.gov.uk/SwordDaggerRing.html. Conversation with Robert Noel, Lancaster Herald, 6 May 2011.
25. Whatton, 'An Inquiry into the probability of a Tradition connected with the Library and Furniture of James IV of Scotland.'
26. Martine, 'I say, could I have a royal digit back.'
27. Lang, *History of Scotland*, vo1. 1, 397.
28. Morkill, 'Notice of a Human Hand and Forearm, pierced with Nail-holes, and a Basket-hilted sword formerly preserved in the Family of Graham of Woodhall, Yorkshire, as Relics of James, First Marquis of Montrose.'
29. The suggestion occurs in Gunnyon, *Illustrations of Scottish History*, 69 and earlier by Lyon, *Ancient and Modern*, 192, and is repeated by other writers. The skull may be older than Flodden and possibly even female. Dr Helen C. Rawson confirms that the skull is still among the medical collections at the University of St Andrews.
30. Rolph, 'A Strange Family Heirloom: the Rib of a Scottish

King in America?'

31. Stow, *A Survey of London*, vol. 1, 297-8. The holy odour of the king's head is rationally explained away as a by-product of the embalming process by Dalrymple, *Remarks on The History of Scotland*, 154. Edward the Confessor is supposed to have died in the odour of sanctity. Evans, 'The Romance of the Dead,' 192.
32. Colquhoun, *Sword of Wisdom*, 113.
33. Lindsay, 'The Testament and Complaynt of our Soverane Lordis Papyngo,' *Poetical Works*, vol. 1, 81.
34. *Ibid.*, 82.
35. Guy, *My Heart Is My Own, The Life of Mary Queen of Scots*, 504.
36. Nicholson, *Scotland, The Later Middle Ages*, 574.
37. Macdougall, *James IV*, 197.
38. Lesley, *Historie*, vol. 2,124.
39. Pitscottie, *History*, 102.
40. Examples include rulers like Alfred the Great, Robert the Bruce on occasion and Hārūn al-Rachīd, whose undercover adventures are found in the *Thousand Nights and One Night*, Westwood and Kingshill, *The Lore of Scotland*, 99. Ironically, the Duke of Albany, considered travelling to Scotland incognito in 1512 to meet his cousin James IV, though it never happened, Stuart, *The Scot Who Was A Frenchman*, 23.
41. Westwood and Kingshill, *The Lore of Scotland*, 98-99.
42. Stevenson, 'The Gudeman of Ballangeich', 196.
43. Rev. Peter Barclay, *Statistical Account of Scotland, 1791-9*, vol.1, number 39, parish of King's Kettle, Fife, http://stat-acc-scot.edina.ac.uk/link/1791-99/Fife/Kings%Kettle/
44. Westwood and Kingshill, *The Lore of Scotland*, 74-75. The story appears in an account of the parish number written by Rev. George Gib, *Statistical Account of Scotland, 1791-99*, vol. 16, number 26, http://stat-acc-scot.edina.ac.uk/link/1791-99/Fife/Wemyss/

45. See the highly coloured version of Bruce, 'The Court Cave: A Legendary Tale of Fifeshire.' Another version of the story was recorded by James Wilkie in *Bygone Fife North of the Lomonds*, and summarised by Katharine M. Briggs, *A Dictionary of British Folk Tales in the English Language, Part B, Folk Legends*, vol. 2, 25.
46. Rankin, *Guide to the Wemyss Caves*, 9. The cave was also credited with being the scene of the escape of Macduff, who fled from Macbeth along the cave leading from Kennoway. Simson, *A History of the Gipsies*,104, follows some others in making James V the hero of the Court Cave tale.
47. Macritchie, *Scottish Gypsies under the Stewarts*, 29. Pinkerton, *History*, vol. 2, 444. Simson, *A History of the Gipsies*, 99-100. Tytler, *Lives of the Scottish Worthies*, vol. 3, 339.
48. Stair-Kerr, *Scotland under James IV*, 65-67.
49. Nicholson, *Scotland, The Later Middle Ages*, 574.
50. Buchanan, *History*, vol. 2, 261.
51. Pitscottie, *History*, 118.
52. Lesley, *Historie*, vol. 2, 107.
53. Barr, *Flodden*, 116-117.
54. Reputed to have been cried by Gordon of Glenbucket at the Battle of Sheriffmuir, Lang, *History of Scotland*, vol. 4, 218.
55. Buchan, *Montrose*, 296.
56. Lang, *A History of Scotland from the Roman Occupation*, vol. 1, 375.
57. Chambers, *The Book of Days*, vol. 2, 327.
58. Brewer, *Reader's Handbook*, 1050.
59. Mackie, *King James IV*, 201. Mackie's accusation is countered by David Dunlop in 'The Politics of Peace-keeping', 139.
60. Polydore Vergil, *History*, 29.
61. Lewis, *English Literature in the Sixteenth Century*, 66.
62. 'The Battle of Maldon', in Bradley, *Anglo-Saxon Poetry*, 519-528.
63. Perry, *Sisters to the King*, 73.

64. Cited by Gerber, *The Search For the Stone of Destiny*, 112.
65. Pittock, *Scottish Nationality*, 108.
66. Dunbar, *Scottish Kings, A Revised Chronology of Scottish History, 1005-1625*, 216.
67. Hutchinson, *The Last Days of Henry VIII*, 131.
68. Comrie, *History of Scottish Medicine*, vol. 1, 151-2, notes half a dozen payments to assorted doctors in 1501-2 alone for unknown services, along with other payments to patients who had received treatment.
69. Mackie, *King James IV*, 279-80.
70. Douglas, *A History of the Border Counties*, 252. The flag was restored in 1984 and placed in Selkirk's Halliwell's House Museum, McCallum, 'The battle to save Flodden flag.'
71. *The Glasgow Herald*, 14 June 1913. *The Straits Times* (Singapore), 18 July 1913. Lang, *The Queen's Scotland, The Border Counties*, 194.
72. Stewart, *King's Memory, An Autobiography*.
73. Stewart, Falcon, *The Autobiography of His Grace James the 4 King of Scots, presented by A. J. Stewart*.
74. Macdougall, *James IV*, viii.
75. Stewart, Falcon, *The Autobiography of His Grace James the 4 King of Scots*, 20.
76. Lesley, *Historie*, vol. 2, 97.
77. She was 'infamous for too close a connexion with her brother'. Buchanan, *History*, vol. 2, 213.
78. Stewart, *Falcon*, 218.
79. *Ibid.*, 21. A more fundamental, domestic error is her confusion over several members of the Home family and their titles, 242-3.
80. *Ibid.*, 130.
81. Wilson, *Mind Out of Time, Reincarnation Investigated*, 223-42.
82. Stewart, *Falcon*, 118. Wilson, *Mind Out of Time, Reincarnation Investigated*, 231-3.
83. Wilson, *Mind Out of Time*, 231.

84. Martine, *Supernatural Scotland*, 189-208. The king himself favoured grey or white coloured steeds, but there is a record of a black horse given to him by Lord Home in 1512, *Accounts of the Lord Treasurer*, vol. 4, 335.
85. Cited by Colquhoun, *Sword of Wisdom*, 112.
86. King, *Modern Ritual Magic*, 49.
87. *Ibid.*,49.
88. *The Daily Telegraph*, 27 April 1911. *The Times*, 27 April 1911.
89. For example, *The Daily News* (Perth, Australia), 27 May 1911. The verdict in favour of the defendents was reported in *The Times*, 27 April, 1911.
90. *The Morning Leader* (Sri Lanka), 27 May, 1911. *Barrier Miner* (Broken Hill, New South Wales) 21 June 1911.
91. Westwood and Kingshill, *The Lore of Scotland*, 265.
92. Lang and Lang, *Highways and Byways in The Border*, 56.
93. Ellis, *Defending English Ground*, 7.
94. Jennings, *Stress Along the Medieval Scottish Border?*, 5.
95. *Ibid.*, 22.

Bibliography

Printed Primary Sources

Abell, Adam, 'Adam Abell's The roit or quheill of tyme: an edition', ed. StephanieThorson, Unpublished Ph.D. thesis (University of St Andrews, 1998).

Accounts of the Lord High Treasurer of Scotland, volume 1, 1473-1498, ed. Thomas Dickson (Edinburgh, 1877).

Accounts of the Lord High Treasurer of Scotland, volume 2, 1500-1504, ed. Sir James Balfour Paul (Edinburgh, 1900).

Accounts of the Lord High Treasurer of Scotland, volume 3, 1506-1507, ed. Sir James Balfour Paul (Edinburgh, 1901).

Accounts of the Lord High Treasurer of Scotland, volume 4, 1507-1513, ed. Sir James Balfour Paul (Edinburgh, 1902).

Accounts of the Lord High Treasurer of Scotland, volume 5, 1515-1531, ed. Sir James Balfour Paul (Edinburgh, 1903).

Anderson, A. O., ed., *Early Sources of Scottish History* (2 vols., 1922, reprinted Stamford, 1990).

----- *Scottish Annals from English Chroniclers* (1908, reprinted Stamford, 1991).

Anglo-Saxon Poetry, ed. S.A.J. Bradley (1982, reprinted London, 1991).

Aubrey, John, *Miscellanies* (1696, reprinted London, 1784).

George Bannatyne, ed., *The Bannatyne Manuscript* (4 vols., Glasgow, 1896).

Barbour, John, *The Brus*, ed. A. A. M. Duncan (Edinburgh, 1997).

Bollard, John K., & Griffiths, Anthony, *Englynion y Beddau, The Stanzas of the Graves* (Llanwrst, 2015).

Brandt, Sebastian, *The Ship of Fools*, translated by Alexander Barclay, ed. T. H. Jamieson (2 vols., Edinburgh, 1874).

Buchanan, George, *The History of Scotland*, ed. James Aikman (4 vols., Glasgow, 1827).

---- *Rerum Scoticarum Historia*. A hypertext critical edition by Dana F. Sutton. http://www.philological.bham.ac.uk/scothist/

Calendar of State Papers and Manuscripts, Milan, ed. A. B. Hinds (London, 1912).

Calendar of State Papers, Spain, volume 1, 1485-1509, ed. G. A. Bergenroth (London, 1862).

Calendar of State Papers, Venice, and Northern Italy, volume 1, 1502-1509, ed. Rawdon Brown (London, 1864).

Calendar of State Papers, Venice, and Northern Italy, volume 2 1509-1519, ed. Rawdon Brown (London, 1867).

Calendar of State Papers and Manuscripts relating to Scotland, volume 4, 1357-1509, ed. Joseph Bain (Edinburgh, 1888).

Camden, William, *Remaines Concerning Britain* (7th impression 1605, reprinted London, 1674).

The Complaynt of Scotlande, with an appendix of contemporary English tracts, ed. J. A.H. Murray, Early English Text Society (1875, reprinted Millwood, 1981).

A Diurnal of Remarkable Occurrents that have passed in Scotland since the death of King James the Fourth till the year MDLXXV (Edinburgh, 1833).

Dolman, Marmaduke, 'Ancient Ballads on the Battle of Flodden Field,' *The Gentleman's Magazine and Historical Review*, 221, 11-16, 154-167 (1866).

Drummond, William, *The Genealogy of the Most Noble and Ancient House of Drummond* (Edinburgh, 1832).

Drummond of Hawthornden, William, *The History of Scotland, from the year 1423, to the year 1542, containing the lives and reigns of James I, II, III, IV and V* (1655, reprinted Glasgow, 1749).

Dunbar, William, *The Poems of William Dunbar*, ed. David Laing (2 vols., Edinburgh, 1834).

Dunbar, William, *The Poems of William Dunbar*, ed. John Small, notes by Æ. J. G. Mackay (3 vols., Edinburgh, reprinted Hildesheim, 1973).

Ellis, Henry, *Original Letters, Illustrative of English History,* volume 1 (2nd. edn., London, 1825).

Erasmus, Desiderius, *The Adages of Erasmus*, selected by William Barker (Toronto, 2001).

Erasmus, Desiderius, *Proverbs, chiefly taken from the Adagia of Erasmus*, ed. Robert Bland (London, 1814).

The Exchequer Rolls of Scotland, volume 7, A.D. 1460-1469, ed. George Burnett (Edinburgh, 1884).

Fowler, Rev. J. T., ed., *Rites Of Durham, Being A Description or Brief Description of All The Ancient Monuments, Rites, & Customs Belonging Or Being Within The Monastical Church Of Durham before The Suppression*, Written 1593, Surtees Society (Durham, 1903).

Fulwell, Ulpian, *The Flower of Fame* (1575), reprinted in Supplement to the *Harleian Miscellany*, volume 9, ed. Thomas Park (London, 1812), 337-374.

Greene, Robert, *The Scottish History of James the Fourth*, ed. Norman Sanders (London, 1970).

------ *The Scottish History of James the Fourth*, ed. A. E. H. Swaen (Oxford, 1921).

Hall, Edward, *The Triumphant Reigne of Kyng Henry the VIII*, ed. Charles Whibley (2 vols., London, 1904).

Henryson, Robert, *Poems*, ed. Charles Elliot (2nd. edn., Oxford, 1974).

Holinshed, Raphael, *Chronicles of England, Scotland, and Ireland*, volume 5, Scotland (London, 1808).

Kirk, Rev. Robert, *The Secret Commonwealth of Elves, Fauns and Fairies*, in *The Occult Laboratory Magic, Science and Second Sight in Late 17th Century Scotland: The Secret Commonwealth and Other Texts*, ed. Michael Hunter (Woodbridge, 2001), 77-106.

Lambe, Rev. Robert, ed., *An Exact and Circumstantial History of the Battle of Flodden in Verse, written about the time of Queen Elizabeth* (London, 1774).

The Chronicle of Lanercost, ed. Sir Herbert Maxwell (1913, reprinted Cribyn, 2001).

Lesley, John, *The Historie of Scotland, John Leslie*, ed. E.G Cody (2 vols., Edinburgh, 1888-1895).

Letters and Papers, Foreign and Domestic, Henry VIII, volume 1, ed. J. S. Brewer (London, 1862).

Letters and Papers, Foreign and Domestic of the Reign of Henry VIII, volume 1, ed. J. S. Brewer, Gairdner and Brodie, vol 1, parts 1 and 2 (revised edn., London, 1920).

Letters and Papers, Foreign and Domestic, Henry VIII, volume 3, ed. J. S. Brewer (London, 1867).

The Letters of King James the Fourth, 1504-1513, calendared R. C. Hannay, ed. R. L. Mackie (Edinburgh, 1953).

Lindsay, Sir David, *The Poetical Works of Sir David Lyndsay of the Mount*, ed. David Laing (new edn., 2 vols., Edinburgh, 1871).

----- *The Historie of Ane Nobil and Wailzeand Squyer, William Meldrum* (Edinburgh, 1594).

Lindsay of Pitscottie, Robert, *The History of Scotland* (Edinburgh, 1728).

------ *The Historie and Cronicles of Scotland, From the Slauchter of King James the First to the Ane Thousand Fyve Hundreith Thrie Scoir Fyftein Zeir*, ed. A. E. G. Mackay, Scottish Text Society (3 vols., Edinburgh, 1899-1911).

Major, John, *A History of Greater Britain as well England as Scotland, Compiled from the Ancient Authorities* (Edinburgh, 1892).

Marwick, J. D., ed., *Extracts From The Burgh Records of Edinburgh, A.D. 1403-1528*, Scottish Burgh Records Society (Edinburgh, 1869).

The Mirror for Magistrates, ed. Lily B. Campbell (1938, reprinted New York, 1960).

Petrie, George, ed., 'A Contemporary Account of the Battle of Flodden, 9 September 1513: Hereafter ensue the Trewe Encountre or Batayle lately don between Englande and Scotlande: In Which Batayle the Scottssh Kynge was slayne', *Proceedings of the Society of Antiquaries of Scotland*, 7 (1866-68), 141-52.

Pollard, A. F., ed., *An English Garner, Tudor Tracts 1532-1588* (New York, 1903).

The Saga of Olaf Tryggwason, trans. J. Sephton (London, 1895).

The Scots Peerage, ed. J. B. Paul (8 vols., Edinburgh, 1904-14).

The Scotichronicon, ed. D.E.R. Watt, volume 5 (Edinburgh, 1990).

Sempill, Robert, *The Sempill Ballates, A Series of Historical, Political, and Satirical Scottish Poems, Ascribed to Robert Sempill, MDLXVII-MDLXXXIII* (Edinburgh, 1872).

Skelton, John, A *Ballade of the Scottysshe Kyng, The Earliest Known Printed English Ballad*, ed. John Ashton (London, 1882).

----- The Complete English Poems, ed. John Scattergood (Harmondsworth, 1983).

----- *The Poetical Works of John Skelton*, ed. Rev. Andrew Dyce (3 vols., Boston, 1862).

Smith, C. Gregory, ed., *The Days of James IV, 1488-1513* (London, 1890).

Spencer, Nathaniel, *The Complete English Traveller, or a New Survey and Description of England and Wales* (London, 1772).

Spont, Alfred, *Letters and Papers Relating to the War with France, 1512-1513*, Navy Records Society (London, 1897).

State Papers, Henry the Eighth, Part IV, Correspondence Relating to Scotland and the Borders, 1513-1534 (London, 1836).

The Statistical Account for Scotland, 1791-9, volume 1. http://stat-acc-scot.edina.ac.uk/link/1791-99.

Stow, John, *A Survey of London, reprinted from the text of 1603*, ed. Charles Lethbridge Kingsford (2 vols., Oxford, 1908).

----- Annales of England (London, 1605).

Strype, John, *A Survey of the Cities of London and Westminster* (London, 1720). www.hrionline.ac.uk/strype

Stuart, John, ed., *Miscellany of the Spalding Club*, volume 1 (Aberdeen, 1841).

Vergil, Polydore, *The Anglica Historia of Polydore Vergil*, A.D. 1485-1537, ed. Denys Hay, Camden Series LXXIV (London, 1950).

---- *Anglica Historia* (1555 version). A hypertext critical edition by Dana F. Sutton. http://www.philological.bham.ac.uk/polverg/

Waldegrave, Robert, ed., *Collection of Ancient Scottish Prophecies in Alliterative Verse: reprinted from Waldegrave's Edition, MDCIII* (Edinburgh, 1833).

----- *The Whole Prophecie of Scotland, England, and some part of France and Denmark, prophesied bee meruellous Merling, Beid, Bertlington, Thomas Rymour, Waldue, Eltraine, Banester, and Sibbilla, all according in one. Containing many strange and meruelous things* (Edinburgh, 1603).

Wendover, Roger of, *Roger of Wendover's Flowers of History*, trans. J. A. Giles (2 vols., London, 1849).

Wyntoun, Andrew of, *The Orygynale Cronykil of Scotland*, ed. David Laing (3 vols., Edinburgh, 1872-9).

Printed Secondary Sources

Aitchison, Nick, *Macbeth, Man and Myth*, Nick Aitchison (Stroud, 1999).

Alexander, Paul J., *The Byzantine Apocalyptic Tradition* (Berkeley, 1985).

'Archaeological Intelligence,' *The Archaeological Journal* 3 (1846), 255-70.

Archer, Harriet, *Unperfect Histories, The Mirror for Magistrates, 1559-1610* (Oxford, 2017).

Armes Prydein, *The Prophecy of Britain*, ed. Sir Ifor Williams, trans. Rachel Bromwich (Dublin, 1982).

Ayton, W. E., 'Edinburgh After Flodden,' *Blackwood's Edinburgh Magazine* 63 (Jan-June 1848), 165-176.

Balfour, *The Historical Works of Sir James Balfour* (2 vols., Edinburgh, 1824).

Barnes, Ishbel, *Janet Kennedy Royal Mistress, Marriage and Divorce at the Courts of James IV and James V* (Edinburgh, 2007).

Barr, Niall, *Flodden* (2001, reprinted London, 2003).

Bates, Cadwallader J., 'Flodden Field,' *Archaeologia Aeliana,* 16 (1894), 351-372.

Beer, Michelle L., 'Practices and Performances of Queenship: Catherine of Aragon and Margaret Tudor', unpublished Ph.D. thesis (Urbana, 2014).

Beveridge, James, and Richardson, J. S., *Linlithgow Palace Official Guide Book* (Edinburgh, 1948).

Bingham, Caroline, *The Stewart Kingdom of Scotland, 1371-1603* (London, 1974).

Brewer, E. C., *The Reader's Handbook* (new edn., London, 1911).

Brewer, J. S., *The Reign of Henry VIII From His Accession to the Death of Wolsey*, ed. James Gairdner (2 vols., London, 1884).

Briggs, Katharine M., *A Dictionary of British Folk Tales in the English Language* (2 vols., London, 1971).

Brown, Michael J., *James I* (Edinburgh, 1984).

Brown, P. Hume, ed., *Early Travellers in Scotland* (Edinburgh, 1891).

Bruce, Drummond, 'The Court Cave: A Legendary Tale of Fifeshire,' in *A Book of Scottish Story* (Edinburgh, 1884), 458-72.

Buchan, John, *Montrose* (London, 1928).

Buchanan, Patricia, *Margaret Tudor, Queen of Scots* (Edinburgh, 1985).

Burnham, Josephine M., 'A Study of Thomas of Erceldoune,' *Publications of the Modern Language Association of America*, 23, New Series, vol. 16 (1908), 375-420.

Burns, J. H., *The True Law of Kingship: concepts of monarchy in early modern Scotland* (Oxford, 1996).

Burton, Richard F., *Camoens: His Life and His Lusiads* (2 vols., London, 1881).

Cardonnel, *Adam de, Numinismata Scotiae, or a series of the Scottish Coinage from William the Lion to the Union* (Edinburgh, 1786).

Carson, Annette, *Richard III, The Maligned King* (Stroud, 2008).

Chadwick, Nora K., 'The Story of Macbeth: A Study in Gaelic and Norse Tradition,' Scottish Gaelic Studies, 6 (1947-9) 189-211, 7 (1951-3), 1-25.

Chambers, Robert, *The Book of Days, A Miscellany of Popular Antiquities* (2 vols., London, 1832).

-----*The Picture of Scotland* (2 vols., Edinburgh, 1827).

-----*The Popular Rhymes of Scotland* (3rd edn., Edinburgh, 1870).

Chapman, Hester, W., *The Sisters of Henry VIII* (Bath, 1974).

Child, Francis James, ed., *English and Scottish Ballads*, volume1 (Boston, 1860).

Cloake, John, *Richmond's Great Monastery, The Charterhouse of Jesus of Bethlehem of Shene*, Richmond Local History Society Paper No. 6 (Richmond, 1990).

Cohn, Norman, *The Pursuit of the Millennium* (London, 1957).

------ *Europe's Inner Demons, An Enquiry Inspired by The Great Witch-hunt* (London, 1975).

Colquhoun, *Ithell, Sword of Wisdom: MacGregor Mathers and 'The Golden Dawn'* (New York, 1975).

Comrie, John D., *History of Scottish Medicine* (2 vols., 2nd edn., London, 1932).

Connolly, M., 'The Dethe of the Kynge of Scotis: A New Edition,' *Scottish Historical Review*, 71 (1992), 46-69.

Cowan, Edward J., 'The Discovery of the Future: Prophecy and Second Sight in Scottish History,' in Henderson, Lizanne (ed.), *Fantastical Imaginations, The Supernatural in Scottish History and Culture* (Edinburgh, 2009), 1-28.

Cowan, Samuel, *The Royal House of Stewart* (2 vols., London, 1908).

Creighton, Charles, *A History of Epidemics in Britain* (2 vols., Cambridge, 1891).

Cunningham, Allan, *Sir Michael Scott, A Romance* (3 vols., London, 1828).

Dalrymple, Sir David, *Remarks On The History of Scotland* (Edinburgh, 1773).

Dalyell, John Graham, *The Darker Superstitions of Scotland, Illustrated From History and Practice* (Edinburgh, 1834).

Dawson, Jane E. A., *Scotland Re-formed, 1488-1587*, The New Edinburgh History of Scotland (Edinburgh, 2007).

'The Dethe of the Kynge of Scotis,' in *The Life and Death of King James the First of Scotland*, ed. John Stevenson (Glasgow, 1837), 47-67.

Dickinson, W. Croft, Donaldson, Gordon & Milne, Isabel, A., eds., *A Source Book of Scottish History*, volume 2, 1424-1567 (2nd edn., London & Edinburgh, 1958).

Disney, A. R., *A History of Portugal and the Portuguese Empire* (2 vols., Cambridge, 2009).

Douglas, Sir George, *A History of the Border Counties* (Roxburgh, Selkirk, Peebles) (Edinburgh, 1899).

Dowden, John, *The Bishops of Scotland*, ed. J. Maitland Thomson (Glasgow, 1912).

Draskau, Jennifer Kewley, *The Tudor Rose, Princess Mary, Henry VIII's Sister* (Stroud, 2013).

Dunbar, Sir Archibald H., *Scottish Kings, A Revised Chronology of Scottish History, 1005-1625* (2nd edn., Edinburgh, 1906).

Dunlop, David, 'The Politics of Peace-keeping: Anglo-Scottish Relations from 1503 to 1511,' *Renaissance Studies*, vol. 8, no. 2, 138-61 (1994).

Edinburgh March Riding Association. http://www.edinburghridingthemarches.co.uk

Edington, Carol, *Court and Culture in Renaissance Scotland, Sir David Lindsay of the Mount* (Amherst, 1994).

Edward de Vere Newsletter, No. 11 (Kelowna, 1990).

Elliot, Fitzwilliam, *The Battle of Flodden and the Raids of 1513* (Edinburgh, 1911).

Ellis, Steven G., *Defending English Ground, War and Peace in Meath and Northumberland, 1460–1542* (Oxford, 2015).

----- *Tudor Frontiers and Noble Power, The Making of the British State* (Oxford, 1995).

Emond, William Kevin, 'The Minority of King James V 1513-1528', Unpublished Ph.D. Thesis (University of St Andrews, 1988).

Etty, Claire, 'Tudor Revolution? Royal Control of the Anglo-Scottish Border, 1483-1530', Unpublished Ph.D. Thesis (University of Durham, 2005).

Evans, Henry Ridgely, 'The Romance of the Dead,' *The Theosophical Path Magazine*, 5, no. 1 (July to December 1913).

Evans, Michael, *The Death of Kings, Royal Deaths in Medieval England* (London, 2003).

Eyre-Todd, George, *Scotland Picturesque and Traditional* (Glasgow, 1921).

'Farce in court. Alice in Wonderland trial. Secret rites.' *Barrier Miner* (Broken Hill, New South Wales, 21 June 1911).

Ferguson, Rev. John, *Ecclesia Antiqua or, the Ancient Church (St Michael's Linlithgow)* (Edinburgh, 1905).

Fitzgibbons, Jonathan, *Cromwell's Head* (Richmond, 2008).

'The Flodden Death-roll,' *The Scottish Antiquary, or Notes and Queries*, vol. XIII (July 1898), 101-11.

'The Flodden Death-roll,' Supplementary, I, II, III, *The Scottish Antiquary, or Notes and Queries*, vol. XIII (April 1899), 168-72.

Fradon-Burg, Louise Olga, City, *Marriage, Tournament: Arts of Rule in Late Medieval Scotland*, Louise Olga Fradon-Burg, (Madison, 1995).

Fraser, George Macdonald, *The Steel Bonnets, The Story of the Anglo-Scottish Border Reivers* (London, 1971).

Fraser, Stephen, 'Standard Life paves the way for Scottish king's memorial.' *Scotland on Sunday* (18 August 2002).

Fraser, Sir William, *The Douglas Book* (4 vols., Edinburgh, 1885).

Fraser, Sir William, *The Elphinstone Family Book of the Lords Elphinstone, Balmerino and Coupar* (2 vols., Edinburgh, 1897).

Galt, John, *The Life of Cardinal Wolsey* (3rd edn., London, 1846).

Garnett, Richard, *Richmond on the Thames* (London, 1896).

Gerber, Pat, *The Search For the Stone of Destiny* (Edinburgh, 1992).

Godwyn, Francis, *Annals of England from the year 1508 to the year 1558*, translated by Morgan Godwyn (London, 1675).

Goodwin, George, *Fatal Rivalry, Flodden 1513* (London, 2013).

Gosman, Martin; Macdonald, Alasdair, A.; Vanderjagt, Arie Johan, *Princes and Princely Culture, 1450-1650*, volume 1 (Leiden, 2005).

Graham, Rev. Patrick, *Sketches of Perthshire* (2nd edn., Edinburgh, 1812).

Gray, Douglas, 'Later Poetry: The Courtly Tradition,' pp. 313-368 in Bolton, W. F. (ed.), *The Middle Ages (Sphere History of Literature)* (revised edn., London, 1986).

Gray, John, 'Lawlessness on the frontier: The Anglo-Scottish borderlands in the fourteenth to sixteenth century', *History and Anthropology*, 12:4, 381-408 (2001).

Green, Mary Anne Everett, *Lives of the Princesses of England from the Norman Conquest*, volume 4 (London, 1857).

Grose, Francis, *The Antiquities of Scotland* (2 vols., London, 1797).

Gunn, George, *The Early History of Stichill, Stichill During the Commonwealth, The Church of Hume, A Century of Life In the Borders* (Alnwick, 1901).

Gunnyon, William, *Illustrations of Scottish History, Life and Superstition from Song and Ballad* (London, 1877).

Guthrie, Douglas, 'The Medical and Scientific Exploits of King James IV of Scotland,' *British Medical Journal* (May 30 1953), 1191-1193.

Guy, John, *My Heart Is My Own, The Life of Mary Queen of Scots* (London, 2004).

Gwyn, Peter, *The King's Cardinal, The Rise and Fall of Thomas Wolsey* (1990, reprinted London, 2002).

Haig, James, *A Topographical and Historical Account of the Town of Kelso, and of the Town and Castle of Roxburgh* (Edinburgh, 1825).

Hendrie, William F., *Linlithgow, Six Hundred Years A Royal Burgh* (Edinburgh, 1989).

Hepburn, William Rendall, 'The Court of James IV, 1488-1513', unpublished Ph. D. thesis (Glasgow, 2013).

Herkless, John and Hannay, Robert, *The Archbishops of St Andrews* (6 vols., Edinburgh, 1907-15).

Herodotus, *Histories,* translated George Rawlinson (1910, reprinted London, 1996).

Harvey, Nancy Lenz, *The Rose and the Thorn, The Lives of Mary and Margaret Tudor* (New York, 1975).

Historical Tales of the Wars of Scotland (2 vols., Edinburgh, 1849).

Hodgkin, Thomas, 'The Battle of Flodden', *Archaeologia Aeliana,* 16 (1892), 1-45.

Hogg, James, 'The Queen of France and James IV,' *Historical Ballads No. 1,* , 17 (1834), 41.

Hudson, Benjamin T., *Prophecy of Berchán: Irish and Scottish High-kings of the Early Middle Ages* (Westport, 1996).

Hume Brown, Peter, *Early Travellers in Scotland* (Edinburgh, 1891).

Hume of Godscroft, David, *The History of the House and Race of Douglas* (2 vols., 4th edn., 1748, reprinted Lavergne, 2010).

Hutchison, Robert, *The Last Days of Henry VIII* (London, 2005).

Illes, Judika, *The Element Encyclopedia of Witchcraft* (London, 2005).

Jack, Ronald, D. S., ed., *Scottish Prose 1150-1700* (London, 1971).

'James IV alive it is asserted.' *The Morning Leader* (Ratmalana, Sri Lanka. 27 May 1911).

Jamieson, Thomas, *Notice of the life and Writings of Alexander Barclay, the translator of Brandt's Ship of Fools* (Edinburgh, 1874).

Jennings, Jaime D., 'Stress Along the Medieval Scottish Border? Skeletal Indicators of Conflict-Zone Health', Unpublished Ph. D. thesis (Durham, 2010).

Jones, Rev. Robert, *The Battle of Flodden Field* (Edinburgh, 1864).

Jones, Thomas, 'The Black Book of Carmarthen Stanzas of the Graves,' *Proceedings of the British Academy* 3 (1967), 87-137.

'King's Bench Division. "An Amazing Sect." Singular Libel Action.' *The Daily Telegraph* (27 April 1911).

'King's Bench Division. "The Equinox." Jones v. The Looking Glass Company (Limited) and Others.' *The Times* (27 April 1911.)

Laing, David, ed., *Early Popular Poetry of Scotland and the Northern Border*, revised by W. Carew Hazlitt (London, 1895).

King, Francis, *Modern Ritual Magic, The Rise of Western Occultism* (Bridport, 1989).

Lang, Andrew, *A History of Scotland from the Roman Occupation*, (4 vols., Edinburgh, 1900).

Lang, Andrew, and Lang, John, *Highways and Byways in the Border* (London, 1913).

Lang, Theo, *The Queen's Scotland, The Border Counties, Tweedale, Merse and Teviotdale* (London, 1957).

Larner, Christina, *Enemies of God, The Witch Hunt in Scotland* (London, 1981).

Leland, John, *Antiquarii de Rebus Britannicis Collectanea* (2nd edn., 6 vols., London, 1770).

'Lessons of Flodden. Lord Rosebery unveils Selkirk Memorial. Quaint and historic ceremonies.' *The Glasgow Herald* (14 June 1913).

Lewis, C. S., *English Literature in the Sixteenth Century Excluding Drama* (Oxford, 1954).

Lindsay, Sir David, *Ane Satyre of The Thre Estatis* (ed. Roderick Lyall) (Edinburgh, 1989).

Luke, Mary M., *Catherine the Queen* (London, 1968).

Lyon, Charles, John, *Ancient and Modern* (Edinburgh, 1838).

McCallum, Andrew, 'The battle to save Flodden flag.' *The Glasgow Herald* (10 July 1984).

McEwan, Rod, *Scotland-upon-Thames, Scotland's Legacy to Richmond and Kew, Richmond Local History Society Papers* (New Series) No. 6 (Richmond, 2007).

McGrigor, *The Other Tudor Princess, Margaret Douglas, Henry*

VIII's Niece (Stroud, 2015).

McNeill, Robert, '1m pound dig will look for the head of James IV.' *The Scotsman* (12 January 2000).

McNeill, Robert and Stevenson, Jill, 'Uneasy lies the king's head.' *The Scotsman* (11 January 2000).

Macdonald, Alasdair A., 'Princely Culture in Scotland under James III and James IV,' in *Princes and Princely Culture,1450-1650,* ed. M. Gosman, A. Macdonald, A. Vanderjagt (eds.), (Leiden, 2013) , pp. 147-171.

Macdougall, Norman, *James IV* (1989, reprinted Edinburgh, 2006).

Macfarlane, Leslie J., *William Elphinstone and the Kingdom of Scotland, 1431-1514: The Struggle for Order* (Aberdeen, 1985).

Mackay, Æneas, 'James IV,' in *The Dictionary of National Biography,* ed. Sidney Lee, Volume 29 (London, 1892), 145-153.

Mackay, Æneas, 'Notice of A Portrait Group of Margaret Tudor, the Regent Albany, and a Third Figure: the Property of the Marquis of Bute, at Cardiff Castle, Glamorganshire,' *Proceedings of the Society of Antiquaries of Scotland,* 27 (1893), 186- 205.

Mackay, Æneas, 'John Stewart, Duke of Albany (1481-1536),' in *The Dictionary of National Biography,* ed. Sidney Lee, volume 54 (1898), 317-322.

Mackenzie, W. Mackay, *The Secret of Flodden* (Edinburgh, 1931).

Macritchie, David, *Scottish Gypsies under the Stewarts* (Edinburgh, 1894).

Mackie, R. L., *King James IV of Scotland* (Edinburgh, 1958).

Mackie, R. L. (ed.), 'The English Army at Flodden,' in *Miscellany of the Scottish History Scoiety,* vol. 8 (Edinburgh, 1951), 85-88.

Marsden, John, *Alba of the Ravens, In Search of the Celtic Kingdom of the Scots* (London, 1997).

Martine, Roddy, 'I say, could I have a royal digit back.' 'Thorns from the Thistle,' *The Scottish Daily Mail* (6 December 1996).

Martine, Roddy, *Supernatural Scotland* (2003, reprinted Anstey,

2004).
Mattingly, Garrett, *Catherine the Queen* (1944, reprinted London, 1952).
Maxwell, Sir Herbert, *Robert the Bruce and the Struggle for Scottish Independence* (London, 1897).
Miller, Peter, 'The Mercat Cross of Edinburgh, From 1365 to 1617 – Its Site and Form,' *Proceedings of the Society of Antiquaries of Scotland*, 20 (1885-6), 377-389.
Moffat, Dr. Ralph, 'Sword and Dagger in the College of Arms, London.' http://www.college-of-arms.gov.uk/SwordDagger Ring.html
Morkill, J. W., 'Notice of a Human Hand and Forearm, pierced with Nail-holes, and a Basket-hilted sword formerly preserved in the Family of Graham of Woodhall, Yorkshire, as Relics of James, First Marquis of Montrose,' *Proceedings of the Society of Antiquaries of Scotland*, 31 (1897), 65-73.
Morton, R. S., 'Some Aspects of the Early History of Syphilis in Scotland,' *British Journal of Venereal Disease*, 38 (1962), 175-180.
Murray, James A. H., ed., *The Romance and Prophecies of Thomas of Erceldoune* (1875, reprinted Felinfach, 1991).
'Mystic Ritual and Incense. Invocation of Saturn.' *The Daily News* (27 May 1911, reprinted 29 May 1911). Perth, Western Australia. http://trove.nla.gov.au/
Newton, Michael, 'Prophecy and Cultural Conflict in Scottish Gaelic Tradition,' *Scottish Studies* 35 (2007-10), 144-73.
Nicholson, Ranald, *Scotland, The Later Middle Ages*, The Edinburgh History of Scotland (Edinburgh, 1974).
Nicol, Donald M., *Immortal Emperor, The Life and Legend of Constantine Palaiologos, Last Emperor of the Romans* (Cambridge, 1992).
Oliver, Stephen, *Rambles in Northumberland and on the Scottish Border* (London, 1835).
Owen, Jonathan, 'A wee bit of Scotland in the heart of Surrey: Flodden 1513 Club to mark James IV's final resting place.' *The*

Independent, 7 September 2013.

Patten, William, 'The Expedition into Scotland In 1547', in *Tudor Tracts 1532-1588*, ed. A. F. Pollard (New York, 1903), 53-158.

Percy, Thomas, *Bishop Percy's Folio MS. Ballads and Romances*, volume 1, ed. John W. Hales and Frederick J. Furnivall (London, 1867).

Perrie, Maureen, *Pretenders and Popular Monarchism in Early Modern Russia, the False Tsars of the Time of Troubles* (Cambridge, 1995).

Perry, Maria, *Sisters to the King - the Tumultuous Lives of Henry VIII's Sisters - Margaret of Scotland and Mary of France* (1998, reprinted London, 2002).

Pinkerton, John, *The History of Scotland from the Accession of the House of Stuart to that of Mary* (2 vols., London, 1797).

Pittock, Murray G., *Scottish Nationality* (London, 2001).

Pollet, Maurice, *John Skelton, Poet of Tudor England*, trans. John Warrington (London, 1971).

The Book of Pluscarden, ed. Felix J. Skene (2 vols., Edinburgh, 1877, 1880).

Previté-Orton, C. W., 'An Elizabethan Prophecy,' *History*, New Series, 2 (April 1917-January 1918), 207-18.

Radcliffe, John, 'The King's Stone At Flodden,' *Notes and Queries*, 9th Series, 2 (August 13, 1898), 131.

Rankin, Frank, *Guide to the Wemyss Caves* (Wemyss, 1993).

Read, Prof. John, 'Alchemy and Alchemists,' *Folklore*, 44 (Sept. 1933), 251-278.

----- 'An Alchemical Airman,' *The New Scientist* (8 February, 1958), 21-32.

Reid, Norman H., 'Alexander III: The Historiography of a Myth', in Norman H. Reid ed., *Scotland in the Reign of Alexander III 1249-1286* (Edinburgh, 1990), 181-213.

'Rex marks the spot.' *The Daily Record* (29 July 2002).

Ridpath, George, *The Border History of England and Scotland From the Earliest Times to the Union of the Two Crowns* (Edinburgh,

London & Berwick, 1776).

Rolph, Daniel N., 'A Strange Family Heirloom: the Rib of a Scottish King in America?' blog entry, http://frontierhistory.blogspot.com. (24 May 2010.)

Routh, C. R. N., *Who's Who in Tudor England* (revised edn., London, 1990).

D. B. S., 'Armour Worn by James IV at Flodden', *The Scottish Historical Review*, 12 (1915), 332.

Salces, Juan E. Tazón, 'Death in northern Africa: The Battle of Alcazar and its theatrical representation,' *SEDERI: yearbook of the Spanish and Portuguese Society for English Renaissance Studies*, 7 (1996), 173-178.

Scott, Sir Walter, *Marmion, A Tale of Flodden Field,* (Edinburgh & London, 1808).

----- *Minstrelsy of the Scottish Border*, 4 volumes (1802-3, reprinted Edinburgh, 1849).

----- *Redgauntlet* (1824, reprinted London, 1918).

----- *Tales of A Grandfather*, vol. 2 (Edinburgh, 1828).

----- *Waverley* (1814, reprinted London, 1906).

Simpkins, John Ewart, *County Folklore Volume VII, Examples of Printed Folk-lore Concerning Fife* (London, 1914).

Simson, Walter, *A History of the Gipsies* (New York and London, 1866).

Sinclair, George, *Satan's Invisible World Discovered* (1685, reprinted Edinburgh, 1871).

Skene, W. F., 'On The Traditionary Accounts of the Death of Alexander the Third,' *Proceedings of The Society of Antiquaries of Scotland*, 20 (1885-6), 177-85.

Small, John, 'Sketches of Early Scottish Alchemists: Michael Scot – King James IV – Sir George Erskine of Innertiel, *Proceedings of the Society of Antiquaries of Scotland*, 11 (1874-76), 179-97.

Stair-Kerr, *Scotland under James IV* (Paisley, 1911).

Steel, David & Paterson, Ian, *The Parish of Linlithgow, St Michael's* (Linlithgow, 2004).

Steven, Moses, ed., *Illustrations of Scottish History, From the Twelfth to the Seventeenth Centuries* (Glasgow, 1834).

Stevenson, David, ' "The Gudeman of Ballangeich": Rambles in the Afterlife of James V,' *Folklore*, vol. 115, issue 2, 187-200 (2004).

Stewart, A. J., Falcon, *The Autobiography of His Grace James the 4 King of Scots, presented by A. J. Stewart* (revised edn., Glasgow, 1982).

Stewart, A. J., *King's Memory, An Autobiography* (Glasgow, 1981).

Stewart, A. M., 'Adam Abell's Roit or quheill of tyme', *Aberdeen University Review*, 44 (1971–2), 386-93.

Strickland, Agnes, *Lives of the Queens of Scotland and English Princesses Connected with the Regal Succession of Great Britain* (8 vols., New York, 1851-59).

'The Stuarts and Their Champions,' in *Folklore, Myths and Legends of Britain* (London, 1973), 527-31.

Stuart, Marie W., *The Scot Who Was A Frenchman, Being the Life of John Stewart, Duke of Albany, in Scotland, France and Italy* (London, 1940).

Taylor, I. A., *The Life of James IV* (London, 1913).

Taylor, Rupert, *The Political Prophecy in England* (New York, 1911).

Tolstoy, Nikolai, *The Quest for Merlin* (London, 1985).

Tytler, Patrick Fraser, *The History of Scotland*, volume 4 (new edn., London, 1866), volume 5 (London, 1834).

Tytler, Patrick Fraser, *Lives of the Scottish Worthies* (3 vols., London, 1833).

Vokes, Susan Elisabeth, 'The Early Career of Thomas, Lord Howard, Earl of Surrey and Third Duke of Norfolk, 1474-c.1525', Unpublished Ph. D. thesis, University of Hull, 1988.

Waterhouse, Thomas, *A Genealogical Account of the Royal House of Stuart* (Grantham, 1816).

Watson, Godfrey, *Bothwell and the Witches* (London, 1975).

Weever, John, *Antient Funeral Monuments of Great Britain, Ireland,*

and the Islands Adjacent (1631, reprinted London, 1776).

Weir, Alison, *Henry VIII, King and Court* (London, 2008).

Westwood, Jennifer, Albion, *A Guide to Legendary Britain* (London, 1985).

----- 'The Road to the Fairy Knowe,' foreword to *Robert Kirk, Walker Between Worlds*, ed. R. J. Stewart, viii-x (Shaftesbury, 1990).

Westwood, Jennifer and Kingshill, Sophia, *The Lore of Scotland, A Guide to Scottish Legends* (London, 2009).

Whatton, William Robert, 'An Inquiry into the probability of a Tradition connected with the Library and Furniture of James IV of Scotland, and of their having been carried off after the Battle of Flodden, and set up at Speke Hall, in the County of Lancaster,' *Archaeologia Scotica: Transactions of the Society of Antiquaries of Scotland*, 4 (1857), 1-14.

White, Robert, 'The Battle of Flodden,' *Archaeologia Aeliana*, 3 (1859), 197-236.

Williams, Janet Hadley, 'James V as Literary Patron,' in *Princes and Princely Culture,1450-1650*, ed. M. Gosman, A. Macdonald, A. Vanderjagt (eds.), (Leiden, 2013), pp. 173-198.

Wilson, Daniel, *Memorials of Edinburgh in the Olden Time* (3rd edn., Edinburgh,
1875).

Wilson, Ian, *Mind Out of Time, Reincarnation Investigated* (London, 1981).

Wood, Marguerite, ed., *Flodden Papers, Diplomatic Correspondence between the Courts of France and Scotland, 1507-1517*, Scottish History Society (Edinburgh, 1933).

Wood Brown, Rev. James, *An Enquiry Into the Life and Legend of Michael Scot* (Edinburgh, 1897).

Wroe, Ann, *Perkin, A Story of Deception* (London, 2003).

Young, Sir Charles, 'Remarks on the Sword, Dagger, and Ring of King James the Fourth of Scotland, preserved in the College of Arms, London,' *Archaeologia*, 33 (1849), 335-340.

Younger, Paul L., 'Crouching enemy, hidden ally: the decisive role of groundwater discharge features in two major British battles, Flodden 1513 and Prestonpans 1745', *Geological Society*, London, Special Publications 2012, v.362, 19-33.

About the Author

I'd like to thank you for buying *The Afterlife of King James IV* and would ask, if you enjoyed the book, to leave a favourable comment on your favourite website!

Further and ongoing details of my research into the folklore of the Scottish monarchy and local history can be found via my blogs:

Legends of the Scottish Kings (https://scottishroyallegends.blogspot.co.uk)

Angus Folklore (https://angusfolklore.blogspot.uk)

The Ghosts of Glamis (https://ghostsofglamis.blogspot.co.uk)

Please feel free to contact me at: keith.j.coleman@gmail.com

HISTORY

Recent bestsellers from Chronos Books are:

Lady Katherine Knollys

The Unacknowledged Daughter of King Henry VIII

Sarah-Beth Watkins

A comprehensive account of Katherine Knollys' questionable paternity, her previously unexplored life in the Tudor court and her intriguing relationship with Elizabeth I.

Paperback: 978-1-78279-585-8 ebook: 978-1-78279-584-1

Cromwell was Framed

Ireland 1649

Tom Reilly

Revealed: The definitive research that proves the Irish nation owes Oliver Cromwell a huge posthumous apology for wrongly convicting him of civilian atrocities in 1649.

Paperback: 978-1-78279-516-2 ebook: 978-1-78279-515-5

Why The CIA Killed JFK and Malcolm X

The Secret Drug Trade in Laos

John Koerner

A new groundbreaking work presenting evidence that the CIA silenced JFK to protect its secret drug trade in Laos.

Paperback: 978-1-78279-701-2 ebook: 978-1-78279-700-5

The Disappearing Ninth Legion

A Popular History

Mark Olly

The Disappearing Ninth Legion examines hard evidence for the foundation, development, mysterious disappearance, or possible continuation of Rome's lost Legion.

Paperback: 978-1-84694-559-5 ebook: 978-1-84694-931-9

Beaten But Not Defeated

Siegfried Moos - A German anti-Nazi who settled in Britain

Merilyn Moos

Siegi Moos, an anti-Nazi and active member of the German Communist Party, escaped Germany in 1933 and, exiled in Britain, sought another route to the transformation of capitalism.

Paperback: 978-1-78279-677-0 ebook: 978-1-78279-676-3

A Schoolboy's Wartime Letters

An evacuee's life in WWII — A Personal Memoir

Geoffrey Iley

A boy writes home during WWII, revealing his own fascinating story, full of zest for life, information and humour.

Paperback: 978-1-78279-504-9 ebook: 978-1-78279-503-2

The Life & Times of the Real Robyn Hoode

Mark Olly

A journey of discovery. The chronicles of the genuine historical character, Robyn Hoode, and how he became one of England's greatest legends.

Paperback: 978-1-78535-059-7 ebook: 978-1-78535-060-3

Readers of ebooks can buy or view any of these bestsellers by clicking on the live link in the title. Most titles are published in paperback and as an ebook. Paperbacks are available in traditional bookshops. Both print and ebook formats are available online.

Find more titles and sign up to our readers' newsletter at http://www.johnhuntpublishing.com/history-home

Follow us on Facebook at https://www.facebook.com/ChronosBooks

and Twitter at https://twitter.com/ChronosBooks